CRUISE PORTS
ALASKA

A GUIDE TO PERFECT DAYS ON SHORE

Brendan Sainsbury, Catherine Bodry,
Adam Karlin, John Lee, Becky Ohlsen

Contents

Plan Your Trip

Totem pole
MIHAI STANCIU/SHUTTERSTOCK ©

Plan Your Trip
Alaska's Top 10

CHECUBUS/SHUTTERSTOCK ©

Seattle

Cutting-edge tech city with impeccable taste

A way-station for Alaska-bound travelers for over a century, Seattle (p35) is the perfect place to acclimatize, both physically and mentally. The city shares a national historical park with Skagway, plus there are cultural similarities between the two regions from their coastal indigenous culture to their penchant for coffee and craft beer. Welcome to the 'Emerald City', a tantalizing taste of what's to come. Left: Pike Place Market (p38); Right: Seattle's Space Needle (p40)

ROMAKOMA/SHUTTERSTOCK ©

KEVIN_HSIEH/SHUTTERSTOCK ©

Vancouver

Canada's sophisticated western metropolis

If you could design the perfect modern city, it would probably look something like Vancouver (p65): culturally diverse, temperate in climate, and encased in a dramatic physical location between mountains and sea. It's hard to imagine a prettier start to an Alaskan cruise than watching the skyscrapers of downtown Vancouver disappear behind the trees of Stanley Park as you glide beneath the Lion's Gate Bridge. Top: Stanley Park (p68); Bottom: Lion's Gate Bridge

Ketchikan

Watery adventure town amid temperate rainforest

Alaska's 'first city' (p93) earns its moniker not from its history, but from its position at the extreme south of the Alaskan Panhandle, making it first port of call for practically every cruise ship tracking up the Inside Passage. It also claims premier position for Alaska Native culture (totem poles abound), kayaking, ziplining and slightly less alluring – rain. Rest assured, the welcome is never damp.
Saxman Native Village (p101)

Sitka

Russian history among tall trees and totems

They came in 1741 and stayed for over 135 years, to occupy, trade and preach their faith. For a compelling glimpse into the history of Russian Alaska, a trip to the attractive wilderness-encased town of Sitka (p113) is practically obligatory. Wander around creepy old cemeteries, visit the site of St Innocent's old Bishop's House, and give thanks for the precious icons preserved in gilded St Michael's Cathedral. Right: St Michael's Cathedral (p120)

Juneau

Culture and wilderness coexist in the state capital

Alaska's busiest cruise port (p127) manages to juggle heavy crowds with a dramatic cusp-of-wilderness location. Not 10 miles from where legislators draft bills in the state capitol building, the Mendenhall Glacier slides stealthily off the Juneau Icefield and hungry bruins snatch salmon out of gurgling streams. It's this juxtaposition of civilized and uncivilized that makes Juneau so compelling. Right: Mendenhall Glacier (p132)

JONATHAN KINGSTON/GETTY IMAGES ©

RUTH PETERKIN/SHUTTERSTOCK ©

RICHARD FITZRERYSHUTTERSTOCK ©

Haines

Small-town port with big cultural attractions

If you want to see a side of Alaska different from the teeming cruise
terminals and ubiquitous jewelry stores that characterize the
bigger ports, pick a ship that docks in Haines (p159). Tourists are
incidental in this low-key, laid-back Panhandle town where Tlingit
traditions are strong and bald eagles patrol the skies nearby. Creep
unannounced into a local bar and see what makes it tick.

Bald eagles

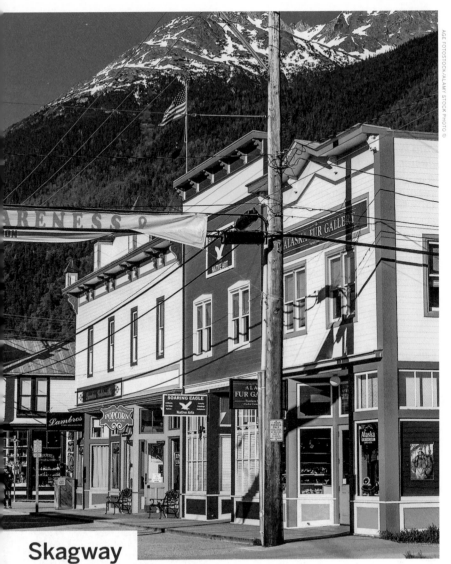

Skagway

A life-sized museum to the gold rush

Skagway (p173) is used to sharing its riches. In the 1890s, it was inundated by over 40,000 hungry Klondike prospectors dreaming of gold. By the 1990s, the 'gold' was in the pockets of holiday makers (over one million annually) intent on reliving the wild drama of the gold rush era now magnificently preserved by the US National Park Service. Broadway Street

Whittier

Cold War conundrum on the cusp of a glacier-fed wilderness

More an oddity than a settlement, Whittier (p191) is worth visiting purely for its weirdness. But, once you've finished photographing its spooky abandoned military installations built for a war that never happened, you'll look around and notice the giant glaciers, abundant wildlife and inlet full of bobbing kayaks and trawling fishing craft. This 'town' merits plenty of independent exploration. Right: Kayaking, Blackstone Bay (p198)

REISEGRAF.CH/SHUTTERSTOCK ©

MARK NEWMAN/GETTY IMAGES ©

Seward

Port on the edge of easily accessible backcountry

The unofficial capital of Alaska's vast wilderness playground, the Kenai Peninsula, Seward (p207) is a small port surrounded by big beauty. Despite its diminutive size, this unashamedly quaint sea-focused town is the main disembarkation point for cruises starting and ending in Alaska. But, with the Kenai Fjords National Park literally around the corner, there are strong reasons to linger.

Left: Exit Glacier, Kenai Fjords National Park (p210)

JON MANJEOT/SHUTTERSTOCK ©

Anchorage

A civilized base for some wild adventures nearby

A revelation to anyone from the lower 48 who thought that Alaska was a uncool backwater full of rural hicks taking potshots at road signs, Anchorage (p219) is a hip, happening, modern metropolis with more coffee bars per head than Seattle. While not a cruise-ship port per se, it acts as the start and end point for many excursions and a link for passengers on land-cruises up to Denali National Park. Right: Anchorage Museum (p222)

10

Plan Your Trip
Need to Know

When to Go

Warm to hot summers, mild winters
Warm to hot summers, cold winters
Mild summers, cold winters
Cold climate

Fairbanks
GO Jun–Sep•

•**Denali National Park**
GO Jun–Aug

Anchorage
GO Jun–Oct•

Homer
GO May–Sep

Juneau
GO May–Sep

High Season (Jun–Aug)

o Solstice festivals and 20-hour days are enjoyed in June.

o Mountain trails and passes are snow-free in August.

o Tour demand is high and prices peak in July.

Shoulder (May & Sep)

o Car-rental rates are 30% lower than in June.

o Southeast Alaska is sunny during May, but rainy in September and October.

o The northern lights begin to appear in late September.

Low Season (Oct–Apr)

o Brrrrr! Bundle up, it's cold.

o Few, if any, cruise companies offer trips.

o Most tour and activity companies close for winter, especially in cruise-orientated towns.

Currencies

US dollar and Canadian dollar

Language

English

Visas

Most international visitors need a visa and should have a multiple-entry one if coming from the lower 48 United States through Canada.

Money

Prices quoted are in US dollars unless otherwise stated. Keep in mind that the Canadian system is also dollars and cents but is a separate currency.

Cell Phones

Coverage is surprisingly good, even in remote areas. Pre-paid SIM cards can be used in some international cell (mobile) phones for local calls and voice mail.

Time

Alaska Time (GMT/UTC minus nine hours)

Costs For a Day in Port

Budget: Less than $75

○ Museum entry: $3–10

○ Cheap restaurant meal: $8–12

○ Kayak rental: $35

Midrange: $75–150

○ Half-day kayaking trip: $125

○ Restaurant mid-afternoon special: $10–15

○ Light coffee-shop breakfast: $5–8

Top End: More than $150

○ Flightseeing tour: $200-plus

○ Dinner main at a top restaurant: $25–35

○ Car rental per day: $60–85

Useful Websites

Travel Alaska (www.travelalaska.com) Alaska's official tourism site.
Cruise Critic (www.cruisecritic.com) Trip reviews, prices, plus ship and port info.
National Park Service (www.nps.gov/alaska) Information on Alaska's national parks, preserves, monuments and historical sites.
Lonely Planet (www.lonelyplanet.com/usa/alaska) Destination information, hotel bookings, traveller forum and more.

Opening Hours

Banks 9am–4pm or 5pm Monday to Friday; 9am–1pm Saturday (main branches)
Bars & Clubs City bars until 2am or later, especially on weekends; clubs to 2am or beyond
Post Offices 9am–5pm Monday to Friday; noon–3pm Saturday (main branches open longer)
Restaurants & Cafes Breakfast at cafes/coffee shops from 7am or earlier; some restaurants open only for lunch (noon–3pm) or dinner (4–10pm, later in cities);

Asian restaurants often have split hours: 11am–2pm and from 4pm.
Shops 10am–8pm/6pm (larger/smaller stores) Monday to Friday; 9am–5pm Saturday; 10am–5pm Sunday (larger stores)

Wi-Fi Access

It's easy to surf the net, make online reservations or retrieve email in Alaska. Most towns, even the smallest ones, have free internet access at libraries. If you have a laptop or phone, free wi-fi is common in Alaska at bookstores, hotels, coffee shops, airport terminals and bars, although reception may be patchier than it is in the lower 48.

Port Access

Ted Stevens Anchorage International Airport There's a people-mover bus to downtown ($2) hourly from the south terminal; the 20-minute taxi ride to the city costs $25.
Sea-Tac International Airport Shuttle Express (p61) links Sea-Tac airport with the Seattle cruise-ship piers ($22).
Vancouver International Airport Situated 13km south of the city in Richmond. Canada Line trains to downtown (for Canada Place cruise terminal) typically take around 25 minutes and cost $7.75 to $10.50. Alternatively, taxis cost up to $45.

Getting Around the Port

Many of Alaska's small port towns are easy to explore on foot.

Train The Alaska Railroad provides a scenic if pricey way of traveling between Seward, Whittier and Anchorage. Some cruise lines include a rail tour in their trip package.

Bus Small free shuttles and/or cheap public buses serve most of Alaska's port towns.

Light Rail Seattle and Vancouver both have good light-rail systems.

Plan Your Trip
Hot Spots for...

ROCKY GRIMES/SHUTTERSTOCK ©

Wildlife

Think of Alaska as the Serengeti of the north, a vast fauna-filled wilderness where majestic beasts roam across land, air and sea. It's a privilege to watch them.

Haines (p159)
Small Alaskan town where abundant salmon runs attract bears and raptors, most notably bald eagles.

Alaska Chilkat Bald Eagle Preserve (p162)
World's best wild bald eagles.

Glacier Bay (p146; pictured above)
An unsullied national park set around a web of bays and inlets with abundant wildlife.

Whale-Watching (p149)
Humpback whales in a spectacular natural show.

Juneau (p127)
Bears wander into the state capital's streets, while whales breach playfully in the surrounding waters.

Pack Creek (p137)
One of the best places in Alaska for bear-viewing.

DIGIDREAMGRAFIX/SHUTTERSTOCK ©

Alaska Native Culture

You'll never fully understand Alaska until you've unraveled its native culture and history, a mix of art, languages, dances and stories that'll dazzle you in every port you dock.

Juneau (p127)
The state capital archives the best elements of Alaska's history, focusing on Alaska Natives culture.

Sealaska Heritage (p140)
Cultural center with mask collection and clan house.

Ketchikan (p93; pictured above)
The capital of northwest totem-pole culture is the best place in the state to see them being made.

Totem Heritage Center (p100)
Diverse collection of poles in a well-kept museum.

Haines (p159)
Home to the Chilkat Tlingits, builders of a new cultural center in the ancient village of Klukwan.

Jilkaat Kwaan Cultural Heritage Center (p164)
Elaborate Alaskan native art.

Kayaking

To many Alaskans in the state's watery southeast, paddling is as natural as walking, and a useful and often necessary means of getting around. Grab an oar and join them.

AMANDA MORTIMER/SHUTTERSTOCK ©

Ketchikan (p93)
A rainforest city with coves and islands where wilderness and wildlife form a rugged natural alliance.

Clover Pass (p96)
Island waters away from Ketchikan's busy waterfront.

Sitka (p113)
Alaska's Russian-tinged former capital sits aside a quiet waterfront ideal for canoeing or kayaking.

Sitka Sound (p121)
An archipelago of islands under volcanic Mt Edgecumbe.

Whittier (p191; pictured above)
The westernmost point of Prince William Sound is the entry point into a world of whales and glaciers.

Blackstone Bay (p197)
Up-close views of icebergs and majestic glaciers.

Hiking

After several days aboard a ship, most people are keen to rediscover their land legs. And what Alaska lacks in roads, it makes up for in trails.

STEVE ESTVANIK/SHUTTERSTOCK ©

Juneau (p127; pictured above)
Hemmed in by mountains, waterfalls and wilderness, Juneau is a trailhead for numerous hikes.

Perseverance Trail (p131)
A walk through Juneau's gold-mining history (above).

Seward (p207)
Explore superb hiking trails both in town and in the nearby Kenai Fjords National Park.

Mt Marathon (p213)
Seward's proverbial 'fitness ladder' attracts many hikers.

Ketchikan (p93)
Don't let the rain that dampen the joy of hiking above the treeline in Alaska's so-called 'first city.'

Deer Mountain (p110)
Enjoy panoramic views climbing this 3000ft summit.

Plan Your Trip
Local Life

Activities

Visiting Alaska is all about answering the call of the wild. Hiking and paddling are the two cheapest and easiest shore-time activities to organize and – if you're lucky – will incorporate some wildlife-watching and glacier viewing into the package. Ziplining and rafting are a step up in price and adrenaline value. Flightseeing is expensive, but usually worth it.

Day hikes, paddles and tours can be organized at every port, but they are popular so it's worth spending a little time planning your activities.

Shopping

Most of Alaska's larger cruise-ship ports have an abundance of shops designed to lure in passengers with itchy credit cards and a couple of hours to kill before the ship leaves. But, to root out some of the more interesting stuff, you'll have to sift through the ubiquitous jewelry stores and gift shops in search of Alaska Native wood-carvers, local fish packers, hole-in-the-wall bookshops and esoteric artists.

Entertainment

Alaska has been enjoying a renaissance of indigenous culture in recent years. Look out for performances of Alaska Native music and dance in refurbished clan houses and heritage centers.

Several big festivals, such as Anchorage's Spenard Jazz Fest, augment an otherwise small and low-key music scene.

Eating

The Alaskan eating scene gets better and more sophisticated by the day, but it's also stridently casual, and while you may experience the occasional wait, reservations are rarely needed.

You'll encounter Pacific Rim cuisines, fresh game, local produce and the occasional sticker shock, but pretension and white-tablecloth attitude are foreign concepts here.

For many visitors, the first glance at the menu in an Alaskan restaurant sends them into a two-day fast. Meals in the 49th state are more expensive than most other places in the country because of the short tourist season and the high labor costs for wait staff and chefs.

Drinking & Nightlife

Rough-and-ready Alaskan bars, where the wallpaper looks radioactive and the conversation centers around gun calibers, are the stuff of legend. Notwithstanding, brewpubs plugging craft beer and microdistilleries plying cocktails have proliferated in the 2010s and most ports will have at least one. Top-notch coffee bars have a longer history. Indeed, Alaska is one of the most caffeinated states in the United States.

★ Microbreweries

Haines Brewing Company (p171)

Baranof Island Brewing Co (p124)

Midnight Sun Brewing Company (p232)

Skagway Brewing Company (p188)

From left: Kayaking, Kenai Fjords National Park (p210); Downtown Skagway (p173)

Plan Your Trip
Month by Month

CARLO EMANUELE BARBI/SHUTTERSTOCK ©

May
🍺 Great Alaskan Craftbeer & Home Brew Festival
In the third week of May, most of the state's microbrews compete for the honor of being named top suds at this festival (p170) in Haines.

✥ Little Norway Festival
To celebrate Norwegian Constitution Day on May 17, the residents of Petersburg dress up in traditional costumes. Events include a foot race, an all-you-can-eat fish dinner, and a long string of craft booths and beer tents.

June
☆ Sitka Summer Music Festival
Since 1972 this festival has been a most civilized gathering, with chamber music, concerts and lots of culture by the sea in beautiful Sitka. You'll need to book tickets in advance.

☆ Spenard Jazz Fest
Alaska is a lightly populated region with a lot of good musicians. Come and see the latest talent improvise with jazz riffs at this rapidly growing festival in Anchorage.

✥ Moose Pass Summer Solstice Festival
At this midsummer festival join in some small-town fun and games, not to mention a short parade and major boogying, down on the Kenai Peninsula in tiny Moose Pass.

July
✥ Fourth of July in Juneau
On the Fourth of July, Juneau residents head to the docks where the cruise ships line up. Dress up in your Mardi Gras finest, build a giant sand castle on Douglas Island, or simply enjoy the colorful parade.

Above: Craft beer

🏃 Mt Marathon Race
Take in the exhausting Fourth of July 3.1-mile run (p215) up Seward's 3022ft-high peak, which started in 1915. Join the fans as they crane their necks at the racers, many of whom make it up and back in well under an hour.

🎪 Southeast Alaska State Fair
Held in late July in Haines, this unique fair (p170) hosts a lively fiddler competition as well as the Ugliest Dog Contest – but make sure you don't miss the pig races.

August
✖ Blueberry Arts Festival
Blue tongues aren't the only thing you'll see at this Ketchikan festival (www.visit-ketchikan.com): slug races, pie-eating contests, a parade and even a poetry slam are all events held at this celebration of everyone's favorite berry.

★ Best Festivals
Spenard Jazz Festival

Mt Marathon Race

Great Alaskan Craftbeer & Home Brew Festival

Sitka Summer Music Festival

September
☆ Seward Music & Arts Festival
This family-friendly festival incorporates artists and more than 20 musical acts and theatrical companies, including circus lessons for the kiddos. Every year the townsfolk get together and paint a mural; come help them.

🏃 Running of the Boots
A half-mile boot race to the harbor, marking the transition from tourism to fishing season.

Above: Mt Marathon, Seward (p207)

Plan Your Trip
Get Inspired

Above: Gold nugget mining

Read

Ordinary Wolves (Seth Kantner; 2004) A tale about a white boy growing up in Bush Alaska, and his struggles to be accepted into the Native culture.

Coming into the Country (John McPhee; 1976) Powerful journalistic storytelling captures the offbeat and eccentric essence of Alaska's wild men and women.

Alaska: A History (Claus Naske and Herman Slotnick; 2011) The definitive back-story of this wonderful wilderness.

Klondike: The Last Great Gold Rush, 1896–1899 (Pierre Berton; 2001) Entertaining story of the north's most infamous gold rush and Alaska's part in it.

Watch

Grizzly Man (2005) Werner Herzog's darkly incisive documentary follows Timothy Treadwell's life (and death) among grizzlies.

30 Days of Night (2007) Vampires invade Utqiaġvik during the sunless days of deep winter.

Into the Wild (2007) Sean Penn's visually stunning adaptation of Jon Krakauer's book about the travels of Christopher McCandless.

Listen

Alaska (Maggie Rogers; 2016) Maggie Rogers may be from Maryland, but this intensely beautiful song perfectly captures the satori of an Alaskan hike.

The Wrangell Mountain Song (John Denver; 1976) Has that flowy, John Denver ballad magic, and it's all about the mountains that dominate the southeast Interior.

Alaska Highway (Dan Bern; 2001) A good roadtrip rocker.

Into the Wild (Eddie Vedder; 2007) The Pearl Jam frontman hits a few folksy notes on the soundtrack to the Sean Penn film.

Plan Your Trip
Choose Your Cruise

With their tightly packed jumble of islands and landscape-molding glaciers, Alaska's waterways hold an obvious allure. Add in the fact that many of Alaska's ports and cities aren't accessible by road, and you've got ample reasons to take to the high seas.

Picking Your Ship

Cruises in Alaska aren't just the preserve of retirees playing bingo on crowded sundecks. Sure, you can meet Mickey Mouse on a Disney cruise or stroll the deck with 3000 others on the *Emerald Princess*, but, for every aquatic skyscraper there's a smaller, cozier option. Some of the state's best and most adventurous cruises take place on boats carrying barely a dozen passengers that sail between little-visited ports stopping off in wilderness areas in between.

Cruise Ships

Some of the world's largest cruise-line companies ply the waters of Alaska, including Princess, Norwegian and Holland America. Most of the bigger ships are

pretty luxurious. However, these so-called resorts on the sea do have limitations. You won't be able to stop at as many places as you can on a smaller ship, and you'll be sharing your Alaska wilderness experience with up to 3000 other vacationers. Most large cruises stop only in the major ports of call, and generally start from Vancouver or Seattle. Excursions range from heli-seeing trips and zipline tours to guided hikes, kayaks and day trips to inland attractions such as Denali National Park. Costs for Alaskan cruises average around $120 a night (per person), but that does not include your flight to the port of embarkation. You can save good money (sometimes as much

Above: Cruise ships docked at Skagway (p173)

MARIDAV/SHUTTERSTOCK ©

as 50%) by hopping on a 'repositioning' cruise, which takes the boat back to its home port.

Check the small print about what's included in the price before you commit. Unless you're on a luxury cruise, you'll likely be paying extra for alcoholic beverages, shore excursions and tips. Then there's the spa, casino, gift shop and so on.

Here's how the big cruise companies break down:

Carnival (☎800-764-7419; www.carnival.com) Young people rule on these ships that aren't known for their environmental stewardship. The bonus: it's one of the cheapest options.

Celebrity (☎877-202-4345; www.celebrity cruises.com; ♠) Family-friendly and laid-back cruises on large 2000-plus-passenger ships.

Disney (☎800-951-3532; www.disneycruise. disney.go.com; ♠) Plenty of family fun and activities on a ship with good environmental credentials. Slightly pricier than other big-name favorites.

Holland America (☎877-932-4259; www. hollandamerica.com) One of the world's largest cruise companies and considered a classy option. It runs seven ships carrying 1500 to 2000 passengers in Alaska and owns the local Westmark Hotel chain.

Norwegian (☎866-234-7350; www.ncl.com) Many modern details make this a top pick for young couples.

Princess (☎800-774-6237; www.princess.com) The largest ship visiting Alaska is the 3082-capacity *Emerald Princess,* one of seven used by the company in the region. It also owns five plush hotels.

Regent Seven Seas Cruises (☎844-437-4368; www.rssc.com) Lauded as one of the most luxurious lines. Its two Alaska ships are smaller than average, carrying between 500 and 700 passengers.

Royal Caribbean (☎866-562-7625; www. royalcaribbean.com) Despite the name, it offers voyages to Alaska each summer on the ship *Radiance of the Seas*.

Small Ships

Just 3% of Alaska cruisers take a small-ship voyage. While you'll have tighter quarters, bumpier seas and fewer entertainment options than on the big boys, these vessels offer better chances of seeing wildlife. There will also be more land and kayak excursions, onboard naturalists (most of the time), good food, a more casual atmosphere (you can leave that blue sports coat at the office where it belongs) and a more intimate portrait of Alaska.

These boats sleep anywhere from 12 to 100 and are more likely to depart from within Alaska. While this is probably your best bet if you are looking to match comfort with quality and authentic experience, it does come with a steeper price tag: anything from $400 to $1200 a night.

Each small cruise ship is different. Here's a breakdown of some of our favorites:

Adventure Life Voyages (☎800-344-6118; www.adventure-life.com; per person 9-day cruise $3555-4965) Specializes in top-end trips up the

★ Best Cruise Lines

Un-Cruise Adventures (www.un-cruise.com)

Discovery Voyages (www.discovery voyages.com)

AdventureSmith Explorations (www. adventuresmithexplorations.com)

Disney (www.disneycruise.disney. go.com)

Inside Passage. Carries 42 to 74 passengers with activities such as snorkeling and paddleboarding.

AdventureSmith Explorations (☎877-620-2875; www.adventuresmithexplorations.com; per person $1595-10,900) This company offsets its carbon emissions and focuses on learning and adventure cruises in Southeast Alaska aboard its fleet of small boats (accommodating from 40 to 50 people). The boats have kayaks and small skiffs for numerous excursions that include

From left: Glacier Bay National Park (p146); Deck of Princess cruises ship

everything from kayaking in Glacier Bay National Park to wildlife-watching near Tracy Arm, the ABC Islands, Icy Straight, Misty Fiords and Frederick Sound. Most trips depart from Juneau.

Discovery Voyages (☏800-324-7602; www. discoveryvoyages.com; per person $2500-7150) Small 12-berth yacht that specializes in wildlife and photography tours of Prince William Sound – including stops in quiet ports like Cordova – an area few cruise ships visit. The yacht's small size enables it to negotiate narrow fjords and land in wilderness areas for hiking and kayaking. It has a good environmental record.

Lindblad National Geographic Expeditions (☏800-397-3348; www.expeditions.com; per person from $8990) Backed by National Geographic, Lindblad offers kayaking, wilderness walks, onboard naturalists and Zodiac excursions during eight-day cruises in the Southeast. Many trips include the airfare from Seattle and take visitors from Juneau through the Inside Passage. Plus you get the unique opportunity of pretending to be a National Geographic explorer for the week.

Un-Cruise Adventures (☏888-862-8881; www. un-cruise.com; per person $2995-8095) Offers themed seven- to 21-day cruises, carrying 22 to 86 passengers, that focus on whale-watching, Glacier Bay, wildlife-watching or adventure travel. The small boats (they call them yachts) have modern, elegant staterooms, and a naturalist is on board to teach you the ways of the Alaska wilderness. Most trips depart from Juneau, but one leaves from Seattle.

Picking Your Route

Inside Passage

This is the classic route, sailing from Seattle or Vancouver. The 'Great Land' coastal views don't start until Prince Rupert Island. Most trips stop in Ketchikan – with about as many bars as people and some fine totem poles – then continue to Juneau,

home to a great glacier and heli-seeing tours; Skagway, a gold-rush port with good hiking close to town; and the granddaddy attraction of Alaska cruises, Glacier Bay, where you'll see 11 tidewater glaciers spilling their icy wares into the sea. The pros: this is classic Alaska and the coast is rarely (if ever) out of sight. The cons: busy ports and ships following a well-trammeled path sometimes kill the wilderness feel.

Gulf of Alaska

This trip includes the Inside Passage but then continues to the Gulf of Alaska, with stops in Seward, the Hubbard Glacier and Whittier in Prince William Sound. While you get a broader picture of coastal Alaska on this one-way cruise and reap the benefit of pulling into some quieter ports, it also comes at a price, as you'll generally need to arrange flights from separate start and end points.

Bering Sea & Northwest Passage

These trips are more expensive and generally focus on natural and cultural history. People who enjoy learning on their vacations will like this trip, with stops in the Pribilof Islands, Nome and, on the really expensive cruises, King Island.

Since the mid-2010s some ships have started to ply the Northwest Passage (now partly ice-free in August and early September), sailing all the way to Greenland or, in some cases, New York. In 2016 the first luxury cruise liner, *Crystal Serenity,* began offering a 32-day Anchorage–New York cruise with stops in Kodiak, Dutch Harbor and Nome en route. Prices start at $22,000. European cruise companies such as Ponant and Hapag-Lloyd send smaller boats on Northwest Passage tours, stopping in Nome and Utqiaġvik (Barrow).

RUBEN M RAMOS/SHUTTERSTOCK ©

Cruisetours

These trips give you the chance to get off the boat for about half of your journey. Most begin with the Inside Passage cruise, then head out on a tour bus or (even better) the Alaska Railroad, with stops in Talkeetna, Denali National Park, Fairbanks, Eagle or the Copper River. Big cruise companies such as Princess and Holland America have all-inclusive hotels in these destinations (basically cruise ships without the rocking).

Less-Visited Ports

Petersburg Few large ships can navigate the Wrangell Narrows, and fewer still can dock in Petersburg's shallow harbor, meaning this wonderful Norwegian-flavored town only welcomes about two small ships a week in season.

Wrangell Rough-and-ready Wrangell is the antithesis of a cruise port. Good job too, as it only gets about one cruise ship docking a week – and a small one at that.

Nome Although it's now included on the pioneering Northwest Passage cruises, this erstwhile gold-rush outpost still only gets a half-dozen cruise ships stopping in any given year.

Dutch Harbor The treeless outpost of the Aleutian Islands, with its Russian church and half-forgotten WWII history, gets a dozen small cruises ships stopping a year, plus twice-a-month visits from the MV *Tustumena* ferry.

Yakutat This tiny fishing town in the Gulf of Alaska gets just one cruise-boat call a year, the equally tiny *Silver Discoverer*, which briefly disgorges its 120 passengers.

Above: Dutch Harbor, Unalaska Island

Plan Your Trip
Sustainable Cruising

FLORIDASTOCK/SHUTTERSTOCK ©

While all travel causes certain environmental and cultural impacts, by their very size, cruise ships leave a heavy wake. But you can make a difference.

The Impact
Pollution

A large cruise liner like the *Queen Mary* emits 1lb (0.45kg) of carbon dioxide per mile, while a long-haul flight releases about 0.6lb (0.27kg). In Alaska, an 11-day cruise from Seattle to Juneau on a small boat with around 100 guests will burn about 71 gallons of fuel per passenger, releasing some 0.77 tons of carbon into the air per passenger. The flight from Seattle to Juneau releases 0.17 tons of carbon per passenger. Cruise ships also release around 17% of total worldwide nitrogen oxide emissions, and create around 50 tons of garbage on a one-week voyage. In 2013, the US Environmental Protection Agency estimated that cruise ships produce about 1 billion gallons of sewage a year.

Cultural Impact

While cruise lines generate money and jobs for their ports of call, thousands of people arriving at once can change the character of a town in a second. Big cruise ports such as Juneau and Ketchikan see six or seven cruise ships a day – that's around 15,000 people, or close to one million visitors in a five-month season. And with such short stays, there is little of that cultural interchange that makes travel an enriching endeavor for both tourist and 'town-y.'

Cruise Ships in Glacier Bay

Glacier Bay has seen several disputes between the cruise-ship industry and environmentalists. After the number of whales seen in the national park dropped dramatically in 1978, the National Park Service (NPS) reduced ship visits during the

JAYLI/SHUTTERSTOCK ©

three-month season. But the cruise-ship industry lobbied the US Congress and the NPS in 1996 to OK a 30% increase in vessels allowed in the bay. Environmentalists sued, and eventually a compromise of two large cruise ships per day was hammered out.

What You Can Do

As consumer pressure grows, more and more ships are being equipped with new wastewater treatment facilities, LED lighting and solar panels. In several Alaska ports (as well as San Francisco, Vancouver and Seattle) 'cold-ironing' allows ships to plug into local power supplies and avoid leaving the engine running while in port. Knowing that customers care about these things has an effect on cruise-ship operations. There are also organizations that review the environmental records of cruise lines and ships. These include the following:

Friends of the Earth (www.foe.org/cruisereport card) Gives out grades for environmental impact.

★ Most Sustainable Cruise Companies

According to Friends of the Earth, the most sustainable large cruise-ship company is Disney, followed by Holland America and Norwegian. See p26 for cruise-company details.

US Centers for Disease Control & Prevention (www.cdc.gov) Follow the travel links to the well-regarded sanitation ratings for ships calling into US ports.
World Travel Awards (www.worldtravelawards. com) Annual awards for the 'World's Leading Green Cruise Line.'

Be mindful of your impact on the communities you visit. Support independently owned businesses and look for opportunities to interact with local culture.

From left: Cruise ship pool deck; Cruise-ship passengers take the Polar Bear Dip

Plan Your Trip
Family Time Ashore

SAM WASSON PHOTOGRAPHY ©

Everybody is a kid in Alaska. Whether it's sitting by a stream full of bright red salmon or watching a bald eagle winging its way across an open sky, encounters with nature's wonders will captivate five-year-olds just as much as their parents.

Outdoor Activities

If your family enjoys the outdoors, Alaska can be a relatively affordable place once you've arrived. A cruise cabin can work out cheaper than a hotel room, and hiking and wildlife-watching are free. Even fishing is free for children, since anglers under 16 years don't need a fishing license in Alaska.

The key to any Alaskan hike is to match it to your child's ability and level of endurance. It's equally important to select one that has an interesting aspect to it – a glacier, a ruined gold mine, waterfalls or a remote cabin to stop at for lunch.

Paddling with children involves a greater risk than hiking due to the frigid temperature of most water in Alaska. You simply don't want to tip at any cost. Flat, calm water should be the rule. Needless to say, all rentals should come with paddles and life jackets that fit your child. If in doubt, hire a guide to go along with you.

Children marvel at watching wildlife in its natural habitat but may not always have the patience for a long wait before something pops out of the woods. In July and August, however, you can count on seeing a lot of fish in a salmon stream, a wide variety of marine life in tidal pools, and bald eagles where the birds are known to congregate. Marine wildlife boat tours work out better than many park shuttles because, let's face it, a boat trip is a lot more fun than a bus ride. Nature tours that are done in vans are also ideal for children as they stop often and usually include short walks.

KONRAD WOTHE/LOOK-FOTO/GETTY IMAGES ©

Eating Out

Like elsewhere in the USA, most Alaskan restaurants welcome families and tend to cater for children, with high chairs and kids' menus that offer smaller portions and reduced prices, and waiters quick with a cloth when somebody spills their drink. Upscale restaurants where an infant would be frowned upon are limited to a handful of places in Anchorage. Salmon bakes are a fun, casual and colorful way to introduce Alaska's seafood, especially since they often come with corn and potatoes – familiar items at any barbecue.

For a Rainy Day

Anchorage Museum (www.anchoragemuseum. org; 625 C St; adult/child $15/7; 9am-6pm summer;) Tons of stuff for kids, including an Imaginarium Discovery Center and planetarium.

Alaska Sealife Center (800-224-2525; www. alaskasealife.org; 301 Railway Ave; adult/child $25/13; 9am-9pm Mon-Thu, 8am-9pm Fri-Sun;) Diving seabirds, swimming sea lions and

★ Best Cruise Lines for Families

Disney (p26)

Carnival (p26)

Celebrity (p26)

Holland America (p26)

a tide-pool touch tank are found in Seward's marine research center.

Dimond Park Aquatic Center (907-586-2782; www.juneau.org/parkrec; 3045 Riverside Dr; adult/child $8/3; 6-10:30am Mon, 6am-8pm Tue-Fri, 9am-6pm Sat, noon-6pm Sun;) Flume slides, bubble benches, tumble buckets and interactive water sprays in Juneau.

Sitka Sound Science Center (www.sitka science.org; 801 Lincoln St; $5; 9am-4pm;) Five aquariums, three touch tanks and a working hatchery.

From left: Anchorage Museum (p222); Alaska Sealife Center (p212), Seward

Explore Ashore

Pike Place Market is 3 miles southeast of Smith Cove cruise ship terminal (Pier 91), easily accessible by taxi or Metro buses 24 and 19. Bus fares are a flat $2.75.

Bell St cruise port (Pier 66) is just a 10-minute walk from the market.

ℹ Need to Know

Map p52; www.pikeplacemarket.org; 85 Pike St; ☺9am-6pm Mon-Sat, to 5pm Sun; 🚉Westlake ⚲

✕ Take a Break

Head to Beecher's Handmade Cheese (p58) for savory snacks. The mac-and-cheese is a Seattle rite of passage.

★ Top Tip

Join a Seattle walking tour; plenty of them start in or around the market.

Corner & Sanitary Market Buildings

Across Pike Pl from the Main Arcade are the 1912 Corner & Sanitary Market Buildings, so named because they were the first of the market buildings in which live animals were prohibited. It's now a maze of ethnic groceries and great little eateries.

Post Alley

Between the Corner Market and the Triangle Building, narrow Post Alley (named for its hitching posts) is lined with shops and restaurants. In Lower Post Alley, beside the market sign, is the **LaSalle Hotel**, which was the first bordello north of Yesler Way. The building, rehabbed in 1977, now houses commercial and residential space. Post Alley continues on the southern side

of Pike St where you'll find the beautifully disgusting **gum wall** (Map p52; Post Alley; 🚉University St).

New MarketFront

In a city as fast-moving as Seattle, not even a historical heirloom like Pike Place Market escapes a makeover. In 2017, a 30,000-sq-ft extension called MarketFront opened showcasing three dozen new stalls, public art, low-income housing and an artisan chocolate maker.

HUYENHOANG/SHUTTERSTOCK ©

Space Needle

Whether you're from Alabama or Timbuktu, your abiding image of Seattle will probably be of the Space Needle, a streamlined, modern-before-its-time tower that has been the city's defining symbol for more than 50 years.

Great For...

☑ Don't Miss

Photograph the Needle reflected in the multi-colored walls of the Museum of Pop Culture.

Space Needle and Seattle skyline

Explore Ashore

The Space Needle is in the downtown area less than 1 mile north of Pier 66 and 2 miles southeast of Pier 99. Metro buses 24 and 19. ($2.75) run from the latter or a taxi costs around $8.

ℹ Need to Know

Map p56; ☎206-905-2100; www.space needle.com; 400 Broad St; adult/child $22/14; ⊙9:30am-11pm Mon-Thu, to 11:30pm Fri & Sat, 9am-11pm Sun; ⑤Seattle Center

In 2017–18, the Space Needle underwent the most expensive renovation in its 55-year history.

Admiring From the Outside

Standing apart from the rest of Seattle's skyscrapers, the Needle often looks taller than it actually is. On its completion in 1962, it was the highest structure west of the Mississippi River, topping 605ft, though it has since been easily surpassed (it's currently the seventh-tallest structure in Seattle).

Zipping Up the Elevators

The part of the Needle that's visible above ground weighs an astounding 3700 tons. Most visitors head for the 520ft-high observation deck on zippy elevators that

Space Needle observation deck

ascend to the top in a mere 41 seconds. The 360-degree views of Seattle and its surrounding water and mountains are suitably fabulous.

Observation Deck

The observation deck has a cafe, copious wall-mounted facts, free telescopes and some interesting touch screens. One takes you on a 'virtual' walk through Pike Place Market, Seattle Aquarium and some of Lake Union's houseboats. Another is a high-powered telescope that you can move around and zoom in and out to see close-up images of the street below.

The Views

New floor-to-ceiling windows fitted in 2017–18 have enhanced views from the observation deck replacing the enclosed wire fence of yore. The vista is broad: on clear days, you can see three Cascade volcanoes (Mts Rainier, Baker and St Helen's), the Olympic range, the jagged coastline of Puget Sound and the sparkling surfaces of Lakes Union and Washington fanning out in the haze.

✕ Take a Break

While the Needle's restaurant is being refurbished, hit the Seattle Center's Armory food court for lunch.

★ Top Tip

Buy a joint ticket ($38) for entry to the wonderful Chihuly Garden & Glass (p51) next door.

VACCLAV/SHUTTERSTOCK ©

Starbuck's Reserve Roastery & Tasting Room

PEPPINUZZO/SHUTTERSTOCK ©

Coffee Culture

Seattle practically invented modern coffee culture. The ground was broken by Starbucks in the 1970s, but has since moved onward and upward with an emerging army of third-wave micro-roasters.

Great For...

☑ Don't Miss

Taking home your favorite blend from the 'scoop bar' at Starbucks Reserve Roastery.

When the first Starbucks opened in Pike Place Market in 1971, Seattle was suddenly the center of the coffee universe.

After Starbucks came the 'third wave': coffee shops that buy fair-trade coffee with traceable origins and concoct it through a micro-managed in-house roasting process that pays attention to everything from the coffee's bean quality to its 'taste notes.' These shops are now as ubiquitous as Starbucks, though they remain independent and adhere strictly to their original manifesto: quality not quantity.

Starbucks

It's practically impossible to walk through the door of the world's oldest **Starbucks** (Map p52; www.1912pike.com; 1912 Pike Pl; ⊙6am-9pm; ⺫Westlake) in Pike Place Market

HAL BERGMAN PHOTOGRAPHY/GETTY IMAGES ©

Explore Ashore

Hit **Seattle Coffee Works** (Map p52; www.seattlecoffeeworks.com; 107 Pike St; ⏱7am-7pm Mon-Fri, 8am-7pm Sat, 9am-6pm Sun; 🛜; 🚊West-lake) where you can taste various local roasts at the 'slow bar'.

❶ Need to Know
Average price for cup of coffee $2.25.

without appearing in someone's Facebook photo, so dense is the tourist traffic.

Almost as popular is the far newer **Starbucks Reserve Roastery & Tasting Room** (Map p52; ☎206-624-0173; http://roastery. starbucks.com; 1124 Pike St; coffees $3-12; ⏱7am-11pm; 🚊Pike & Boren) in Capitol Hill, a huge, hip high church to the joys of coffee drinking that is the antithesis of everything Starbucks-y that has gone before.

Uptown Espresso

Some say latte art owes much of its early inspiration to the velvet foam developed at Uptown Espresso, the Seattle coffee veteran that opened its first **cafe** (Map p56; ☎20 6-285-3757; 525 Queen Anne Ave N; ⏱5am-10pm Mon-Thu, 5am-11pm Fri, 6am-11pm Sat, 6am-10pm Sun; 🛜; 🚊13) in Lower Queen Anne in the

mid-1980s. It now has eight locations and is known for its generous opening hours.

Zeitgeist Coffee

Possibly Seattle's best (if also busiest) indie coffee bar, **Zeitgeist** (Map p52; ☎206-583-0497; www.zeitgeistcoffee.com; 171 S Jackson St; ⏱6am-7pm Mon-Fri, 7am-7pm Sat, 8am-6pm Sun; 🛜; 🚊Occidental Mall) brews smooth doppio macchiatos to go with its sweet almond croissants and other luscious baked goods. The atmosphere is trendy industrial, with brick walls and large windows for people-watching. Soups, salads and sandwiches are also on offer.

Coffee Chains

Look out for excellent Seattle-only coffee chains like **Storyville** (Map p52; ☎206-780-5777; www.storyville.com; 94 Pike St; ⏱6:59am-6pm; 🛜; 🚊Westlake), **Espresso Vivace** (www. espressovivace.com; 532 Broadway E; ⏱6am-11pm; 🛜; 🚊Capitol Hill) and **Victrola** (Map p52; www.victrolacoffee.com; 310 E Pike St; ⏱6:30am-8pm Mon-Fri, 7:30am-8pm Sat & Sun; 🚊10).

Historical Pioneer Square Circuit

Pioneer Square is Seattle's historic red-bricked quarter, the original downtown that was saved from the demolition ball by conservationists in the 1960s. This circular walk starts next to the transport hub of King Street.

Start King Street Station
Distance 1 mile
Duration 1 hour

Classic Photo

The decorative facade of the Pioneer Building with a totem pole in the foreground.

2 Admire urban beauty at **Pioneer Square Park** with its Eiffel-esque iron pergola and the Richardsonian Romanesque Pioneer Building.

3 Yesler Way holds the dubious distinction of being the nation's original 'skid row.'

5 Surrounded by ivy-covered edifices, **Occidental Park** is an outdoor emporium of food carts and old-fashioned games.

James St

2nd Ave

Yesler Way

1st Ave S

Occidental Ave S

S Main St

Nord Al

Occidental Square

S Jackson St

Occidental Mall

Alaskan Way Viaduct

S King St

1st Ave S

Occidental Ave S

Ⓝ

0
0
200 m
0.1 miles

4 Smith Tower (p50) was erected by LC Smith, a man who built his fortune on typewriters (Smith-Corona) and guns (Smith & Wesson).

6 Fill in your historical gaps at the intellectually stimulating **Klondike Gold Rush National Historical Park** (p51).

④

Yesler Way

2nd Ave S

S Washington St

2nd Ave Extended S

3rd Ave S

4th Ave S

PIONEER SQUARE

S Main St

1 Start at **King Street Station**, Seattle's main railway terminus, recently returned to its Gilded Age glory.

⑥

S Jackson St

2nd Ave S

START   FINISH

①

S King St

King St Station (Amtrak)

Take a Break...
Plug into the spirit of the times at **Zeitgeist Coffee** (p45).

Downtown Architecture

Downtown Seattle isn't the city's most buzzing neighborhood, but its tall, modern edifices contain some fascinating architectural details rarely spared a glance by the area's office workers.

Start Arctic Building
Distance 2 miles
Duration 1 hour

6 The **Cobb Building** is one of downtown's more ornate edifices, decorated with sculpted heads of a Native American chief.

5 Walk into the glass-enclosed lobby of **Benaroya Concert Hall** and look up at the two giant 20ft-long Chihuly chandeliers.

4 1201 Third Avenue, nicknamed 'the Spark Plug,' acts like a mirror to the surrounding mountains.

7 Rainier Tower, with its precarious-looking inverted base, has been nicknamed the 'Beaver Building.'

8 Enter the domain of the Jazz Age **Fairmont Olympic Hotel**, with its plush lobby replete with chandeliers and marble.

3 Pop inside the post-modern **Seattle Central Library** to see how good architecture can combine practicality and beauty.

2 Ascend to the 73rd floor of the **Columbia Center**, the tallest building on the West Coast.

Take a Break...

There's a branch of **Top Pot Hand-forged Doughnuts** next to the Arctic Building. Say no more!

1 Kick off at the **Arctic Building** built in 1917 as a club for Klondike Gold Rush veterans.

◉ SIGHTS

◉ Downtown

Seattle Art Museum   Museum

(SAM; Map p52; ☑206-654-3210; www.seattle
artmuseum.org; 1300 1st Ave; adult/student
$24.95/14.95; ☉10am-5pm Wed & Fri-Sun, to
9pm Thu; ℞University St) While not compa-
rable with the big guns in New York and
Chicago, Seattle Art Museum is no slouch.
Always re-curating its art collection with
new acquisitions and imported temporary
exhibitions, it's known for its extensive
Native American artifacts and work from
the local Northwest school, in particular
by Mark Tobey (1890–1976). Modern
American art is also well represented, and
the museum gets some exciting traveling
exhibitions (including Yayoi Kusama's
infinity mirrors).

◉ Pioneer Square

Pioneer Square
Historical District   Area

(Map p52; btwn Alaskan Way S, S King St, 5th
Ave S, 2nd Ave ext & Columbia St; ℞Pioneer Sq)

Many important architectural heirlooms
are concentrated in Pioneer Sq, the
district that sprang up in the wake of the
1889 Great Fire. Instantly recognizable
by its handsome redbrick buildings, the
neighborhood's predominant architectural style is Richardsonian Romanesque,
strongly influenced by America's Chicago
School.

Smith Tower   Landmark

(Map p52; ☑206-622-4004; www.smithtower.
com; 506 2nd Ave; observatory tickets from $12;
☉10am-10pm; ℞Pioneer Sq) A mere dwarf
amid Seattle's impressive modern stash
of skyscrapers, the 42-story neoclassical
Smith Tower was, for half a century after
its construction in 1914, the tallest building
west of Chicago. The beaux arts–inspired
lobby is paneled in onyx and marble, and
the brass-and-copper elevator is still man-
ually operated by a uniformed attendant.
You can visit the observation deck in the
35th-floor Observatory (formerly called
the Chinese Room), which has an ornate
wooden ceiling.

Chihuly Garden & Glass

Understand

The Klondike Gold Rush Started Here

Ironically, the event that propelled Seattle from a peripheral frontier town into the undisputed capital of the Pacific Northwest was sparked thousands of miles away in the frozen wastes of the Yukon in Canada. When gold was discovered in Klondike Creek in 1896, Seattle quickly established itself as the supply center and embarkation point for tens of thousands of optimistic prospectors heading north through the Inside Passage to Alaska. Outfitters sprang up all over Pioneer Square as the port heaved daily with ships full of starry-eyed dreamers (and scoundrels). Engrained in the national consciousness like no other gold rush before or since, the spirit of Klondike has been preserved in a unique US National Historic Park split between dual outposts in Seattle and Skagway, Alaska. The park's Seattle museum in Pioneer Square is a cerebral feast that follows the stories of five stampeders from rags to (occasional) riches in fascinating detail.

State building in Pioneer Square Historical District
NEELSKY/SHUTTERSTOCK ©

◎ Belltown & Seattle Center

Chihuly Garden & Glass Museum
(Map p56; ☑206-753-4940; www.chihulygarden andglass.com; 305 Harrison St; adult/child $24/14; ◷10am-8pm Sun-Thu, to 9pm Fri & Sat; ⑤Seattle Center) Opened in 2012 and reinforcing Seattle's position as the Venice of North America, this exquisite exposition of the life and work of dynamic local sculptor Dale Chihuly is possibly the finest collection of curated glass art you'll ever see. It shows off Chihuly's creative designs in a suite of interconnected dark and light rooms before depositing you in an airy glass atrium and – finally – a landscaped garden in the

shadow of the Space Needle. Glassblowing demonstrations are a highlight.

Museum of Pop Culture Museum
(Map p56; ☑206-770-2700; www.mopop.org; 325 5th Ave N; adult/child $25/16; ◷10am-7pm Jun-Aug, to 5pm Sep-May; ⑤Seattle Center) The Museum of Pop Culture (formerly EMP, the 'Experience Music Project') is an inspired marriage between super-modern architecture and legendary rock-and-roll history that sprang from the imagination (and pocket) of Microsoft co-creator Paul Allen. Inside its avant-garde frame, designed by Canadian architect Frank Gehry, you can tune into the famous sounds of Seattle

Downtown Seattle

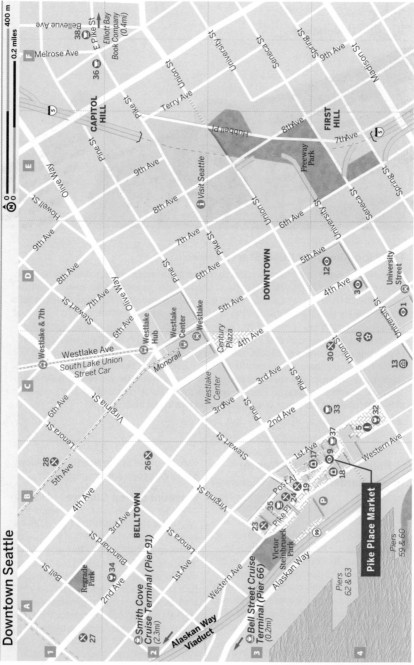

Pike Place Market

0 ━━━ 400 m
0 ━━━ 0.2 miles

Elliott Bay Book Company (0.4mi)

CAPITOL HILL

DOWNTOWN

FIRST HILL

Freeway Park

Visit Seattle

Westlake & 7th

Westlake Ave
South Lake Union Street Car

Westlake Hub

Westlake Center

Monorail

Century Plaza

Westlake Center

BELLTOWN

Smith Cove Cruise Terminal (Pier 91) (2.3mi)

Bell Street Cruise Terminal (Pier 66) (0.2mi)

Alaskan Way Viaduct

Regrade Park

Victor Steinbrueck Park

Post Alley

Pike Pl

Piers 62 & 63

Piers 59 & 60

University Street

Melrose Ave
Bellevue Ave
E Pike St

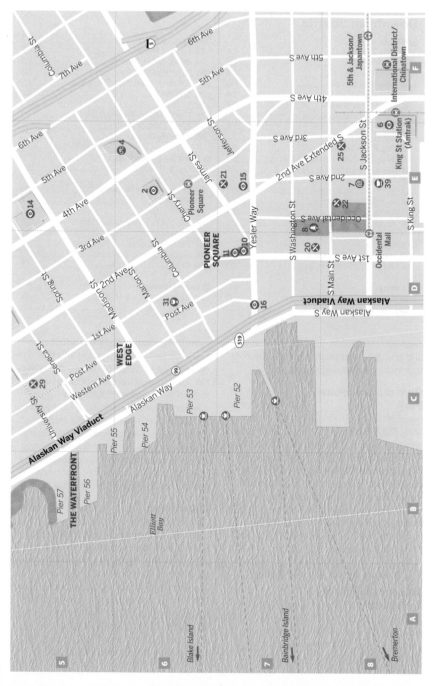

Downtown Seattle

(with an obvious bias toward Jimi Hendrix and grunge) or attempt to imitate the masters in the Interactive Sound Lab.

Olympic Sculpture Park
Park, Sculpture

(Map p56; 2901 Western Ave; ◎sunrise-sunset; 🚍13) FREE This smart urban-renewal project and outpost of the Seattle Art Museum was inaugurated in 2007 to widespread local approval. The terraced park is landscaped over railway tracks and overlooks Puget Sound with the distant Olympic Mountains winking on the horizon. Joggers and dog walkers meander daily through its zigzagging paths, enjoying over 20 pieces of modern sculpture.

◎ Queen Anne & Lake Union

Museum of History & Industry
Museum

(MOHAI; Map p56; ☎206-324-1126; www. mohai.org; 860 Terry Ave N; adult/child under 14yr $19.95/free; ◎10am-5pm, 10am-8pm 1st Thu of month; 🚻; 🚍Lake Union Park) Almost

everything you need to know about erstwhile Seattle is crammed into the refurbished Museum of History & Industry (MOHAI), the centerpiece of Lake Union Park in the emerging South Lake Union neighborhood. In operation since the early 1950s, and with an astounding archive of over four million objects to draw upon, MOHAI displays its rich stash of historical booty in an impressively repurposed naval armory building. If only school history lessons could've been this riveting.

Lake Union
Lake

(Map p56; 🚍Lake Union Park) Unifying Seattle's various bodies of water, freshwater Lake Union was carved by glacial erosion 12,000 years ago. Native American Duwamish tribes once subsisted on its then-isolated shores, but 21st-century Lake Union is backed by densely packed urban neighborhoods and is linked to both Lake Washington and Puget Sound by the Lake Washington Ship Canal (built as part of a huge engineering project in the 1910s).

Lake Union

ⓖ TOURS

Seattle Free
Walking Tours   Walking
(www.seattlefreewalkingtours.org) `FREE` A nonprofit set up by a couple of world travelers
and Seattle residents who were impressed
with the free walking tours offered in various
European cities. An intimate two-hour walk
takes in Pike Pl, the waterfront and Pioneer
Square. Each tour has different starting
times and meeting places; check online. If
you have a rip-roaring time, there's a sug-
gested $15 donation. Reserve online.

Savor Seattle   Food & Drink
(☑206-209-5485; www.savorseattletours.com)
These guys lead a handful of gastronomic
tours, the standout being the two-hour
Booze-n-Bites, which runs daily at 4pm
from the corner of Western Ave and Virginia
St. It costs $65 and visits such culinary bas-
tions as **Von's 1000 Spirits** (Map p52; ☑206-
621-8667; www.vons1000spirits.com; 1225 1st
Ave; pizzas $19; ⊙11am-midnight Sun-Thu, 11am-
1am Fri & Sat; ⺫University St). Prepare yourself
for some sublime cocktails, wine and food.

ⓐ SHOPPING

REI   Outdoor Equipment, Clothing
(Map p56; ☑206-323-8333; www.rei.com; 222
Yale Ave N; ⊙9am-9pm Mon-Sat, 10am-7pm Sun;
⺫70) As much an adventure as a shopping
experience, the state-of-the-art megastore
of America's largest consumer co-op has
its own climbing wall – a 65ft rock pinnacle
to the side of the store's entryway. The wall
offers various climbing options from open
climbs to private instruction. Check the
website for details.

Elliott Bay
Book Company   Books
(☑206-624-6600; www.elliottbaybook.com; 1521
10th Ave; ⊙10am-10pm Mon-Thu, to 11pm Fri &
Sat, to 9pm Sun; ⺫Broadway & Pine) Seattle's most beloved bookstore offers over
150,000 titles in a large, airy, wood-beamed
space with cozy nooks that can inspire
hours of serendipitous browsing. Biblio-
philes will be further satisfied with regular
book readings and signings.

Seattle Center

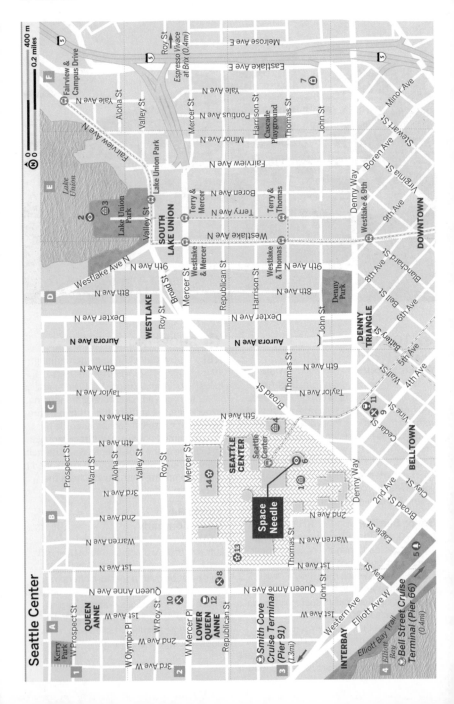

Kerry Park

QUEEN ANNE

LOWER QUEEN ANNE

Smith Cove Cruise Terminal (Pier 91) (1.3mi)

INTERBAY

Bell Street Cruise Terminal (Pier 66) (0.4mi)

Elliott Bay Trail

SEATTLE CENTER

Seattle Center

Space Needle

WESTLAKE

AURORA AVE N

Lake Union

Lake Union Park

SOUTH LAKE UNION

Fairview & Campus Drive

Espresso Vivace at Brix (0.4mi)

Roy St

Melrose Ave E

Eastlake Ave E

Cascade Playground

DENNY TRIANGLE

Denny Park

DOWNTOWN

BELLTOWN

400 m
0.2 miles

Seattle Center

Old Seattle Paperworks
Posters, Magazines

(Map p52; 1501 Pike Place Market, downstairs; ◷10:30am-5pm; 🚇Westlake) If you like decorating your home with old magazine covers from *Life, Time* and *Rolling Stone,* or have a penchant for art-deco tourist posters from the 1930s, or are looking for that rare Hendrix concert flyer from 1969, this is your nirvana. It's in Pike Place Market's Down Under section.

Made in Washington
Gifts & Souvenirs

(Map p52; 📞206-467-0788; www.madeinwash ington.com; 1530 Post Alley; ◷10am-6pm; 🚇Westlake) If you're looking for something authentically Northwest, head to Made in Washington. One of several locations around the city, this one in Pike Place Market stocks arts and crafts, T-shirts, coffee and chocolate, smoked salmon, regional wines, books and other creative ephemera made in the Evergreen state.

🅧 EATING

If you want to get a real taste for eating in Seattle, dip your metaphorical finger into Pike Place Market. This clamorous confederation of small-time farmers, artisan bakers, cheese producers, fishers and family-run fruit stalls is the gastronomic bonanza that every locavore dreams about, and its cheap, sustainable, locally produced food ends up on the tables of just about every Seattle restaurant that matters.

🅧 Downtown

Beecher's Handmade Cheese
Deli $

(Map p52; www.beechershandmadecheese.com; 1600 Pike Pl; snacks $3-5; ◷9am-6pm; 🚇Westlake) ✔ Artisan beer, artisan coffee...next up, Seattle brings you artisan cheese and it's made as you watch in this always-crowded Pike Place nook, where you can buy all kinds of cheese-related paraphernalia. As for that long, snaking, almost permanent queue – that's people lining up for the wonderful homemade mac 'n' cheese that comes in two different-sized tubs and is simply divine.

Piroshky Piroshky
Bakery $

(Map p52; www.piroshkybakery.com; 1908 Pike Pl; snacks $3-6; ◷8am-6pm; 🚇Westlake) Piroshky knocks out its delectable sweet and savory Russian pies and pastries in a space about the size of a walk-in closet. Get the savory smoked-salmon pâté or the sauerkraut with cabbage and onion, and follow it with the chocolate-cream hazelnut roll or a fresh rhubarb piroshki.

Wild Ginger
Asian $$

(Map p52; 📞206-623-4450; www.wildginger. net; 1401 3rd Ave; mains $19-34; ◷11:30am-11pm Mon-Sat, 4-9pm Sun; 🚇University St) All around the Pacific Rim – via China, Indonesia, Malaysia, Vietnam and Seattle, of course – is

Pioneer Square Historical District (p50)

the wide-ranging theme at this highly popular downtown fusion restaurant. The signature fragrant duck goes down nicely with a glass of Riesling. The restaurant also provides food for the swanky Triple Door (p57) dinner club downstairs.

Pink Door Ristorante
Italian $$$

(Map p52; ☏206-443-3241; www.thepinkdoor. net; 1919 Post Alley; mains $18-29; ⊙11:30am-10pm Mon-Thu, 11:30am-11pm Fri & Sat, 4-10pm Sun; ☒Westlake) A restaurant like no other, the Pink Door is probably the only place in the US (the world?) where you can enjoy fabulous *linguine alle vongole* (pasta with clams and pancetta) and other Italian favorites while watching live jazz, burlesque cabaret, or – we kid you not – a trapeze artist swinging from the 20ft ceiling.

✪ Pioneer Square

Salumi Artisan Cured Meats
Sandwiches $

(Map p52; ☏206-621-8772; www.salumicured meats.com; 309 3rd Ave S; sandwiches $10-14;

⊙11am-1:30pm Mon for takeout only, to 3:30pm Tue-Fri; ☒International District/Chinatown) With a shopfront as wide as a smart car and a following as large as the Seattle Mariners, Salumi is a well-known vortex of queues. But it's worth the wait for the legendary Italian-quality salami and cured-meat sandwiches (grilled lamb, pork shoulder, meatballs) that await you at the counter. Grab one and go! Fresh homemade gnocchi is available most Tuesdays.

Il Corvo Pasta
Italian $

(Map p52; ☏206-538-0999; www.ilcorvopasta. com; 217 James St; pasta $10; ⊙11am-3pm Mon-Fri; ☒Pioneer Sq) A unique hole-in-the-wall, pasta-only place with limited seating and a high turnover of office workers on their lunch breaks. Join the perennial queue, order one of three daily pastas with sauces and grab a seat (if there's one available). You have to bus your own table, Seattle-style, at the end. Wine and bread provide welcome accompaniments.

Grand Central Baking Co
Soup, Sandwiches $

(Map p52; ☑206-622-3644; www.grandcentral bakery.com; Grand Central Arcade, 214 1st Ave S; sandwiches $4-10; ☺7am-5pm Mon-Fri, 8am-4pm Sat; ⓠOccidental Mall) Grand Central (located in the eponymous building) is considered one of the best bakeries in Seattle. Its artisan breads can be bought whole or sliced up for sandwiches in its cafe and enjoyed in the redbrick confines of the Grand Central mall, or at a Euro-chic table in Occidental Park outside. Beware the lunchtime queues.

London Plane
Cafe, Deli $$

(Map p52; ☑206-624-1374; www.thelondonplane seattle.com; 300 Occidental Ave S; small plates $7-20; ☺8am-5pm Mon-Tue, 8am-9pm Wed-Fri, 9am-9pm Sat, 9am-5pm Sun; ⓠOccidental Mall) ✐ Matt Dillon (the Seattle chef, not the Hollywood actor) moved less than a block from his established restaurant, Bar Sajor, to open London Plane, a hybrid cafe, flower shop, deli and breakfast spot that maintains the French country kitchen feel that has become Dillon's trademark.

ⓧ Belltown & Seattle Center

Top Pot Hand-Forged Doughnuts
Cafe $

(Map p52; www.toppotdoughnuts.com; 2124 5th Ave; doughnuts from $1.50; ☺6am-7pm Mon-Fri, 7am-7pm Sat & Sun; ⓠ13) Sitting pretty in a glass-fronted former car showroom with art-deco signage and immense bookshelves, Top Pot's flagship cafe produces the Ferraris of the doughnut world. It might have morphed into a 20-outlet chain in recent years, but its hand-molded collection of sweet rings are still – arguably – worth visiting Seattle for alone. The coffee's pretty potent too.

Tavolàta
Italian $$

(Map p52; ☑206-838-8008; 2323 2nd Ave; pasta dishes $17-21, mains $24-28; ☺5-11pm; ⓠ13) Owned by top Seattle chef Ethan Stowell, Tavolàta is a dinner-only, Italian-inspired eatery emphasizing homemade pasta dishes. Keeping things simple with venison-

stuffed ravioli and *linguine nero* (clams with black pasta), the results are as good as those found in Italy – and there's no praise finer than that!

Serious Pie
Pizza $$

(Map p52; ☑206-838-7388; www.tomdouglas. com; 316 Virginia St; pizzas $17-19; ☺11am-11pm; ⓠWestlake) In the crowded confines of Serious Pie you can enjoy beautifully blistered pizza bases topped with such unconventional ingredients as clams, potatoes, nettles, soft eggs, truffle cheese and more. Be prepared to share a table and meet a few Seattleites. There's another location at 401 Westlake Ave N.

Tilikum Place Cafe
Bistro, Brunch $$

(Map p56; ☑206-282-4830; www.tilikumplace cafe.com; 407 Cedar St; brunch mains $9-14; ☺11am-10pm Mon-Fri, 8am-10pm Sat & Sun; ⓠ3) Sometimes old Belltown and new Belltown sit bumper to bumper, and the juxtaposition is never more marked than on Cedar St, where the suave, pseudo-Parisian Tilikum Place lies next door to 90-year-old dive bar, the **Five Point Café** (Map p56; ☑206-448-9993; www.the5pointcafe.com; 415 Cedar St; ☺24hr; ⓠ3). Tilikum has the words 'European bistro' written all over it and is particularly popular for lunch (quiche, sardine sandwiches) and brunch (baked pancakes).

ⓧ Queen Anne & Lake Union

Dick's Drive-in
Burgers $

(Map p56; ☑206-285-5155; www.ddir.com; 500 Queen Anne Ave N; burgers from $1.40; ☺10:30am-2am; ⓠ13) If you're down to your last few dollars and dying for something to eat, don't panic! Dick's is calling you. Welcome to the only fast-food joint in Seattle where you can still buy a burger for $1.40, along with $1.75 fries (hand cut, no less) and $2.50 milkshakes.

Toulouse Petit
Cajun, Creole $$

(Map p56; ☑206-432-9069; www.toulousepetit. com; 601 Queen Anne Ave N; dinner mains $17-45; ☺9am-2am Mon-Fri, from 8am Sat & Sun; ⓠ13)

Hailed for its generous happy hours, cheap brunches and rollicking atmosphere, this perennially busy Queen Anne eatery has the common touch. The menu is large and varied, offering choices such as blackened rib-eye steak, freshwater gulf prawns and house-made gnocchi with artichoke hearts.

🍸 DRINKING & NIGHTLIFE

Pike Pub & Brewery   Brewery
(Map p52; ☎206-622-6044; www.pikebrewing. com; 1415 1st Ave; ⊙11am-midnight; ℝUniversity St) ✦ Leading the way in the US microbrewery revolution, this brewpub was an early starter, opening in 1989 underneath Pike Place Market. Today it continues to serve good pub food (mains $11 to $20) and hop-heavy, made-on-site beers in a busily decorated but fun multilevel space. Free tours of the brewery are available.

Owl & Thistle   Irish Pub
(Map p52; ☎206-621-7777; www.owlnthistle. com; 808 Post Ave; ⊙11am-2am; ℝPioneer Sq) One of the best Irish pubs in the city, the dark, multiroomed Owl & Thistle is located slap-bang downtown but misses most of the tourist traffic (which homes in on the more 'themed' Fado) because it's hidden in Post Ave.

Shorty's   Bar
(Map p52; ☎206-441-5449; www.shortydog.com; 2222 2nd Ave; ⊙noon-2am; 🚌13) Increasingly shabby but seemingly (hopefully?) eternal, Shorty's is one of the best hold-overs from grungy old Belltown. It's all about pinball, hotdogs, cheap beer and loud music. Pinball machines are built into some of the tables, and the back room is basically a church for flipper devotees.

✪ ENTERTAINMENT

McCaw Hall   Opera
(Map p56; ☎206-684-7200; 321 Mercer St; ⑤Seattle Center) Home of the **Seattle Opera** (Map p56; www.seattleopera.org; ⑤Seattle Center) and **Pacific Northwest Ballet** (Map p56; www.pnb.org; ⑤Seattle Center), this

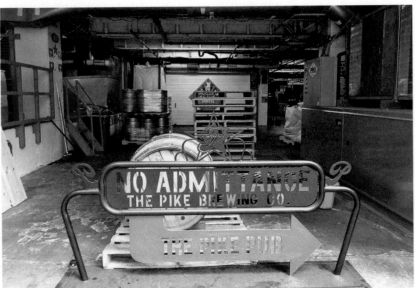

ERIC BRODER VAN DYKE/SHUTTERSTOCK ©

Pike Pub & Brewery

magnificent structure in the Seattle Center was given a massive overhaul in 2003.

KEXP — Live Performance

(Map p56; ☎206-520-5800; www.kexp.org; 472 1st Ave N; ☐Rapid Ride D-Line) The new KEXP radio headquarters opened in the Seattle Center in December 2015 and provides a central gathering space for live music and parties, a see-through DJ booth and a live recording studio with room for audiences of up to 75 people.

Triple Door — Live Performance

(Map p52; ☎206-838-4333; www.thetripledoor. net; 216 Union St; ☐University St) This club downstairs from the Wild Ginger (p58) restaurant is a Seattle mainstay with a liberal booking policy that includes country and rock as well as jazz, gospel, R&B, world music and burlesque performances. There's a full menu and a smaller lounge upstairs called the Musicquarium with an aquarium and free live music.

❶ GETTING THERE & AWAY

Seattle is served by **Sea-Tac International Airport** (SEA; ☎206-787-5388; www.portseattle. org/Sea-Tac; 17801 International Blvd; ☎), located 13 miles south of downtown Seattle. It's one of the top 20 airports in the US with numerous domestic flights and good direct connections to Asia and a handful of European cities, including Paris and London.

Three railway arteries converge in Seattle from the east (the Empire Builder to Chicago), south (the Coast Starlight to Oregon and California) and north (the Cascades to Vancouver, Canada). These land-based journeys through the watery, green-tinged, mountainous Pacific Northwest landscape are spectacular and often surprisingly cheap.

Seattle's main road highway is the mega-busy I-5, which flows north–south along the West Coast. Points east are best served by cross-continental I-90, which crosses the Cascade Mountains via Snoqualmie Pass. Regular boats arrive in Seattle from Victoria, Canada.

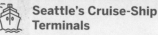

Seattle's Cruise-Ship Terminals

Nearly 200 cruise ships call in at Seattle annually. They dock at either Smith Cove Cruise Terminal (Pier 91), in the Magnolia neighborhood two miles north of downtown, or Bell Street Cruise Terminal (Pier 66). The latter is adjacent to downtown and far more convenient. Many cruise lines pre-organize land transportation for their passengers. Check ahead.

Metro buses 24 and 19 connect Pier 91 in Magnolia with downtown via the Seattle Center. Fares are a flat $2.75.

Shuttle Express links the piers with Sea-Tac airport ($22) or downtown ($12).

Bell Street Cruise Terminal
JW_PNW/SHUTTERSTOCK ©

❶ GETTING AROUND

There is a large and growing network of public transportation in Seattle.

Bus A wide number of routes. Pay as you enter the bus; there's a peak-time flat fee of $2.50/1.50 per adult/child.

Light rail Regular all-day service on one line between Sea-Tac Airport and the University of Washington via downtown.

Streetcar Two lines; the South Lake Union line runs from Westlake Center to South Lake Union every 15 minutes, and the First Hill line runs from Pioneer Square to Capitol Hill. Fares are $2.25/1.50 per adult/child.

Water taxi Runs between Pier 50 on the waterfront to West Seattle; daily in summer, weekdays only in winter.

Taxi Initial charge $2.60, then $2.70 per mile.

Where to Stay

Room prices can vary wildly depending on: season (peak season is generally May through August); day of the week (weekends are usually cheaper); and time of booking (earlier is usually better).

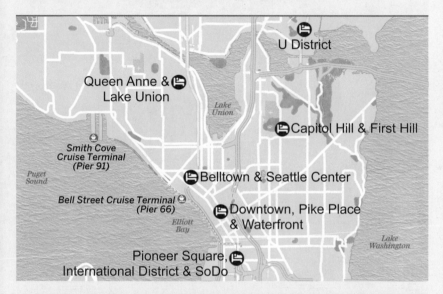

U District

Queen Anne & Lake Union

Lake Union

Capitol Hill & First Hill

Smith Cove Cruise Terminal (Pier 91)

Puget Sound

Belltown & Seattle Center

Bell Street Cruise Terminal (Pier 66)

Elliott Bay

Downtown, Pike Place & Waterfront

Lake Washington

Pioneer Square, International District & SoDo

Neighborhood	
Downtown, Pike Place & Waterfront	Highest concentration of hotels of all types, best neighborhood for absolute luxury and fantastic central location. But, many places are expensive, driving can be a nightmare and parking usually costs extra.
Pioneer Square, International District & SoDo	Close to sports grounds, downtown and the waterfront. But a noisy, rambunctious neighborhood at night that's a bit edgy for some.
Belltown & Seattle Center	Plenty of economical hotel options within close walking distance of Seattle's main sights. But, noisy at night with a boozy bar scene and some panhandling.
Queen Anne & Lake Union	Some great midrange options in Lower Queen Anne a stone's throw from the Seattle Center. But lacking options in Queen Anne proper.
Capitol Hill & First Hill	Excellent selection of high-quality, well-run B&Bs that are adjacent to Seattle's most exciting nightlife. But, a lack of hotel choices in Capitol Hill which is little removed from downtown.
U District	Three affordable boutique hotels adjacent to the pulsating life of 'the Ave.' But, a little isolated from the downtown core and other major sights.

Left: Pike Place Market (p38)

Science World (p83)

VANCOUVER

Vancouver at a Glance...

Walkable neighborhoods, drink-and-dine delights and memorable cultural and outdoor activities framed by dramatic vistas – there's a glassful of great reasons to love this lotusland metropolis.

In a city studded with sandy beaches, forest trails, kayaking routes, seawall bike lanes and the mighty and highly beloved Stanley Park, Vancouver's downtown is just a primer. Whether discovering the coffee shops of Commercial Dr or the heritage-house beachfronts and browsable stores of Kitsilano, you'll find this city perfect for easy-access urban exploration.

Two Days in Vancouver

o Visit the **Vancouver Art Gallery** (p78) in the morning, before strolling down to **English Bay Beach** (p78) and entering the leafy domain of **Stanley Park** (p68) until dusk falls.

o On day two, warm up on Granville Island, an excellent place for breakfast and lunch. After eating your fill, walk it off with a hike over to **Kitsilano Beach** (p82), visiting the **Museum of Vancouver** (p82) on the way.

Four Days in Vancouver

o Get a bus out to the **Museum of Anthropology** (p82) at UBC. Heading back into town, stop at **Science World** (p83); then walk up the road in SoMa for an insight into Vancouver's craft beer universe.

o Dedicate your last day to the North Shore by traversing the **Capilano Suspension Bridge** (p83) and climbing up **Grouse Mountain** (p83) via the infamous 'grind.'

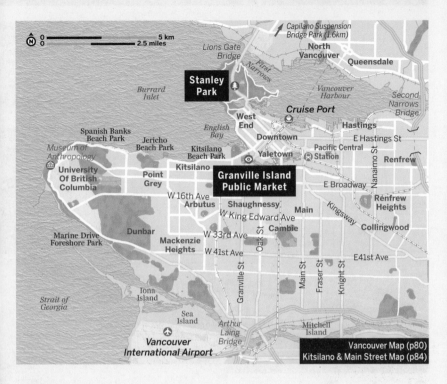

Arriving in Vancouver

Vancouver International Airport
Situated 8 miles (13km) south of the city. Canada Line trains to downtown typically take around 25 minutes and cost C$7.75 to C$10.50.

Pacific Central Station Most trains and buses arrive at this station just five minutes from downtown (C$2.75).

BC Ferries Arrive at Tsawwassen, one hour south of Vancouver, or Horseshoe Bay, 30 minutes from downtown.

Fast Facts

Currency Canadian dollar (C$)

Language English

Money ATMs are widely available. Credit cards are accepted and widely used.

Visas Not required for visitors from the US, the Commonwealth and most of Western Europe for stays up to 180 days.

Tourist Information (www.tourism vancouver.com)

Free Wi-fi Most libraries and cafes.

Stanley Park's Seawall

ROMAKOMA/SHUTTERSTOCK ©

Stanley Park

One of North America's largest urban green spaces, Stanley Park is revered for its dramatic forest-and-mountain oceanfront views.

This 1000-acre (400-hectare) woodland is studded with nature-hugging trails, family-friendly attractions and places to eat.

Seawall

Built in stages between 1917 and 1980, the park's 5.5-mile (8.8km) seawall trail is Vancouver's favorite outdoor hangout. Encircling the park, it offers spectacular waterfront vistas on one side and dense forest on the other. The seawall delivers you to some of the park's top highlights. You'll pass alongside the stately **HMCS Discovery** (Map p80; 1200 Stanley Park Dr; 🚍19) naval station and, about a mile (1.5km) from the W Georgia St entrance, you'll come to the Totem Poles. Remnants of an abandoned 1930s plan to create a First Nations 'theme village,' the poles were joined by the addition of three Coast Salish welcome arches.

Great For...

☑ Don't Miss

The family of beavers that currently reside on Beaver Lake; you'll likely spot them swimming around their large den.

Explore Ashore

Stanley Park is around 2.5km from the cruise-ship port. Bus 19 runs into Stanley Park. It typically takes around three hours to walk the 5.5-mile (8.8km) seawall, but bike rentals are also available on nearby Denman St.

✗ Take a Break

The park's **Stanley's Bar & Grill** (Map p80; ☎604-602-3088; www.stanleypark pavilion.com; 610 Pipeline Rd; ⊘9am-8pm Jul & Aug, 9am-5pm Sep-Jun; 🚍19) is a great spot for a patio beer among the trees.

Lost Lagoon

A few steps from the park's W Georgia St entrance lies Lost Lagoon, which was originally part of Coal Harbour. After a causeway was built in 1916, the new body of water was renamed, transforming itself into a freshwater lake. Today it's a bird-beloved nature sanctuary – keep your eyes peeled for blue herons – and its perimeter pathway is a favored stroll for wildlife nuts. The **Stanley Park Nature House** (Map p80; ☎604-257-8544; www.stanleypark ecology.ca; north end of Alberni St, Lost Lagoon; ⊘10am-5pm Tue-Sun Jul & Aug, 10am-4pm Sat & Sun Sep-Jun; 🚼; 🚍19) **FREE** here has exhibits on the park's wildlife, history and ecology – ask about the fascinating and well-priced guided walks.

Beaches & Views

Second Beach is a family-friendly area on the park's western side, with a grassy playground, an ice-cream stand and a huge outdoor **swimming pool** (Map p80; ☎604-257-8371; cnr N Lagoon Dr & Stanley Park Dr; adult/child $5.86/2.95; ⊘10am-8:45pm mid-Jun–Aug, reduced hours low-season; 🚼; 🚍19). For a little more tranquility, try Third Beach, a favored summer-evening destination for Vancouverites.

Perhaps the most popular vista is at Prospect Point. One of Vancouver's best lookouts, this lofty spot is located at the park's northern tip. In summer, you'll be jostling for elbow room with the crowds; heading down the steep stairs to the viewing platform usually shakes them off. Also look out for scavenging raccoons here (don't pet them).

JULIEN HAUTCOEUR/SHUTTERSTOCK ©

Granville Island Public Market

A multisensory smorgasbord of fish, cheese, fruit and bakery treats, this is one of North America's finest public markets.

Great For...

☑ Don't Miss

The alfresco farmers market outside (June to September) with BC cherries, peaches and blueberries.

Forgotton Past

The Public Market is the centerpiece of one of Canada's most impressive urban regeneration projects. Built as a district for small factories in the early part of the last century, Granville Island – which has also been called Mud Island and Industrial Island over the years – had declined into a paint-peeled, no-go area by the 1960s. But the abandoned sheds began attracting artists and theater groups by the 1970s, and the old buildings slowly started springing back to life with some much-needed repairs and upgrades. Within a few years, new theaters, restaurants and studios had been built and the Public Market quickly became an instantly popular anchor tenant. One reason for the island's popularity? Only independent, one-of-a-kind businesses operate here.

Granville Island
**Granville Island
Public Market**

False Creek
Ferries

Broker's
Bay

Granville
Bridge

Aquabus

Granville
Island

Johnston St

Granville St

False Creek

Explore Ashore

Granville Island Public Market is around 4km southwest of the cruise-ship terminal. Arrive or depart from Granville Island via one of the tiny miniferries that not only transport passengers from the north side of False Creek to the market on the south side but have several additional ports of call around the shoreline.

ℹ Need to Know

Map p84; 604-666-6655; www.granville island.com/public-market; Johnston St; 9am-7pm; 50, miniferries

Taste-Tripping

Come hungry: there are dozens of food stands to weave your way around at the market. Among the must-see stands are Oyama Sausage Company, replete with hundreds of smoked sausages and cured meats; Benton Brothers Fine Cheese, with its full complement of amazing curdy goodies from BC and around the world (look for anything by Farm House Natural Cheese from Agassiz, BC); and Granville Island Tea Company (Hawaiian rooibos recommended), with its tasting bar and more than 150 steep-tastic varieties to choose from. Baked goodies also abound: abandon your diet at Lee's Donuts and Siegel's Bagels, where the naughty cheese-stuffed baked bagels are not to be missed.

And don't worry: there's always room for a wafer-thin album-sized 'cinnamon record' from Stuart's Baked Goods. French-themed L'Epicerie Rotisserie and Gourmet Shop has also been a popular addition to the market in recent years. It sells vinegars, olive oils and Babapapa pop bottles with delicious, fresh-cooked, picnic-friendly takeout chicken and sausages.

If you're an incurable foodie, the delicious market tour organized by **Vancouver Foodie Tours** (604-295-8844; www.foodie tours.ca; tours from $50) is the way to go.

For a fancy lunch stop, dine at Bistro 101 (p87), the reasonably priced training restaurant of the Pacific Institute of Culinary Arts.

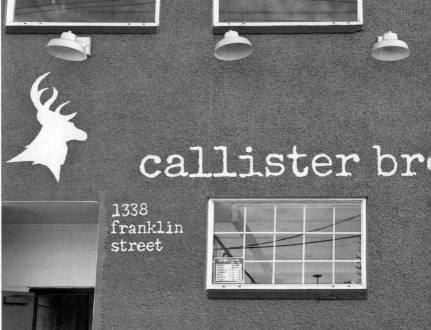

MORGANA/ALAMY STOCK PHOTO ©

Craft Beer Experience

Vancouver is one of Canada's craft-beer capitals. You can plan an easy stroll (or stumble) around inviting clusters of microbrewery tasting rooms on Main St, or around the northern end of Commercial Dr.

Great For...

☑ Don't Miss

The microbrewery district accessible from the north end of Commercial Dr; it's the city's best.

Brassneck Brewery

Vancouver's favorite **microbrewery** (Map p84; 604-259-7686; 2184 Main St; 2-11pm Mon-Fri, noon-11pm Sat & Sun; 3) concocted more than 50 different beers in its first six months of operating and continues to win new fans with an ever-changing chalk-board of intriguing libations with names like Bivouac Bitter, Stockholm Syndrome and Magician's Assistant. Our recommendation? The delicious Passive Aggressive dry-hopped pale ale. Arrive early for a seat in the small tasting bar, especially on weekends.

Off the Rail

A firm favorite among the locals. Nip upstairs to the compact **tasting room** (604-563-5767; www.offtherailbrewing.com;

Explore Ashore

The craft breweries here are several kilometers south as east of the Canada Place cruise ship terminal. Book a taxi to journey between tasting rooms and allow at least a few hours.

ℹ Need to Know

www.camravancouver.ca

✕ Take a Break

Sober up at **Cannibal Cafe** (☏604-558-4199; www.cannibalcafe.ca; 1818 Commercial Dr; mains $11-16; ⊙11:30am-10pm Mon-Thu, 11:30am-midnight Fri, 10am-midnight Sat, 10am-10pm Sun; ☐20), a punk-tastic diner for fans of seriously real burgers.

★ Top Tip

Ask your server what's local and/or seasonal on the draft list.

1351 Adanac St; ⊙noon-8pm Sun-Thu, to 10pm Fri & Sat; ☐14) and snag a stool at the bar to try everything from Crazy Train IPA to Derailer Pale Ale. Need some non-liquid sustenance? Hit the cured sausages in the corner before returning to the beer list; there's often a dozen or so to try, including plenty of seasonals.

Callister Brewing Company

One of the most exciting of East Van's beer-district microbreweries, Callister has a red-painted former industrial space exterior housing a Spartan **tasting room** (☏604-569-2739; www.callisterbrewing.com; 1338 Franklin St; ⊙2-9pm Mon-Thu, 2-10pm Fri, 1-10pm Sat, 1-8pm Sun; ☐14) with beer-barrel tables on a bare concrete floor. But there's

nothing austere about the booze selection; four onsite nano-breweries share the same equipment to produce a wide array of differing brews. Order a selection of small-glass samples and dive right in.

Main Street Brewing

Tucked into an historic old brewery building, **Main Street Brewing** (Map p84; ☏604-336-7711; www.mainstreetbeer.ca; 261 E 7th Ave; ⊙2-11pm Mon-Thu, noon-11pm Fri-Sun; ☐3) has a great, industrial-chic little tasting room and a booze roster divided into regular beers and casks. Start with a four-flight tasting sampler then dive in with a larger order. The Westminster Brown Ale is our favorite but there's usually an IPA or two worth quaffing here as well.

Downtown Grand Tour

The bustling heart of central Vancouver is an eminently walkable street grid of stores, coffeeshops and places to eat. There are also more than a few grand buildings and scenic sights worth whipping out your camera for. Keep your eye out for many lesser-known public artworks and historic stops.

Start Canada Place
Distance 3km
Duration 1 hour

1 Check out the towering **Olympic Cauldron**, a landmark reminder of the 2010 Olympic and Paralympic Winter Games.

8 There were 1970s moves to demolish 19th-century **Christ Church Cathedral** but these were mercifully rejected. Check out the new stained-glass bell tower alongside.

7 Duck into the grand **Fairmont Hotel Vancouver**. There are photos on one wall showing the historic building's construction and its former incarnations.

6 Visit the **Vancouver Art Gallery** (p78) for a culture fix.

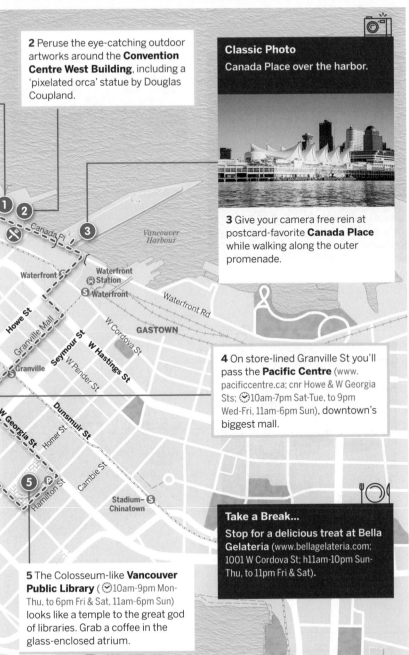

2 Peruse the eye-catching outdoor artworks around the **Convention Centre West Building**, including a 'pixelated orca' statue by Douglas Coupland.

Classic Photo
Canada Place over the harbor.

3 Give your camera free rein at postcard-favorite **Canada Place** while walking along the outer promenade.

Vancouver Harbour

Waterfront

Canada Pl

Waterfront
Station
Waterfront

Waterfront Rd

Howe St

Granville Mall

GASTOWN

Seymour St

W Cordova St

W Hastings St

Granville

W Pender St

Dunsmuir St

4 On store-lined Granville St you'll pass the **Pacific Centre** (www.pacificcentre.ca; cnr Howe & W Georgia Sts; ◷10am-7pm Sat-Tue, to 9pm Wed-Fri, 11am-6pm Sun), downtown's biggest mall.

W Georgia St

Homer St

Cambie St

Hamilton St

Stadium–
Chinatown

Take a Break...
Stop for a delicious treat at Bella Gelateria (www.bellagelateria.com; 1001 W Cordova St; h11am-10pm Sun-Thu, to 11pm Fri & Sat).

5 The Colosseum-like **Vancouver Public Library** (◷10am-9pm Mon-Thu, to 6pm Fri & Sat, 11am-6pm Sun) looks like a temple to the great god of libraries. Grab a coffee in the glass-enclosed atrium.

Chinatown Culture & History Crawl

Stroll the streets of one of North America's largest Chinatown districts and immerse yourself in culture and heritage.

Start Chinatown Millennium Gate
Distance 1 mile (1.5km)
Duration one hour

4 Turn right onto **Pender St** passing rows of antique Chinatown buildings – some of the city's oldest storefronts.

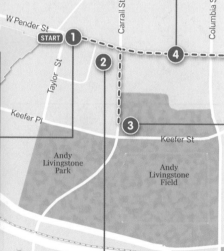

Classic Photo
Stand well back to get a zoom-in close-up of the elaborate Millennium Gate.

1 Enter Chinatown by the **Millennium Gate** erected in 2002 to replace an earlier 1912 model.

2 Examine the quirky **Jack Chow Building**, reputedly the world's narrowest office block.

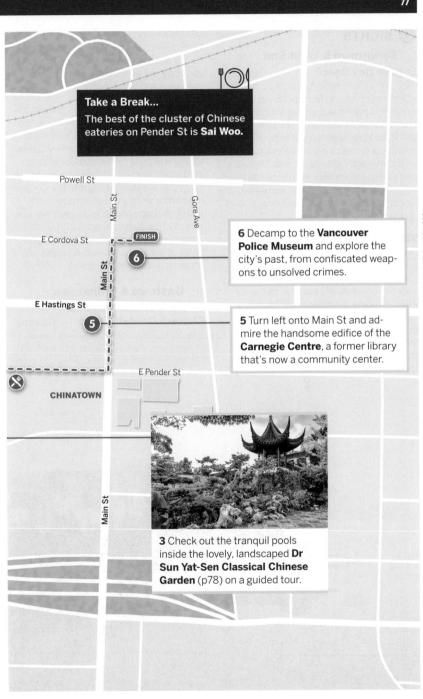

Take a Break...
The best of the cluster of Chinese eateries on Pender St is **Sai Woo**.

Powell St

Main St

Gore Ave

E Cordova St

FINISH

6 Decamp to the **Vancouver Police Museum** and explore the city's past, from confiscated weapons to unsolved crimes.

Main St

E Hastings St

5 Turn left onto Main St and admire the handsome edifice of the **Carnegie Centre**, a former library that's now a community center.

E Pender St

CHINATOWN

Main St

3 Check out the tranquil pools inside the lovely, landscaped **Dr Sun Yat-Sen Classical Chinese Garden** (p78) on a guided tour.

◉ SIGHTS
◉ Downtown & West End
English Bay Beach   Beach
(Map p80; cnr Denman St & Beach Ave; ☐5)
Wandering south on Denman St, you'll spot
a clutch of palm trees ahead announcing
one of Canada's best urban beaches. Then
you'll see Vancouver's most popular public
artwork: a series of oversized laughing figures that makes everyone smile. There's a
party atmosphere here in summer as locals
catch rays and panoramic ocean views...or
just ogle the volleyballers prancing around
on the sand.

Vancouver Art Gallery   Gallery
(VAG; Map p80; ☑604-662-4700; www.vanart
gallery.bc.ca; 750 Hornby St; adult/child $20/6;
⊘10am-5pm Wed-Mon, to 9pm Tue; ☐5) The
VAG has dramatically transformed since
2000, becoming a vital part of the city's
cultural scene. Contemporary exhibitions – often showcasing Vancouver's
renowned photoconceptualists – are now
combined with blockbuster international
traveling shows. Check out **FUSE** (Map p80;

☑604-662-4700; www.vanartgallery.bc.ca/fuse;
Vancouver Art Gallery; $24; ⊘8pm-midnight;
☐5), a quarterly late-night party where you
can hang out with the city's young arties
over wine and live music.

Canada Place   Landmark
(Map p80; ☑604-775-7063; www.canadaplace.
ca; 999 Canada Place Way; P; ⑤Waterfront)
Vancouver's version of the Sydney Opera
House – judging by the number of post-
cards it appears on – this iconic landmark
is shaped like sails jutting into the sky over
the harbor. Both a cruise-ship terminal
and convention center (next door's grass-
roofed expansion opened in 2010), it's also
a stroll-worthy pier, providing photogenic
views of the North Shore mountains and
some busy floatplane action.

◉ Gastown & Chinatown
Dr Sun Yat-Sen Classical
Chinese Garden & Park   Gardens
(Map p80; ☑604-662-3207; www.vancouver
chinesegarden.com; 578 Carrall St; adult/child
$14/10; ⊘9:30am-7pm mid-Jun–Aug, 10am-6pm

English Bay Beach

BIGWORLD/GETTY IMAGES ©

Understand

Outdoor Activities

Vancouver's variety of outdoorsy activities is a huge hook: you can ski in the morning and hit the beach in the afternoon; hike or bike scenic forests; windsurf along the coastline; or kayak to your heart's content – and it will be content, with grand mountain views as your backdrop. There's also a full menu of spectator sports to catch here.

Hiking

Hiking opportunities abound in local parks and Vancouverites are ever-keen to partake – especially on the infamous **Grouse Grind** (p86). Lighthouse Park and Whytecliff Park are also scenic gems with gentle trails to tramp around. If you're heading to any of the North Shore parks, be prepared for continually changing mountain conditions – the weather can alter suddenly here and a warm sunny day in the city might not mean it's going to be the same, or stay the same, in the mountains. For more information on area hiking trails, visit www.vancouvertrails.com.

Biking

Vancouver is a cycle-friendly city with a network of designated urban routes and a new public bike-share scheme. For maps and resources, see www.vancouver.ca/cycling. There's also a very active mountain-biking community on the North Shore; start your research via www.nsmba.ca and consider the forested runs at **Mt Seymour** (☑604-986-2261; www.mountseymour.com; 1700 Mt Seymour Rd, North Vancouver; adult/youth 13-18yr/child $51/44/24; ⊙9:30am-10pm Mon-Fri, 8:30am-10pm Sat & Sun Dec-Apr), including the 6-mile (10km) Seymour Valley Trailway.

Paddling

It's hard to beat the joy of a sunset kayak around the coastline here; it's a signature outdoor activity that many Vancouverites enjoy. But hitting the water isn't only about paddling: there are also plenty of opportunities to surf, kiteboard and stand-up paddleboard, especially along the shoreline of Kitsilano. Why not join the locals at the **Jericho Sailing Centre** (☑604-224-4177; www.jsca.bc.ca; 1300 Discovery St; ⊙9:30am-9pm; ☑4) to find out what's available?

Lighthouse Park
EB ADVENTURE PHOTOGRAPHY/SHUTTERSTOCK ©

Vancouver

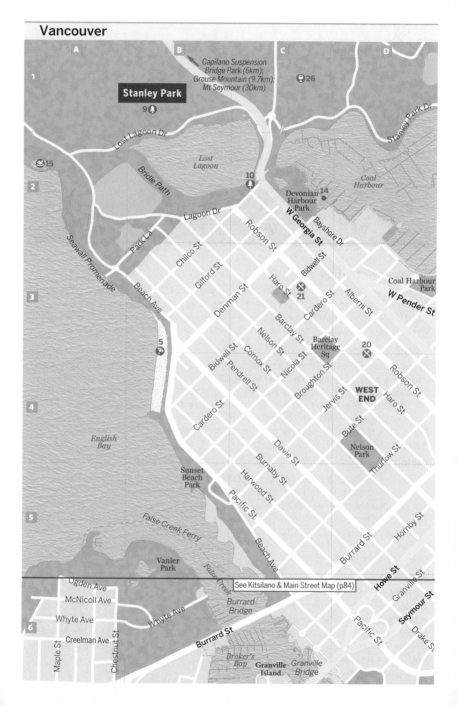

Stanley Park

9

Capilano Suspension
Bridge Park (6km);
Grouse Mountain (9.7km);
Mt Seymour (30km)

26

15

Lost Lagoon Dr

Lost
Lagoon

10

Coal
Harbour

Devonian
Harbour
Park

14

Bridle Path

Lagoon Dr

W Georgia St

Bayshore Dr

Seawall Promenade

Park La

Robson St

Chilco St

Gilford St

Bidwell St

Coal Harbour
Park

Beach Ave

Denman St

Haro St

21

Cardero St

Alberni St

W Pender St

Barclay St

Nelson St

Nicola St

Barclay
Heritage
Sq

20

Bidwell St

Cornox St

Broughton St

Robson St

5

Pendrell St

Jervis St

WEST
END

Haro St

Cardero St

Bute St

Nelson
Park

Thurlow St

English
Bay

Davie St

Burnaby St

Sunset
Beach
Park

Harwood St

Hornby St

Pacific St

Beach Ave

Burrard St

False Creek Ferry

Vanier
Park

Ogden Ave

McNicoll Ave

Whyte Ave

Creelman Ave

Maple St

Chestnut St

Whyte Ave

False Creek

Howe St

Granville St

Seymour St

See Kitsilano & Main Street Map (p84)

Burrard St

Burrard
Bridge

Pacific St

Drake St

Broker's
Bay

Granville
Island

Granville
Bridge

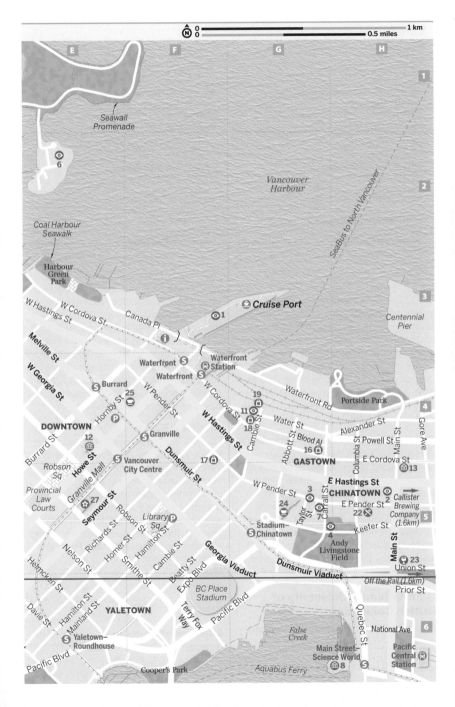

E

Seawall
Promenade

6

Coal Harbour
Seawalk

Harbour
Green
Park

F

N 0   1 km
   0   0.5 miles

Vancouver
Harbour

G

SeaBus to North Vancouver

H

1

2

Centennial
Pier

3

W Cordova St
W Hastings St

Canada Pl

1

Cruise Port

Melville St

W Cordova St

W Hastings St

Waterfront Rd

Portside Park

4

W Georgia St

Burrard

W Pender St

Waterfront
Waterfront

Waterfront
Station

25

W Cordova St

19

Water St

Alexander St

Powell St

E Cordova St

Gore Ave

Main St

Portside Park

DOWNTOWN

Hornby St

Granville

W Hastings St

11

18

Cambie St

Abbott St

Blood Al

16

Columbia St

GASTOWN

13

Burrard St

12

Howe St

Granville

Vancouver
City Centre

Dunsmuir St

17

W Pender St

3

E Hastings St

CHINATOWN

Carrall St

2

Callister
Brewing
Company
(1.6km)

Robson
Sq

Provincial
Law
Courts

27

Seymour St

Granville Mall

Richards St

Robson St

Homer St

Hamilton St

Library
Sq

24

Taylor St

7

E Pender St

22

Keefer St

Andy
Livingstone
Field

5

Nelson St

Cambie St

Beatty St

Expo Blvd

Georgia Viaduct

Stadium–
Chinatown

Dunsmuir Viaduct

Main St

23

Union St

Off the Rail (1.6km)

Prior St

Helmcken St

Smithe St

BC Place
Stadium

Terry Fox Way

Pacific Blvd

Quebec St

National Ave

6

Davie St

Hamilton St

Mainland St

YALETOWN

Pacific Blvd

Yaletown–
Roundhouse

Pacific Blvd

Cooper's Park

False
Creek

Main Street–
Science World

8

Aquabus Ferry

Pacific
Central
Station

Vancouver

Sep & May–mid-Jun, 10am-4:30pm Oct-Apr; Ⓢ Stadium-Chinatown) A tranquil break from bustling Chinatown, this intimate 'garden of ease' reflects Taoist principles of balance and harmony. Entry includes a 45-minute guided tour, in which you'll learn about the symbolism behind the placement of the gnarled pine trees, winding covered pathways and ancient limestone formations. Look out for the lazy turtles bobbing in the jade-colored water.

Steam Clock　　　　　Landmark
(Map p80; cnr Water & Cambie Sts; Ⓢ Waterfront) Halfway along Water St, this oddly popular tourist magnet lures the cameras with its tooting steam whistle. Built in 1977, the clock's mechanism is actually driven by electricity; only the pipes on top are fueled by steam (reveal that to the patiently waiting tourists and you might cause a riot). It sounds every 15 minutes, and marks each hour with little whistling symphonies.

◎ Kitsilano & University of British Columbia

Museum of Anthropology Museum
(☎604-822-5087; www.moa.ubc.ca; 6393 NW Marine Dr; adult/child $18/16; ⊙10am-5pm, to 9pm Thu (closed Mon Oct-May); Ⓟ; ☐99B-Line)

Vancouver's best museum is studded with spectacular First Nations totem poles and breathtaking carvings – but it's also teeming with artifacts from cultures around the world, from Polynesian instruments to Cantonese opera costumes. Take one of the free daily **tours** (check ahead for times) for some context, but give yourself at least a couple of hours to explore on your own. It's easy to immerse yourself here.

Kitsilano Beach　　　　　Beach
(Map p84; cnr Cornwall Ave & Arbutus St; ☐22) Facing English Bay, Kits Beach is one of Vancouver's favorite summertime hangouts. The wide, sandy expanse attracts buff Frisbee tossers and giggling volleyball players, and those who just like to preen while catching the rays. The ocean is fine for a dip, though serious swimmers should consider the heated **Kitsilano Pool** (Map p84; ☎604-731-0011; www.vancouverparks. ca; 2305 Cornwall Ave; adult/child $5.86/2.95; ⊙7am-evening mid-Jun–mid-Sep; ⊞; ☐22), one of the world's largest outdoor saltwater pools.

Museum of Vancouver　　　Museum
(MOV; Map p84; ☎604-736-4431; www.museum ofvancouver.ca; 1100 Chestnut St; adult/child $15/5; ⊙10am-5pm, to 8pm Thu; Ⓟ⊞; ☐22)

The MOV has hugely improved in recent years, with cool temporary exhibitions and evening events aimed at culturally minded adults. It hasn't changed everything, though. There are still superbly evocative displays on local 1950s pop culture and 1960s hippie counterculture – a reminder that 'Kits' was once the grass-smoking center of Vancouver's flower-power movement – plus a shimmering gallery of vintage neon signs from around the city.

◎ Main Street

Science World   Museum

(Map p80; ☑604-443-7440; www.scienceworld.ca; 1455 Quebec St; adult/child $25.75/17.75; ⊙10am-6pm, to 8pm Thu Jul & Aug, reduced hours off-season; ℗ ♿; Ⓢ Main St-Science World) Under Vancouver's favorite geodesic dome (OK, it's the only one), this ever-popular science and nature showcase has tons of exhibition space and a cool outdoor park crammed with hands-on fun (yes, you can lift 2028kg). Inside, there are two floors of educational play, from a walk-in hamster wheel to an air-driven ball maze.

◎ North Shore

Grouse Mountain   Amusement Park

(☑604-980-9311; www.grousemountain.com; 6400 Nancy Greene Way, North Vancouver; Skyride adult/child $44/15; ⊙9am-10pm; ℗ ♿; ☐236) On the self-proclaimed 'Peak of Vancouver,' this mountain-top playground offers smashing views of downtown glittering in the water below. In summer, Skyride gondola tickets include access to lumberjack shows, alpine hiking, bird-of-prey displays and a grizzly bear refuge. Pay extra for ziplining and Eye of the Wind, a 20-story, elevator-accessed turbine tower with a panoramic viewing pod that will have your camera itching for action.

Capilano Suspension
Bridge Park   Park

(☑604-985-7474; www.capbridge.com; 3735 Capilano Rd, North Vancouver; adult/child $40/12; ⊙8:30am-8pm Jun-Aug, reduced hours off-season; ℗ ♿; ☐236) As you walk gingerly onto one of the world's longest (460ft, 140m) and highest (230ft, 70m) suspension bridges, swaying gently over the roiling

Capilano Suspension Bridge Park

Kitsilano & Main Street

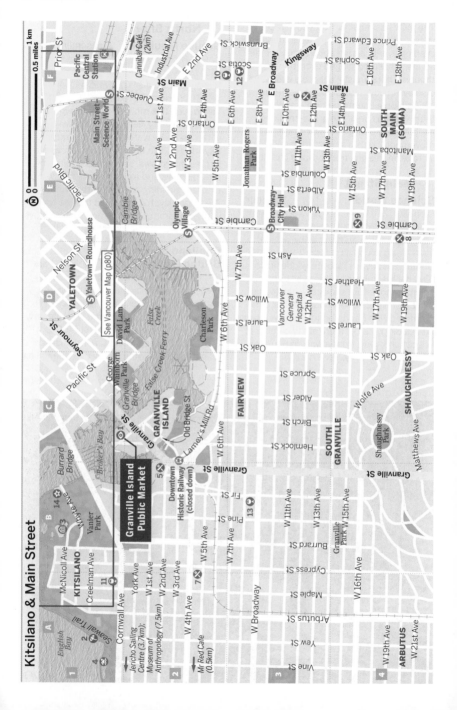

Granville Island Public Market

E Broadway

Kingsway

SOUTH MAIN (SOMA)

Main St

Pacific Central Station

Main Street–Science World

Cannibal Café (2km)

YALETOWN

See Vancouver Map (p80)

Yaletown–Roundhouse

Olympic Village

Broadway–City Hall

Vancouver General Hospital

FAIRVIEW

SOUTH GRANVILLE

SHAUGHNESSY

Shaughnessy Park

GRANVILLE ISLAND

Downtown Historic Railway (closed down)

KITSILANO

Vanier Park

English Bay

Seawall Trail

Jericho Sailing Centre (3.7km); Museum of Anthropology (7.5km)

Mr Red Cafe (0.5km)

ARBUTUS

Burrard Bridge

Granville Park

Broker's Bay

Charleson Park

David Lam Park

False Creek

False Creek Ferry

Jonathan Rogers Park

Cambie Bridge

Pacific Blvd

Kitsilano & Main Street

Capilano Canyon, remember that its thick steel cables are embedded in concrete. That should steady your feet – unless there are teenagers stamping across. Added park attractions include a glass-bottomed cliffside walkway and an elevated canopy trail through the trees.

✪ TOURS

Sins of the City Walking Tour   Walking

(Map p80; ☎604-665-3346; www.sinsofthecity. ca; 240 E Cordova St, Vancouver Police Museum; adult/student $20/16; ☐14) If your criminal interests are triggered by the Vancouver Police Museum, take one of their excellent Sins of the City walking tours, which weave through Gastown and Chinatown in search of former brothels, opium dens and gambling houses. The tours last around two hours and are a great way to see the far less salubrious side of the metropolis.

Harbour Cruises   Boating

(Map p80; ☎604-688-7246; www.boatcruises. com; 501 Denman St; adult/child from $35/12; ☺May–mid-Oct; ☐19) View the city – and some unexpected wildlife – from the water on a 75-minute narrated harbor tour, weaving past Stanley Park, Lions Gate Bridge and the North Shore mountains. There's also a lovely 2½-hour sunset dinner cruise (adult/child C$83/69) plus a long, languid lunch trek to lovely Indian Arm (C$72) that makes you feel as if you're a million miles from the city.

🛍 SHOPPING

Paper Hound   Books

(Map p80; ☎604-428-1344; www.paperhound. ca; 344 W Pender St; ☺10am-7pm Sun-Thu, to 8pm Fri & Sat; ☐14) Proving the printed word is alive and kicking, this small but perfectly curated secondhand bookstore opened a couple of years ago and has already become a dog-eared favorite among locals. It is a perfect spot for browsing your day away. You'll find tempting tomes (mostly used but some new) on everything from nature to poetry to chaos theory. Ask for recommendations: they really know their stuff here.

Six Hundred Four   Gallery

(Map p80; ☎604-424-0859; www.sixhundred four.com; 101-123 Cambie St; ☺11am-7pm; Ⓢ Waterfront) Steps from Gastown's Steam Clock, this slender, white-walled gallery has an intriguing approach: seven distinctive paintings from local artists adorn its walls, and under each painting are four sneaker-shoe designs digitally printed with the artwork above. The result is a limited run of 604 shoes per artwork – and the chance to buy the perfect wearable souvenir from your Canada visit.

Salmagundi West   Vintage

(Map p80; ☎604-681-4648; 321 W Cordova St; ☺11am-6pm Mon-Sat, noon-5pm Sun; Ⓢ Waterfront) For that one stubborn person on your souvenir list who defies the usual salmon or maple cookies gifts from Canada, try this beloved local gem: a browser's paradise.

Grouse Grind

If you really want a workout, try North Vancouver's **Grouse Grind** (www.grouse mountain.com; 🚌236), a steep, sweat-triggering slog up the side of Grouse Mountain that's been nicknamed 'Mother Nature's Stairmaster.' Reward yourself at the top with free access to Grouse Mountain Resort's facilities – although you'll have to pay C$10 to get down via the Skyride gondola.

Hiking the Grouse Grind trail
ZENNIE/GETTY IMAGES/ISTOCKPHOTO ©

You'll find everything from reproduction old-school toys to oddly alluring taxidermy and sparkling Edwardian-style jewelry.

Community Thrift & Vintage
Vintage

(Map p80; 🕿604-682-1004; www.community thriftandvintage.ca; 41 W Cordova St; ⊙11am-7pm Mon-Sat, noon-5pm Sun; 🚌14) There are two branches of this popular vintage clothing store just around the corner from each other. This one focuses on clothes for men and women, while the other (311 Carrall St) is dedicated to womenswear and is lined with dresses from every conceivable era.

✖ EATING
Downtown & West End
Forage
Canadian **$$**

(Map p80; 🕿604-661-1400; www.forage vancouver.com; 1300 Robson St; mains $16-29; ⊙6:30-10am & 5pm-midnight Mon-Fri, 7am-2pm & 5pm-midnight Sat & Sun; 🚌5) 🍴 A champion of the local farm-to-table scene, this

sustainability-friendly restaurant is the perfect way to sample the flavors of the region. Brunch has become a firm local favorite (turkey-sausage hash recommended), and for dinner the idea is to sample an array of tasting plates. The menu is innovative and highly seasonal, but look out for the seafood chowder with quail's egg. Reservations recommended.

Guu with Garlic
Japanese **$$**

(Map p80; 🕿604-685-8678; www.guu-izakaya. com; 1698 Robson St; small plates $4-9, mains $8-16; ⊙11:30am-2:30pm & 5:30pm-12:30am Mon-Sat, 11:30am-2:30pm & 5:30pm till midnight Sun; 🚌5) One of Vancouver's best *izakayas* (Japanese pubs), this welcoming, wood-lined joint is a cultural immersion. Hotpots and noodle bowls are available but it's best to experiment with some Japanese bar tapas, including black cod with miso mayo, deep-fried egg and pumpkin balls or finger-lickin' *tori-karaage* fried chicken. Garlic is liberally used in most dishes.

✖ Yaletown & Granville Island
Bistro 101
Canadian **$$**

(Map p84; 🕿604-724-4488; www.picachef.com; 1505 W 2nd Ave; ⊙11:30am-2pm & 6-9pm Mon-Fri; 🚌50) Vancouver's best-value gourmet dining option, the training restaurant of the **Pacific Institute of Culinary Arts** is popular with in-the-know locals, especially at lunchtime, when C$22 gets you a delicious three-course meal (typically three options for each course) plus service that's earnestly solicitous.

✖ Fairview & South Granville
Pronto
Italian **$$**

(Map p84; 🕿604-722-9331; www.prontocaffe.ca; 3473 Cambie St, Cambie Village; mains $14-22; ⊙11:30am-9pm Sun, Tue & Wed, to 10pm Thu-Sat; 🚌15) A delightful neighborhood eatery, this charming Cambie Village trattoria combines woodsy candlelit booths, perfectly prepared housemade pasta and the kind of welcoming service few restaurants manage to provide. Drop by for a lunchtime *porchetta* sandwich, or head here for

ANDRE RINGUETTE/CONTRIBUTOR/GETTY IMAGES ©

The Famous Players Band perform at the Commodore Ballroom (p89)

dinner, when the intimate, wood-floored space feels deliciously relaxed. Check the blackboard specials or head straight for the gnocchi with pesto and pancetta.

Vij's   Indian $$$
(Map p84; ☑604-736-6664; www.vijsrestaurant.ca; 3106 Cambie St, Cambie Village; mains $19-27; ◷5:30-10pm; ☑; ☐15) A sparkling (and far larger) new location for Canada's favorite East Indian chef delivers a warmly sumptuous lounge coupled with a cavernous dining area and cool rooftop patio. The menu, a high-water mark of contemporary Indian cuisine, fuses BC ingredients, global flourishes and classic ethnic flavors to produce many inventive dishes. Results range from signature 'lamb popsicles' to flavorful meals such as sablefish in yogurt-tomato broth.

🌐 Kitsilano & University of British Columbia

Mr Red Cafe   Vietnamese $
(☑604-559-6878; 2680 W Broadway; mains $6-14; ◷11am-9pm; ☑; ☐9) Serves authentic northern Vietnamese homestyle dishes that look and taste like there's a lovely old lady making them out back. Reservations are not accepted; dine off-peak to avoid waiting for the handful of tables, then dive into shareable gems such as pork baguette sandwiches, *cha ca han oi* (spicy grilled fish) and the ravishing pyramidical rice dumpling, stuffed with pork and a boiled quail's egg.

Fable   Canadian $$
(Map p84; ☑604-732-1322; www.fablekitchen.ca; 1944 W 4th Ave; mains $19-31; ◷11:30am-2pm Mon-Fri, 5:30-10pm Mon-Sat, brunch 10:30am-2pm Sat & Sun; ☐4) One of Vancouver's favorite farm-to-table restaurants is a lovely rustic-chic room of exposed brick, wood beams and prominently displayed red rooster logos. But looks are just part of the appeal. Expect perfectly prepared bistro dishes showcasing local seasonal ingredients such as duck, lamb and halibut. It's great gourmet comfort food with little pretension – hence the packed room most nights. Reservations recommended.

CANADA/ALAMY STOCK PHOTO ©

Forage restaurant (p86)

❌ Main Street

Dock Lunch International $$

(Map p84; ☎604-879-3625; 152 E 11th Ave; mains $10-14; ⊗11:30am-5pm Mon-Fri, 11am-3pm Sat & Sun) Like dining in a cool hippie's home, this utterly charming room in a side-street house serves a daily-changing menu of one or two soul-food mains (think spicy tacos or heaping weekend brunches). Arrive early and aim for one of the two window seats and you'll soon be chatting with the locals or browsing the cookbooks and Huxley novels on the shelves.

🍷 DRINKING & NIGHTLIFE

Mario's Coffee Express Coffee

(Map p80; 595 Howe St; mains $4-8; ⊗6:30am-4pm Mon-Fri; Ⓢ Burrard) A java-lover's favorite that only downtown office workers seem to know about. You'll wake up and smell the coffee long before you make it through the door here. The rich aromatic brews served up by the man himself are the kind of ambrosia that makes Starbucks drinkers weep.

Storm Crow Alehouse Pub

(Map p84; ☎604-428-9670; www.stormcrowale house.com; 1619 W Broadway, South Granville; ⊗11am-1am Mon-Thu, 11am-2am Fri, 9am-2am Sat, 9am-1am Sun; ☐9) The larger sibling of Commercial Dr's excellent nerd bar (Storm Crown Tavern), this pub welcomes everyone from the Borg to beardy *Lord of the Rings* dwarfs. They come to peruse the memorabilia-studded walls (think Millennium Falcon models and a Tardis washroom door), play the board games and dive into apposite refreshments including Romulan Ale and Pangalactic Gargleblasters. Hungry? Miss the chunky chickpea fries at your peril.

Brickhouse Pub

(Map p80; 730 Main St; ⊗8pm-2am Mon-Sat, 8pm-midnight Sun; ☐3) Possibly Vancouver's most original pub, this old-school hidden gem is a welcoming, windowless tavern lined with Christmas lights, fish tanks and junk-shop couches. It's like hanging out in someone's den, and is popular with artsy locals and in-the-know young hipsters. Grab an ale at the bar, slide onto a chair and start chatting: you're bound to meet someone interesting.

Catfe — Cafe

(Map p80; ☑778-379-0060; www.catfe.ca; International Village Mall, 88 Pender St; with/without cafe purchase $5/8; ☑11am-9pm Fri- Wed; ♿; Ⓢ Stadium-Chinatown) Vancouver's only cat cafe; book online for your time slot (walk-ins may also be available), buy a coffee and then meet the moggies in the large feline play room, where at least a dozen whiskered wonders await. All the cats come from the SPCA (Society for the Prevention of Cruelty to Animals) and are available for adoption via their usual procedures.

Corduroy — Bar

(Map p84; ☑604-733-0162; www.corduroy restaurant.com; 1943 Cornwall Ave; ☑4pm-2am Mon-Sat, 4pm-midnight Sun; ☑22) Handily located near the first bus stop after the Burrard Bridge (coming from downtown), this tiny spot is arguably Kitsilano's best haunt. Slide onto a bench seat and peruse the oddball artworks – junk-shop pictures and carved masks – then order a house beer from the shingle-covered bar: if you're lucky, it'll be served in a boot-shaped glass.

ⓧ ENTERTAINMENT

Bard on the Beach — Performing Arts

(Map p84; ☑604-739-0559; www.bardonthe beach.org; Vanier Park, 1695 Whyte Ave; tickets $20-57; ☑Jun-Sep; ☑22) Watching a Shakespearean play performed while the sun sets against the mountains beyond the tented stage is a Vancouver summer-time highlight. There are usually three of Shakespeare's plays, plus one Bard-related work (*Rosencrantz and Guildenstern are Dead,* for example), to choose from during the run. Q&A talks are staged after Tuesday-night performances, and there are opera, fireworks and wine-tasting nights throughout the season.

Commodore Ballroom — Live Music

(Map p80; ☑604-739-4550; www.commodore ballroom.com; 868 Granville St; ☑10) Local

Vancouver's Cruise-Ship Terminal

From May to September, Alaska-bound cruise ships dock at downtown's Canada Place cruise ship terminal. The modern, full-service terminal can hold up to four cruise ships at a time and receives close to a million passengers a year. The terminal is within easy walking distance of downtown shops and restaurants, as well as public transportation.

bands know they've made it when they play Vancouver's best mid-sized venue, a restored art-deco ballroom that still has the city's bounciest dance floor – courtesy of tires placed under its floorboards.

ⓘ GETTING THERE & AWAY

Most visitors will arrive by air at Vancouver International Airport, south of the city on Sea Island in Richmond. Alternatively, US trains trundle in from Seattle to Pacific Central Station, located on the southern edge of Vancouver's Chinatown district. Cross-border intercity bus services also arrive at this terminal. Vancouver is only an hour or so from several US border crossings, so driving is a popular way to access the city from the US. Cross-Canada rail, bus and flight operations also service the city, which is the main gateway for accessing destinations throughout British Columbia (BC).

ⓘ GETTING AROUND

Transit in Vancouver is cheap, extensive and generally efficient.

Bus Extensive network in central areas with frequent services on many routes.

Train SkyTrain system is fast but limited to only a few routes. Especially good for trips from the city center.

SeaBus A popular transit ferry linking downtown Vancouver and North Vancouver.

Where to Stay

Metro Vancouver is home to more than 25,000 hotel, B&B and hostel rooms – many in or around the downtown core. Book ahead in summer. Rates peak in July and August, but there are good spring and fall deals.

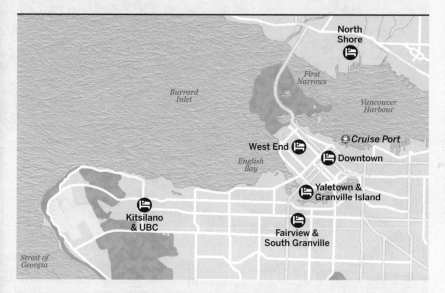

Neighborhood	For
Downtown	A good range of hotels with great transit links, walking distance to stores, restaurants, nightlife and some attractions. But, accommodations can be pricey and streets are often noisy and clamorous.
West End	In the heart of the gay district amid quiet residential streets and within walking distance of Stanley Park. But, accommodations are mostly high-end B&Bs with a couple of additional chain hotels.
Yaletown & Granville Island	A paucity of accommodation options, although the district is close to shops and restaurants with good transport links to other areas.
Fairview & South Granville	Quiet residential streets, well-priced heritage B&B sleepovers, and good bus and SkyTrain access to downtown.
Kitsilano & UBC	Comfy heritage houses and good UBC budget options are on the doorstep of several beaches. But, the local nightlife is poor.
North Shore	Better hotel rates than the city center, but set away from the heart of the action. Grouse Mountain and Capilano Suspension Bridge are nearby.

Left: Totem polem, Stanley Park (p68)

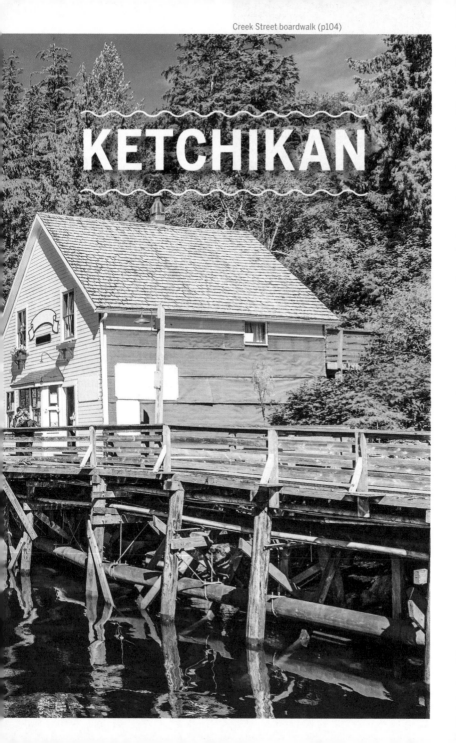

Creek Street boardwalk (p104)

KETCHIKAN

Ketchikan at a Glance...

Close to Alaska's southern tip, where the Panhandle plunges deep into British Columbia, lies rainy Ketchikan, the state's fourth-largest city, squeezed onto a narrow strip of coast on Revillagigedo Island abutting the Tongass Narrows. Ketchikan is known for its commercial salmon fishing and indigenous Haida and Tlingit heritage – there is no better place in the US to see totem poles in all their neck-craning, colorful glory. Every year between May and September, Ketchikan receives around one million cruise-ship passengers. It retains a notable historical heritage, exemplified by the jumbled clapboard facades of Creek St, perched on stilts above a river.

With a Day in Port

○ Orientate yourself in the multifarious **tour center** (p104) which peddles a multitude of day- and half-day trips.

○ Spend the morning investigating the **totem poles** (p100) north and south of town, and the afternoon enjoying a flightseeing tour of **Misty Fjords National Monument** (p102).

○ If there's any time left over, explore **Creek St** (p104) and have a snack in the **New York Cafe** (p110).

Best Places for...

Local fish Bar Harbor Restaurant (p109)

Beer with the locals Hole in the Wall Bar & Marina (p110)

Quick lunch Pioneer Cafe (p109)

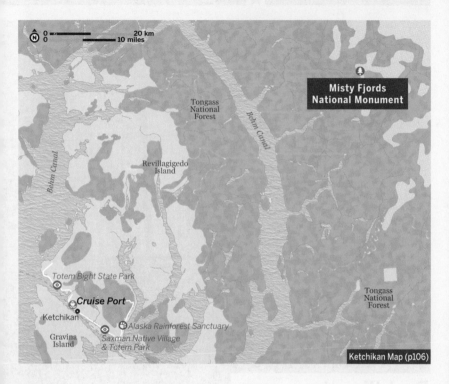

Misty Fjords
National Monument

Tongass
National
Forest

Behm Canal

Revillagigedo
Island

Behm Canal

Tongass
National
Forest

Totem Bight State Park

Cruise Port

Ketchikan

Gravina
Island

Alaska Rainforest Sanctuary

Saxman Native Village
& Totem Park

Ketchikan Map (p106)

Getting from the Port

Ketchikan's waterfront is the main
cruise-ship port and can accommo-
date up to four large ships at once.
Passengers simply step off the ship and
walk straight into downtown.

Fast Facts

Money First Bank and Wells Fargo have
24-hour ATMs.

Free Wi-fi Readily available around
town; note the signs in windows adver-
tising it. Ketchikan's modern library has
free wi-fi and internet computers.

Tourist Information Ketchikan Visitor
Information & Tour Center (p104)

Ketchikan rainforest

Paddling in the Rainforest

The drippy rainforest that practically envelops Ketchikan might have been invented with kayaking in mind. Paddle between lonely beaches, uninhabited islands and shorelines stalked by bears.

It's easy to organize short three- to five-hour guided kayaking trips out of Ketchikan that will transport you, via a short bus or boat transfer, to quiet, quintessential Pacific Northwest waters. Sheltered coves and islands that are located north and south of the town remain the domain of eagles, starfish, salmon, seals and whales. For visitors who have less time on their hands, a quick paddle beneath the wooden trestles of historic Creek St is an interesting alternative to explore.

Great For...

☑ Don't Miss

Circumnavigating one of the small rocky islands in Clover Pass.

Kayaking near the Blank Islands, Ketchikan

IVAN LIAN/GETTY IMAGES ©

Explore Ashore

Most of the local kayak companies have offices downtown and offer half-day trips lasting four hours dock-to-dock, transportation included.

❶ Need to Know

Kayak rental from $35 per day; kayak tours from $89 for 2½ hours

✕ Take a Break

Sink a drink in Hole in the Wall Bar & Marina (p110).

Clover Pass & Betton Island

West of Settler's Cove State Park at the northern terminus of the N Tongass Hwy (18.2 miles north of Ketchikan) are forested Betton Island and several smaller islands sheltering the western shores of Revilla-gigedo Island, making it an excellent day paddle. Although Clover Pass is a highly trafficked area, the backside of Betton Island offers a more genuine wilderness setting. Locally based **Ketchikan Kayak Company** (☑907-225-1272; www.ketchikan kayakco.com; 407 Knudson Cove Rd; 4hr tours $129) offers day trips in these waters with bus transfers from the cruise-ship terminal.

Orcas Cove

Orcas Cove is a short boat ride from the hive of Ketchikan's waterfront. Speckled with islands, home to copious wildlife (including orca whales) and backed by old-growth rainforest it offers a spirit-reviving slice of wilderness tranquility for those relishing a break from the clamor of cruise-ship life. **Southeast Sea Kayaks** (☑907-225-1258; www.kayakketchikan.com; 3 Salmon Landing; 🚻), based right next to the cruise terminal, organizes trips with boat transfers, waterproof clothing and guides included.

Ziplining in Ketchikan

LIANE HARROLD/ALAMY STOCK PHOTO ©

Ziplining

Ketchikan has the two main requirements to be the zipline capital of Alaska: lush rainforests and elevation. Three different ziplines catapult you like an eagle (or low-flying seaplane) over trees, creeks and roaming wildlife.

Great For...

☑ Don't Miss

Zipping over open water and scaling a 50ft climbing wall at Knudson Cove.

Adventure Tours

Two of Ketchikan's ziplines are operated by the fun but professional **Alaska Canopy Adventures** (📞907-225-5503; www.alaska canopy.com; 116 Wood Rd; per person $189; 🚶). The zip sites are both at Herring Cove, 8 miles south of Ketchikan via the S Tongass Hwy. The Bear Creek canopy has seven lines, a skybridge above a waterfall, a 250ft slide and a 4WD vehicle to transport you up the mountain. It is more suitable for beginners and appropriate for kids. The Rainforest Canopy at Eagle Creek is more advanced and enables you to view wildlife, including salmon runs in Herring Creek and the bears that feast on them. The company maintains a desk in the downtown tour center or you can book online. Transport is included.

LIANE HARROLD/ALAMY ©

⚓ Explore Ashore

All three zipline tours take around 3½ hours including 20- to 25-minute bus transfers at either end. They are riotously popular with cruise passengers and thus easy to organize either through your ship or independently online.

❶ Need to Know

Zipline tours, including transfers, cost from $125 to $189.

✕ Take a Break

Load up before you go with a takeout sandwich from Sweet Mermaids (p109).

Knudson Cove

Southeast Exposure (☎907-225-8829; www.southeastexposure.com; 37 Potter Rd) operates a Zipline Adventure Park at Knudson Cove, 16 miles north of Ketchikan with a slightly more varied stash of rainforest thrills. As well as eight ziplines, there are a couple of balance-testing rope and log bridges, a zipline over the water and a 50ft climbing tower.

Alaska Rainforest Sanctuary

The two Alaska Canopy Adventure ziplines are strung high above the **Alaska Rainforest Sanctuary** (www.alaskarainforest.com; South Tongass Hwy; tours adult/child $89/59), a 40-acre wildlife reserve at Herring Cove where you can go on a naturalist-led walk (with the chance of spotting bears), visit a raptor center and old sawmill, and see a working Native totem-carving house. It's particularly popular with cruise-ship passengers, who are whisked here straight off the ships.

Totem poles, Totem Bight State Park

KERI OBERLY/GETTY IMAGES ©

Totem Poles & Alaska Native Culture

Ketchikan vies with Sitka as Alaska's totem-pole capital. Striking examples of the skillful art evoke powerful echoes of Haida, Tlingit and Tsimshian history and culture.

Great For...

☑ Don't Miss

Watching skilled Alaska Native carvers at work at Saxman Native Village.

Totem Heritage Center

For a crash course in Southeast Alaska's impressive totem art look no further than the **Totem Heritage Center** (☏907-225-5900; 601 Deermount St; adult/child $5/free; ☺8am-5pm May-Sep, 1-5pm Mon-Fri Oct-Apr), where old poles brought from deserted Tlingit and Haida communities are kept to prevent further deterioration. Inside the center, over a dozen poles, some more than 100 years old, are on display in an almost spiritual setting that accentuates the reverence Alaska Natives attach to them. More are erected outside, and the entire center is shrouded in pines and serenaded by the gurgling Ketchikan Creek.

Totem pole, Saxman Native Village & Totem Park

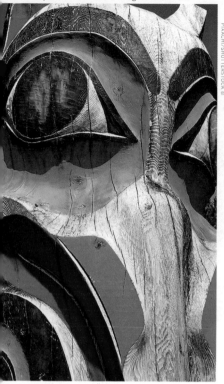

PIXACHI/SHUTTERSTOCK ©

⚓

Explore Ashore

All of Ketchikan's totem sights are accessible by local bus from the cruise dock. Trip times one-way are Totem Heritage Center (five minutes), Saxman Native Village (10 minutes), Totem Bight State Park (25 minutes). For organized trips inquire at the Tour Center (p104).

❶ Need to Know

Ketchikan's totem sights are generally open from 8am to 5pm.

✖ Take a Break

Grab a quick lunch in the locals' favorite diner, Pioneer Cafe (p109).

Saxman Native Village & Totem Park

On S Tongass Hwy, 2.5 miles south of Ketchikan, is this incorporated Tlingit village of 475 residents. It's best known for **Saxman Totem Park** (☏907-225-4421; www.capefoxtours.com; $5; ⊗8am-5pm), which holds 24 totem poles from abandoned villages around the Southeast, restored or recarved in the 1930s. Among them is a replica of the Lincoln Pole (the original is in the Alaska State Museum in Juneau), which was carved in 1883, using a picture of Abraham Lincoln, to commemorate the first sighting of white people.

You can wander around the Totem Park on your own or, by prior appointment (and an extra $32), join an Alaska Native–led two-hour village tour. There are several a day in peak season.

Totem Bight State Park

Ten miles north of downtown Ketchikan is this seaside **park** (☏907-247-8574; 9883 North Tongass Hwy) FREE that contains 14 restored totem poles, a colorful community house and a viewing deck overlooking Tongass Narrows. There are various interpretive boards explaining the importance of this attractive site, which was one of the earliest attempts to revive the dying art of totem carving in the 1930s.

LEE PRINCE/SHUTTERSTOCK ©

Misty Fjords National Monument

This spectacular, 3570-sq-mile national monument, just 22 miles east of Ketchikan, is a natural mosaic of sea cliffs, steep fjords and rock walls jutting 3000ft straight out of the ocean.

Great For...

☑ Don't Miss

A water landing in a floatplane in Rudyerd Bay or Punchbowl Cove.

Brown and black bears, mountain goats, Sitka deer, bald eagles and a multitude of marine mammals inhabit Misty Fjords' drizzly realm. The monument receives 150in of rainfall annually, and many people think the fjord is at its most beautiful when the granite walls and tumbling waterfalls are veiled in fog and mist. Walker Cove, Rudyerd Bay and Punchbowl Cove – the preserve's most picturesque areas – are reached via Behm Canal, the long inlet separating Revillagigedo Island from the mainland. Well off the road network, the monument is best accessed via floatplane or boat, neither of which are cheap. Close to a dozen rustic United States Forest Service (USFS) cabins attract adventurous overnighters.

USA
Misty Fjords National Monument
Prince of Wales Island   Revillagigedo Island
Ketchikan
Gravina Island
CANADA

Explore Ashore

If you're pushed for time, a flightseeing trip is more efficient, filling an action-packed 90 minutes (or less), compared to the 4½ hours required for boat trips – plus, they are only marginally more expensive.

ⓘ Need to Know

A 90-minute flightseeing trip costs $189–249; a 4½-hour boat trip costs $200.

Flightseeing

The most practical way to view the Misty Fjords is on a sightseeing flight. Flightseeing may be the only option if you're in a hurry – most tours operate out of Ketchikan and last 90 minutes including a landing on a lake. Keep in mind that this is a big seller and when the weather is nice there is an endless stream of floatplanes flying to the same area: Rudyerd Bay and Walker Cove. Popular operators include **Family Air Tours** (☏907-247-1305; www.familyairtours.com; 1285 Tongass Ave, Ketchikan), **Seawind Aviation** (☏907-225-1206; www.seawindaviation.com; Front St, Berth 2, Ketchikan) and **Southeast Aviation** (☏907-225-2900; www.southeast aviation.com).

Boat Trips

The best and most comfortable way to see Misty Fjords National Monument is on a boat with mega-experienced **Allen Marine Tours** (☏907-225-8100; www.allenmarinetours. com; 5 Salmon Landing, Suite 215; adult/child $200/127). The 4½-hour fjords tour on an 80ft catamaran includes narration, snacks and use of binoculars to look at wildlife. It's understandably popular. Book online.

◎ SIGHTS

Creek Street Historic Site

Departing from Stedman St is Creek St (a boardwalk built over Ketchikan Creek on pilings), a history book of misshapen wood-paneled houses painted in bright colors to deflect the heaviness of the oft-sodden climate. This was Ketchikan's famed red-light district until prostitution became illegal in 1954. During Creek St's heyday, it supported up to 30 brothels and became known as the only place in Alaska where 'the fishermen and the fish went upstream to spawn.'

Southeast Alaska
Discovery Center Museum

(www.alaskacenters.gov; 50 Main St; adult/ child $5/free; ☺8am-4pm; ♿) Three large totems greet you in the lobby of this NPS-run center, while a school of silver salmon suspended from the ceiling leads you toward a slice of re-created temperate rainforest. Upstairs, the exhibit hall features sections on Southeast Alaska's ecosystems and Alaska Native traditions. You can even view wildlife here: there's a spotting scope trained on Deer Mountain for mountain goats, while underwater cameras in Ketchikan Creek let you watch thousands of salmon struggling upstream to spawn.

Tongass Historical
Museum Museum

(☏907-225-5600; 629 Dock St; adult/child $3/ free; ☺8am-5pm) Houses a collection of local historical and Alaska Native artifacts, many dealing with Ketchikan's fishing industry. More interesting is the impressive Raven Stealing the Sun totem just outside and an observation platform overlooking the Ketchikan Creek falls.

Dolly's House Museum

(24 Creek St; adult/child $10/free; ☺when cruise ships are in) Dolly's House looks like a dollhouse from the outside, but it once operated as a bastion of the world's oldest profession (read: prostitution). These days it's a slightly over-theatrical museum dedi-

cated to a notorious era when the whole of Creek St served as a giant den of iniquity.

The house is the erstwhile parlor of the city's most famous madam, Dolly Arthur. Tours include a look at the brothel, including its bar, which was placed over a trapdoor to the creek for quick disposal of bootleg whiskey.

Waterfront Promenade Street

Ketchikan's newest boardwalk is the Waterfront Promenade, which begins near Berth 4, passes Harbor View Park (a city park that is composed entirely of decking and pilings), follows the cruise-ship docks and then wraps around Thomas Basin Harbor. Along the way there are plenty of whale-tail and halibut benches where you can take a break and admire the maritime scenery.

✪ ACTIVITIES

Rainbird Trail Hiking

Dedicated in 2010, this 1.3-mile trail is within town, stretching from the University of Alaska Southeast campus off 7th Ave to a trailhead off Third Ave Bypass. You can ride the bus to UAS and follow this delightful trail as it winds through a rainforest along a bluff before giving way to striking views of the city and Tongass Narrows below.

Ward Lake Nature Walk Hiking

The easy 1.5-mile Ward Lake Nature Walk is a favorite with local dog owners and accessible year-round. The interpretive loop encircles the peaceful lake and begins near the parking area at the lake's north end. Beavers, birds and the occasional black bear might be seen. To reach the lake, follow N Tongass Hwy, 7 miles north from downtown to Ward Cove; turn right on Revilla Rd and continue to Ward Lake Rd.

✪ TOURS

Ketchikan, with its cruise-ship economy, is well set up for guided tours, especially day trips. The **Ketchikan Visitor**

⚓ **Understand**

Ports Less-Visited: Wrangell

Wrangell, 100 nautical miles north of Ketchikan, is Southeast Alaska's rough, gruff, coastal outpost, a small boom-bust fishing community colored by centuries of native Tlingit settlement and more recent incursions by the Russians and British. Posh it isn't. Lacking the fishing affluence of Petersburg or the cruise-ship-oriented economy of Ketchikan, the town nurtures a tough outback spirit more familiar to Alaska's frigid north than its drizzly Panhandle. A collapse in the lumber industry in the 1990s hit the town hard, a blow from which it has only recently recovered.

Only a few small cruise ships stop in Wrangell (around 20 per season). Passengers who disembark normally use it as a launchpad for excursions to the Anan bear-watching observatory and the incredible Stikine River delta nearby. However, the countryside around town, a mishmash of boggy 'muskeg' and tree-covered mountains, offers fine hiking, a fact not lost on Scottish American naturalist John Muir, who decamped here in 1879 on the first of four Alaska visits.

The town has an impressive **museum** (☑907-874-3770; 296 Campbell Dr; adult/child/family $5/2/12; ☺10am-5pm Mon-Sat late Apr–mid-Sep, 1-5pm Tue-Sat mid-Sep–late Apr) and some important Tlingit history preserved in a rebuilt clan house on **Chief Shakes Island** (Shakes St) FREE. But, Wrangell's oldest attractions are the primitive rock carvings, believed to date back at least 1000 years, on nearby **Petroglyph Beach** (Evergreen Ave; ♿) FREE.

Rock carving at Petroglyph Beach
ERNEST MANEWAL/GETTY IMAGES ©

Information & Tour Center (☑907-225-6166; www.visit-ketchikan.com; 131 Front St, City Dock; ☺7am-6pm) building on City Dock has a whole wing devoted to a gauntlet of 20 tour providers touting their services. Flightseeing, wildlife-watching, kayaking, and boat tours to Misty Fjords are all well represented.

Bering Sea Crab Fishermen's Tour Boating
(☑907-247-2721; www.56degreesnorth.com; Berth 3; tours adult/child $179/115) This fantastically popular and highly original tour employs a veteran crabbing boat, the F/V *Aleutian Ballad* (that once featured in the Discovery Channel's *Deadliest Catch*

Ketchikan

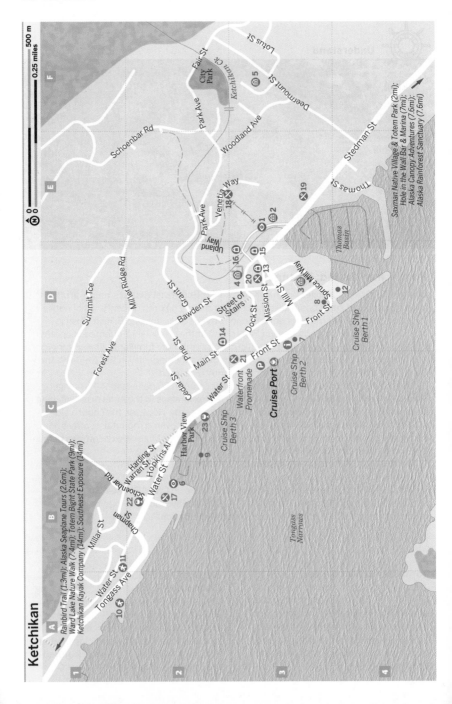

0 2 N

0 500 m
0 0.25 miles

Rainbird Trail (1.3mi); Alaska Seaplane Tours (2.6mi);
Ward Lake Nature Walk (7.4mi); Totem Bight State Park (9mi);
Ketchikan Kayak Company (14mi); Southeast Exposure (14mi)

Saxman Native Village & Totem Park (2mi);
Hole in the Wall Bar & Marina (7mi);
Alaska Canopy Adventures (7.6mi);
Alaska Rainforest Sanctuary (7.6mi)

Tongass Narrows

Thomas Basin

Cruise Ship Berth 1
Cruise Ship Berth 2
Cruise Ship Berth 3

Cruise Port

Waterfront Promenade

Harbor View Park

City Park

Ketchikan Ck

Fair St
Lotus St
Park Ave
Schoenbar Rd
Woodland Ave
Deermount St
Stedman St
Thomas St
Venetia Way
Upland Way
Park Ave
Summit Tce
Miller Ridge Rd
Forest Ave
Bawden St
Grant St
Pine St
Cedar St
Main St
Water St
Street of Stairs
Dock St
Mission St
Mill St
Spruce Mill Way
Front St
Harding St
Warren St
Hopkins Al
Water St
Schoenbar Rd
Chapman St
Millar St
Water St
Tongass Ave

10
11
22
17
6
9
23
14
21
7
3
8
12
13
20
15
16
4
1
2
19
18
5

Ketchikan

television series) to take people out on an authentic Alaskan crab-fishing trip. Watch the masters at work as they haul in crustaceans and listen to their incredible stories from the tempestuous waters of the Bering Sea. The trip lasts three hours and the boat has a 100-seat heated amphitheater for on-deck viewing. Wildlife-watching is an added bonus, as are the complimentary hot drinks and snacks.

Alaska Seaplane Tours Wildlife
(☑907-225-1974; www.alaskaseaplanetours.com; 4743 North Tongass Hwy) As well as offering Misty Fjords excursions, these guys fly to Prince of Wales Island to observe bruins on a two-hour bear-watching tour ($289).

Alaska Amphibious Tours Driving
(☑907-225-9899; www.akduck.com; Ketchikan Visitors Bureau, booth 10; tours adult/child $49/29; ⌖) The 'Ketchikan Duck Tour' runs a part-land, part-water-based history tour of the town in large amphibious buses. The 1½-hour excursion is popular with families but heavy on the tourist cliches.

⊕ SHOPPING

Ketchikan has a rich artists' community, meaning you're better off bypassing the predictable trinket shops in search of the real thing. The city is home to Ray Troll,

whose distinctive and instantly recognizable work you'll see all over Southeast Alaska.

Soho Coho Arts & Crafts
(www.trollart.com; 5 Creek St; ⊘9am-5:30pm Mon-Sat, to 4pm Sun) The must-see home gallery of one of Alaska's most noted contemporary artists, Ray Troll, whose salmon- and fish-inspired work is seen all around town, including on the sides of buses. Treat yourself to a Star Wars–inspired 'Return of the Sockeye' screen-printed T-shirt.

Crazy Wolf Studio Arts & Crafts
(✆907-225-9653; 633 Mission St; ⊘8am-6pm) In a town full of tourist-orientated trinket shops, the locally run Crazy Wolf provides an authentic alternative. It is owned by a native Tsimshian artist and stocks interesting crafts, which include drums, baskets, jewelry and screen prints.

Main Street Gallery Arts & Crafts
(www.ketchikanarts.org; 330 Main St; ⊘9am-5pm Mon-Fri, 11am-3pm Sat) Operated by the Ketchikan Area Arts & Humanities Council, this small but wonderful gallery stages a reception on the first Friday of every month, unveiling the work of a selected local or regional artist. It's an evening of refreshments and presentations by the artist, and of extended hours by other galleries downtown, too.

⚓ **Understand**

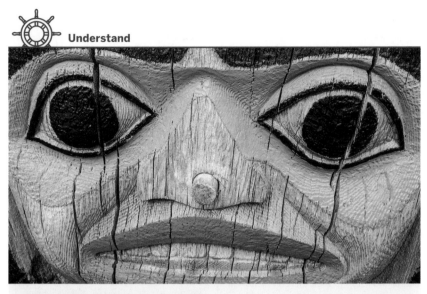

Totem Poles: A Beginner's Guide

There is no finer manifestation of coastal Alaska's indigenous culture than its intricately carved totem poles adorned with ravens, killer whales and carved countenances from native mythology.

Totem poles are peculiar to the Pacific Northwest region, in particular coastal British Columbia and Southeastern Alaska, where they have been sculpted for centuries by the Haida, Tlingit and Tsimshian people. Although the presence of totems predates the arrival of European explorers, the poles became grander and more artistically accomplished when native people gained access to iron tools in the late 18th century.

Usually fashioned out of mature cedars found deep in the forest, totems have a natural lifespan of around 75 years before the sodden Pacific Northwest climate takes its toll. Traditionally poles are rarely touched up. Progressive deterioration is seen as a part of the natural life cycle. Ideally, they are left to rot and return to the earth.

Totems were never intended as objects of worship. Instead, they serve several nonreligious functions: 'welcome poles' are designed to greet visitors to houses and communities, 'memorial poles' honor the dead, 'mortuary poles' contain the remains of deceased ancestors and 'house poles' have a structural function, while 'shame poles' ridicule public figures accused of a transgression.

Totem poles reached their artistic zenith in the mid-19th century. However, by the beginning of the 20th century, their presence had nearly died out. Carving was first rediscovered during the Great Depression when the Civilian Conservation Corps were tasked with carrying out work relief programs in Alaska's national forests. The practice was revived more enthusiastically in the 1960s amid a renewed appreciation of America's indigenous culture, primarily as a means of artistic expression.

Ketchikan, Wrangell, Haines and Prince of Wales Island are the best places to immerse yourself in totem art.

Parnassus Books Books

(105 Stedman St; ⊗8am-6pm Mon-Fri, 10am-5pm Sat & Sun) This unexpectedly encyclopedic bookstore is a delightful place to spend a rainy afternoon (and there will be many!) browsing Alaskan books, cards and local art.

🍴 EATING

If Ketchikan's your first stop in Alaska, you'll quickly discover that it makes sense to become a temporary pescatarian here. Fish rules in these parts, especially salmon and halibut, whether it comes in tacos, with chips or in a chowder. Ketchikan doesn't do much in the way of gourmet cuisine. That said, it has one of the Panhandle's widest selection of restaurants outside Juneau.

Sweet Mermaids Cafe $

(☏907-225-3277; 340 Front St; lunch $8-11; ⊗7am-4pm) Marketing itself as a *shoppe* as opposed to a shop (think home-baked cakes and staff in flowery aprons), Ketchikan's prime source of sugar replenishment plies the best sweet morsels in town, if the frosted banana and Nutella cake is any-

thing to go by. Also on offer are giant deli sandwiches, smoothies and coffee.

Pioneer Café Cafe $$

(619 Mission St; mains breakfast $8-14, lunch $9-14, dinner $11-20; ⊗6am-10pm Sun-Thu, 24hr Fri & Sat) Substantial portions of no-frills, filling food served in a plain but traditional diner with fast service, automatic coffee refills and a plain-speaking cross-section of the local populace. Generous opening hours.

Bar Harbor Restaurant Modern American $$$

(☏907-225-2813; 55 Schoenbar Ct, Berth 4; mains $22-42; ⊗11am-2pm & 5-8pm Tue-Fri, 9am-2pm & 5-8pm Sat, 9am-2pm Sun) This slightly pricey fish-biased restaurant, usually touted among locals as the best in town, opened for the 2017 season in a new cruise-dock location on Berth 4. Expect larger than normal crowds descending on its modern ocean-themed interior to feast on creative seafood and chowder renditions.

For a taster, draw lots between the impressive fish tacos, coconut prawns, ahi tuna, and crab and pesto gnocchi.

Pioneer Café

RUBEN M RAMOS/SHUTTERSTOCK ©

Climbing
Deer Mountain

Within walking distance of downtown, Ketchikan's most popular hike is a well-maintained 2.5-mile climb to the 3000ft summit of Deer Mountain. Along the way lookouts provide panoramic views – the first only a mile up the trail. To reach the trail, take the Bus' Green Line to the corner of Deermount and Fair Sts and then head south on Ketchikan Lakes Rd. Toward the top of the mountain are more trails that extend into the alpine region and a free-use shelter. But keep in mind this is a steady climb and a more challenging hike beyond the shelter.

Deer Mountain trail
RAMUNAS BRUZAS/SHUTTERSTOCK ©

Heen Kahidi
Restaurant   American $$$

(📞907-225-8001; www.capefoxlodge.com; 800 Venetia Way; mains $19-42; ⊘7am-9pm) The hilltop dining in Cape Fox Lodge is about as posh as Ketchikan gets and certainly worth the short climb to get here. Food is split between surf and turf, with the former being slightly better in terms of style and sauce. Choose the pecan-crusted halibut or the blackened rockfish in a mango and pineapple salsa. The views are good and the on-site hotel is replete with native art.

New York Cafe   Breakfast $$$

(📞907-225-0246; www.thenewyorkhotel.com; 207 Stedman St; breakfast $8-12, dinner mains $28-35; ⊘7:30am-8:30pm Tue-Thu & Sun, to 9pm Fri & Sat) Beneath the historic New York Hotel is this wood-paneled cafe which doesn't seem to have changed much decor-wise since its Roaring 1920s opening – if you don't count the food, which has doffed its hat to modern trends (ceviche and falafel included). The breakfast eggs are good, while the lunch and dinner menus are anchored by seafood including crabs legs.

🍷 DRINKING & NIGHTLIFE

Most of Ketchikan's dive-y bars don't (thankfully) stand on ceremony for tourists. Be prepared to dive in with the locals.

Hole in the Wall
Bar & Marina   Pub

(7500 S Tongass Hwy; ⊘noon-2am) A funky little hangout that feels light years away from the tourist madness of Ketchikan in summer. There's not much inside other than a handful of stools, a woodstove, a pool table and a lot of friendly conversation, usually centered on fishing. But the bar is in a beautiful location, perched above a small marina in a narrow cove 7.5 miles south of Ketchikan.

Arctic Bar   Bar

(509 Water St; ⊘8am-2am) Just past the tunnel on downtown's northwest side, this local favorite has managed to survive 70 years by poking fun at itself and tourists. On the back deck overlooking the Narrows is a pair of fornicating bears. And hanging below the wooden bruins, in full view of every cruise ship that ties up in front of the bar, is the sign 'Please Don't Feed the Bears.'

49'er Bar   Bar

(1010 Water St; ⊘9am-2am) A Jurassic bar that preserves more than 100 years of cigarette smoke in a wood-paneled, Wild West–flavored building located just north of the main cruise-ship terminal. Beer, darts and hot dogs satisfy old-fashioned appetites.

Downtown Ketchikan

❶ GETTING AROUND

BICYCLE

Ketchikan has an expanding system of bike paths that head north and south of downtown along Tongass Ave. Rent Trek hybrids at **Southeast Exposure** (✆907-225-8829; www.southeast exposure.com; 1224 Tongass Ave; 4hr/full-day rentals $20/30), which has a summer rental near the cruise-ship docks.

BUS

Ketchikan's excellent public bus system is called **the Bus** (✆907-225-8726; one way $1). There are two main lines: the Green Line runs from downtown and then north past the airport ferry.

The Silver Line heads south past Saxman Village to Rotary Beach and north all the way past Totem Bight State Park.

There's also a free downtown loop. You can't miss the bus: famed artist Ray Troll painted spawning salmon all over it. The 20-minute loop goes from Berth 4 of the cruise-ship dock to the Totem Heritage Center.

TAXI

Cab companies in town include **Sourdough Cab** (✆907-225-5544) and **Yellow Taxi** (✆907-225-5555). The fare from the ferry terminal or the airport ferry dock to downtown costs from $11 to $15.

SUPAPIX/SHUTTERSTOCK ©

SITKA

In This Chapter

Sitka at a Glance...

It's not always easy to uncover reminders of Alaska's 135-year-long dalliance with the Russian Empire – until you dock in Sitka. This sparkling gem of a city, which kisses the Pacific Ocean on Baranof Island's west shore, is one of the oldest non-native settlements in the state and the former capital of Russian Alaska. The bonus for visitors is that Sitka mixes wonderfully preserved history with out-standing natural beauty. Looming on the horizon, across Sitka Sound, is impressive Mt Edgecumbe, an extinct volcano with a graceful cone similar to Japan's Mt Fuji. Closer in, myriad small, forested islands turn into beautiful ragged silhouettes at sunset.

With a Day in Port

○ Warm up in the **Back Door Cafe** (p124) and its **bookshop** (p124).

○ Explore Russian history with visits to **St Michael's Cathedral** (p120), the **Russian Bishop's House** (p117) and **Sitka National Historical Park** (p124).

○ Spend the afternoon admiring birds in the **raptor center** (p121) and finish with a beer in **Baranof Island Brewing Co** (p124) nearby.

Best Places for...

Pizza Mean Queen (p124)

Coffee Back Door Cafe (p124)

Craft Beer Baranof Island Brewing Co (p124)

Wine & Appetizers Ludvig's Wine Bar and Gallery (p125)

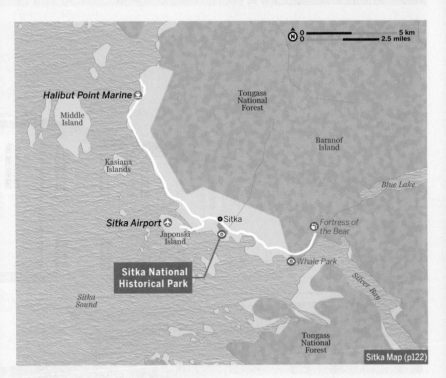

Sitka Map (p122)

Getting from the Port

○ Large cruise ships dock at **Halibut Point Marine**, 6 miles north of town. Special cruise company buses run passengers into town.

○ Smaller ships dock offshore in Sitka Sound and take passengers into Crescent Harbor in water taxis.

Fast Facts

Money First National Bank of Anchorage (318 Lincoln St) has a 24-hour ATM.

Best for free Wi-fi Available throughout the downtown area. It can be picked up in most cafes, stores, bars and hotels along Lincoln St and Harbor Dr.

Tourist Information Sitka Information Center is opposite the Westmark hotel downtown.

The Old School

Sitka National Historical Park

This mystical juxtaposition of tall trees and totems is Alaska's smallest national park and the site where the Tlingits were finally defeated by the Russians in 1804.

Great For...

☑ Don't Miss

Free tours of the upper floor in the Bishop's House.

Visitors Center

The visitors center (8am to 5pm) displays Russian and indigenous artifacts, along with a 12-minute video on the Tlingit–Russian battle waged here in 1804. There's also a workshop where you can observe and talk to native wood-carvers.

Totem Trail

A mile-long Totem Trail winds its way past 18 totems first displayed at the 1904 Louisiana Exposition in St Louis and then moved to the park. These intriguing totems, standing in a thick rainforest setting by the sea and often enveloped in mist, have become synonymous with the national park and, by extension, the city itself.

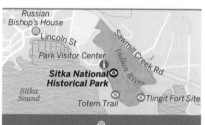

Explore Ashore

From the **Harigan Centennial Hall**, where cruise-ship transfer buses and water taxis arrive and depart, it is a five-minute walk to the Russian Bishop's House and a 15-minute walk to Sitka National Historical Park. You'll need around 2½ hours to see both.

❶ Need to Know

(www.nps.gov; Lincoln St; ⊘6am-10pm) FREE

✕ Take a Break

Close to the Russian Bishop's House, the **Bayview Pub** (www.sitkabayviewpub.com; 407 Lincoln St; sandwiches $12-16; ⊘11am-late) serves good sandwiches and drinks.

Tlingit Fort Site

Halfway around the Totem Trail, you arrive at the site of the Tlingit fort near Indian River with its outline still clearly visible.

Back in 1804, the Tlingits defended their wooden fort for a week. The Russians' cannons did little damage to the walls of the fort and, when the Russian soldiers stormed the structure with the help of Aleuts, they were repulsed in a bloody battle.

Russian Bishop's House

East of downtown along Lincoln St, the **Russian Bishop's House** (☎907-747-0135; Lincoln St; ⊘9am-5pm) FREE is the oldest intact Russian building in Sitka. Built in 1843 by Finnish carpenters out of Sitka spruce,

the two-story log house is one of only four surviving examples of Russian colonial architecture in North America. The National Park Service has restored the building to its 1853 condition, when it served as residence for Russian bishop, Innocent (Ivan Veniaminov).

You can wander the ground-floor museum, with its rescued exhibits, at will. Access to the top floor, home to re-created living quarters and the private chapel of Bishop Innocent, is by guide only.

Sitka's Russian & Tlingit Past

There's no better place to rediscover the relics and relevance of Russian Alaska than at Sitka, one of the state's oldest colonial settlements and its erstwhile capital.

Start Totem Square
Distance 2 miles
Duration 1½ hours

4 Head into the foliage-covered **Russian Cemetery** (p120) for a poignant, sometimes eerie, window into the past

3 Investigate another cleverly re-imagined part of the erstwhile Russian defenses at the octagonal wooden **Blockhouse**.

1 Get oriented in windswept **Totem Square** with its unusual Russian-Tlingit totems.

2 Try to picture the Russian fortifications of yore high above the harbor on **Castle Hill** (p120).

Take a Break ...

Coffee goes down well with a piece of homemade pie at **Back Door Cafe** (p124).

Erler St
Kogwanton St
Katlian St
Marine St
Observatory St
Lake St
Seward St
Cathedral Way
Harbor Dr
ANB Harbor
START
Lincoln St
Harbor Rd
Barracks St
O'Connell Bridge

N 0 — 500 m
0 — 0.25 miles

6 Stop by the **Russian Bishop's House** (p117), one of Alaska's few bricks-and-mortar relics from the Russian era.

7 Admire the trimmed lawns of the former Sheldon Jackson College and peruse its scholarly **museum** (p120).

Sawmill Creek Rd

Monastery St

Baranof St

Etolin St

Finn Al

Jeff Davis St

College Dr

Indian River

Lincoln St

6

Crescent Harbor

7

FINISH 8

5 Drop back into town for an eyeful of ecclesial gold in icon-filled **St Michael's Cathedral** (p120).

8 Lengthen your pace on a wooded trail punctuated by totems in **Sitka National Historical Park** (p124).

⊙ SIGHTS

Russian Cemetery — Cemetery

(⊙6am-10pm) Old headstones and Russian Orthodox crosses lurk in the overgrown and quintessentially creepy Russian Cemetery (located at the north end of Observatory St), where the drippy verdure seems poised to swallow up the decaying graves. Rarely will you find a more atmospheric graveyard.

St Michael's Cathedral — Church

(240 Lincoln St; adult/child $5/free; ⊙9am-4pm Mon-Fri or by appointment) Built between 1844 and 1848, this church stood for more than 100 years as Alaska's finest Russian Orthodox cathedral. When a fire destroyed it in 1966, the church had been the oldest religious structure from the Russian era in Alaska. Luckily the priceless treasures and icons inside were saved by Sitka's residents, who immediately built a replica of their beloved church. The interior is rich in detail and iconography.

Castle Hill — Historic Site

Walk west on Lincoln St for the walkway to Castle Hill. Kiksadi clan houses once covered the hilltop site, but in 1836 the Russians built 'Baranov's Castle' atop the hill to house the governor of Russian America. It was here, on October 18, 1867, that the official transfer of Alaska from Russia to the USA took place. The castle burned down in 1894. A US administrative building briefly took its place, but was demolished in 1955.

Sitka Historical Museum — Museum

(www.sitkahistory.org; 330 Harbor Dr; ⊙9am-5pm) Within Sitka's recently rebuilt Harigan Centennial Hall, the town history museum was undergoing a full renovation at last visit. It was due to reopen in late 2017 with plenty of relics from Russian Alaska.

Sheldon Jackson Museum — Museum

(104 College Dr; adult/child $5/free; ⊙9am-4:30pm) East along Lincoln St on the former campus of Sheldon Jackson College is Sheldon Jackson Museum. The college may be gone, but this fine museum, housed in

St Michael's Cathedral

Alaska's oldest concrete building (1895), survives. The unusual building is home to a small but excellent collection of artifacts from all of Alaska's indigenous groups gathered by Dr Sheldon Jackson, a federal education agent, in Alaska in the 1890s.

Among the artifacts is a raven helmet worn by a Tlingit warrior named Katlian in the 1804 Battle of Sitka, along with rescued totem poles dating from the 1820s to the 1880s.

Sitka Sound
Science Center
Aquarium

(www.sitkascience.org; 801 Lincoln St; $5; ☉9am-4pm; 👪) Sitka's best children's attraction is this hatchery and science center. Outside, the facade is being restored to its original appearance. Inside the science center are five aquariums, including the impressive 800-gallon 'Wall of Water' and three touch tanks where kids can get their hands wet handling anemones, sea cucumbers and starfish.

Alaska Raptor
Center
Wildlife Reserve

(☎907-747-8662; www.alaskaraptor.org; 101 Sawmill Creek Rd; adult/child $12/6; ☉8am-4pm; 🅿👪) ✈ This is no zoo, or bird show for gawping kids. Rather, think of it more as a raptor hospital and rehab center – and a good one at that. The 17-acre center treats 200 injured birds a year, with its most impressive facility being a 20,000-sq-ft flight-training center that helps injured eagles, owls, falcons and hawks regain their ability to fly. In the center eagles literally fly past you, only 2ft or 3ft away, at eye level.

Fortress of
the Bear
Animal Sanctuary

(☎907-747-3550; www.fortressofthebear.com; adult/child $10/5) If you haven't seen a bear in the wild – or don't want to – this rescue facility offers an opportunity to observe brown bears that were abandoned as cubs. The walls of the 'fortress' are actually wastewater treatment pools left over after the lumber mill near the end of Sawmill Creek Rd closed in 1993.

 **Kayaking in
Sitka Sound**

The mini-archipelago of tiny islets that crowds Sitka's harbor, coupled with the fact that big ferries and cruise ships dock several miles to the north, make the town's waters ideal for safe kayaking. Just be sure to keep an eye out for motorized fishing and pleasure boats entering and exiting the harbor.

Sitka Sound Ocean Adventures (☎907-752-0660; www.kayaksitka.com) rents kayaks (single/double $75/95 per day) and runs guided trips appropriate for visitors on cruise-ship schedules; its office is a blue bus outside the **Harigan Centennial Hall**. The great value 2½-hour 'Harbor & Islands' paddle (adult/child $79/54) takes you on a voyage through the mini-archipelago that decorates Sitka's harbor.

EDMUND LOWE PHOTOGRAPHY/GETTY IMAGES ©

The setting is a little strange and these are captive bears, but they are incredibly active – swimming, wrestling and just being bears. It's 5.5 miles south of Sitka.

😊 ACTIVITIES

Hiking

Sitka offers superb hiking in the beautiful and tangled forest surrounding the city. A complete hiking guide is available from the **USFS Sitka Ranger District office** (☎907-747-6671, recorded information 907-747-6685; 2108 Halibut Point Rd; ☉8am-4:30pm Mon-Fri).

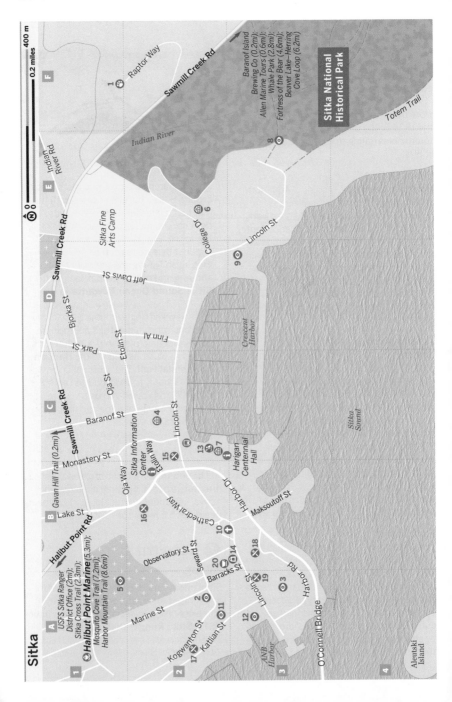

Sitka

A | 1

◎ Halibut Point Marine

USFS Sitka Ranger
District Office (2mi);
Sitka Cross Trail (2.3mi);
Mosquito Cove Trail (7.2mi);
Harbor Mountain Trail (8.6mi)

Halibut Point Rd

Gavan Hill Trail (0.2mi);

Sawmill Creek Rd

Lake St

Marine St

Observatory St

Kogwanton St

Katlian St

ANB
Harbor

O'Connell Bridge

Aleutski
Island

Monastery St

Baranof St

Sawmill Creek Rd

Bjorka St

Park St

Oja St

Etolin St

Sitka Fine
Arts Camp

Jeff Davis St

Sawmill Creek Rd

College Dr

Raptor Way

Indian River

Indian
River Rd

Lincoln St

Crescent
Harbor

Sitka
Sound

Totem Trail

Sitka National
Historical Park

Baranof Island
Brewing Co (0.2mi);
Allen Marine Tours (0.6mi);
Whale Park (2.8mi);
Fortress of the Bear (4.6mi);
Beaver Lake–Herring
Cove Loop (6.2mi)

Oja Way

Sitka Information
Center

Etolin Way

Cathedral Way

Harbor Dr

Lincoln St

Maksoutoff St

Seward St

Barracks St

Lincoln St

Harbor Rd

Harrigan
Centennial
Hall

0   400 m
0   0.2 miles

Sitka

Scared of bears, or lacking a walking companion? **Sitka Trail Works** (www.sitkatrailworks.org), a nonprofit group that raises money for trail improvements, has additional trail information on its website and arranges guided hikes on weekends throughout the summer.

Gavan Hill Trail   Hiking

Close to town, this popular mountain climb ascends 2500ft over 1.6 miles mainly by the use of wooden staircases. The trail, which breaks into alpine terrain higher up, offers excellent views of Sitka and the surrounding area. From the summit, the adventurous can continue to the peaks of the Three Sisters Mountains.

**Beaver Lake–Herring
Cove Loop**   Hiking

(◪) Dedicated in 2010, the Herring Cove Trail is a 1.3-mile route that extends north to Beaver Lake Trail, which loops around the lake from Sawmill Creek Campground. Together the two trails make for a 3.6-mile hike from the Herring Cove Trailhead, featuring three waterfalls.

Mosquito Cove Trail   Hiking

At the northwest end of Halibut Point Rd, 0.7 miles past the ferry terminal, **Starrigavan Recreation Area** (☑518-885-3639, reservations 877-444-6777; www.recreation.gov; Mile 7.8, Halibut Point Rd; tent & RV sites $12-16)

offers a number of short but sweet trails. One of them, Mosquito Cove Trail, is an easy 1.5-mile loop over gravel and boardwalk, with a little beach-walking as well.

Sitka Cross Trail   Hiking

This easy, well-used, 3-mile trail runs roughly from one end of town to the other. The west end starts at Kramer Ave but you can pick it up on Verstovia Rd. The trail heads east, crossing Gavan Hill Trail and ending at Indian River Trailhead.

Whale-Watching

Many companies in Sitka offer boat tours to view whales and other marine wildlife, and most of them swing past **St Lazaria Island National Wildlife Refuge**, home to 1500 pairs of breeding tufted puffins.

You can often spot whales from shore at **Whale Park** (Sawmill Creek Rd). The town also has a whale **festival** (☑907-747-7964; www.sitkawhalefest.org; ⊙early Nov) in November.

Allen Marine Tours   Cruise

(☑907-747-8100; www.allenmarinetours.com; 1512 Sawmill Creek Rd; adult/child $130/84) Experienced operator with offices in Ketchikan, Juneau and Sitka offering wildlife-focused boat cruises. On the three-hour 'Sea Otter & Wildlife Quest' tthere's a $100 refund if you don't sea a whale, sea otter or bear!

☺ TOURS

Sitka Tours
Bus

(📞907-747-5800; www.sitkatoursalaska.com) If you're only in Sitka for as long as the ferry stopover, don't despair: Sitka Tours runs one-hour express bus tours and 3½-hour historic tours just for you. The tour bus picks up passengers from and returns them to the ferry terminal, making brief visits to Sitka National Historical Park (p116) and St Michael's Cathedral (p120).

🅰 SHOPPING

Old Harbor Books
Books

(201 Lincoln St; ⊙10am-6pm Mon-Fri, to 5pm Sat) One of the loveliest bookstores in the Southeast with a large Alaska section, featured local authors, and the pie-selling Back Door Café adjoining. Browsing heaven.

✖ EATING

Highliner Coffee
Cafe $

(www.highlinercoffee.com; 327 Seward St, Seward Sq Mall; light fare up to $5; ⊙6am-5pm Mon-Sat, 7am-4pm Sun; 🛜) At the Highliner they like their coffee black and their salmon wild, which explains why the walls are covered with photos of local fishing boats and political stickers like 'Invest in Wild Salmon's Future: Eat One!'. The baked goods are highly edible too.

Sitka Hotel Bar & Restaurant
International $$

(📞907-747-3288; 118 Lincoln St; mains $15-29; ⊙11am-9pm Mon-Sat, 9am-9pm Sun) Wood decor covers the interior of this recently remodeled gathering spot, although, with its open kitchen and charismatic bar, the atmosphere is far from wooden. Welcome to Sitka's second-best restaurant – nowhere can yet challenge Ludvig's – where casual atmospherics meet the kind of creative food you once had to jump on a plane to Seattle to enjoy. No more!

Mean Queen
Pizza $$

(📞907-747-0616; www.meanqueensitka.com; 205 Harbor Dr; pizzas $18-22; ⊙11am-2pm) New-ish pizza joint trying hard to be hip in a bright modish space on an upstairs floor close to Castle Hill. There's a pleasant rectangular bar, several booths and plenty of young punters. The thin-crust pizzas come in large shareable sizes.

Ludvig's Bistro
Mediterranean $$$

(📞907-966-3663; www.ludvigsbistro.com; 256 Katlian St; mains $28-40; ⊙4:30-9:30pm Mon-Sat) Sophistication in the wilderness! Sitka's boldest restaurant has only seven tables, and a few stools at its brass-and-blue-tile bar. Described as 'rustic Mediterranean fare,' almost every dish is local, even the sea salt. If seafood paella is on the menu, order it. The traditional Spanish rice dish comes loaded with whatever fresh seafood the local boats have netted that day.

There's an equally salubrious wine bar (p125) upstairs. Reservations necessary.

🅾 DRINKING & NIGHTLIFE

Baranof Island Brewing Co
Brewery

(www.baranofislandbrewing.com; 1209 Sawmill Creek Rd; ⊙2-8pm; 🚼) Encased in a handsome new taproom since July 2017, the Baranof is a local legend providing microbrews for every pub and bar in town. For the real deal, however, the taproom's the place. Line up four to six tasters and make sure you include a Halibut Point Hefeweisen and a Redoubt Red Ale.

Back Door Café
Coffee

(104 Barracks St; snacks $1-5; ⊙6:30am-5pm Mon-Fri, to 2pm Sat) Enter this small coffeehouse through either Old Harbor Books on Lincoln St or via the...you guessed it...which is off Barracks St. The cafe is as local as it gets, with strong, potent joe and fantastic home-baked snacks including pies.

Tlingit mask carver

Ludvig's Wine Bar & Gallery
Wine Bar

(www.ludvigsbistro.com; 256 Katlian St; ⏱5-9pm Mon-Sat) Follow the stairs that are located next to Ludvig's Bistro (p124) up to a parquet-floored art gallery furnished with tall bar tables. You will find excellent tapas, homemade ice cream and a diverse wine list. Enjoy live music three times per week and occasional salsa dancing. It's a great place to have dessert after dinner downstairs or appetizers while you're waiting for a table.

✪ ENTERTAINMENT

Sheet'ka Kwaan Naa Kahidi Dancers
Dance

(☎907-747-7137; 204 Katlian St; adult/child $10/5) Tlingit dancers perform in the Tlingit Clan House, situated next to the Pioneers Home, with half-hour performances. The place has excellent acoustics and a beautifully decorated house screen.

ⓘ GETTING AROUND

BICYCLE

Yellow Jersey Cycle Shop (☎907-747-6317; www.yellowjerseycycles.com; 329 Harbor Dr; per 2hr/day $20/25), across the street from the library, rents quality mountain bikes for economical prices.

BUS

Sitka's public bus system, **Ride Sitka** (☎907-747-7103; www.ridesitka.com; adult/child $2/1; ⏱6:30am-7:30pm Mon-Fri), runs on three lines and serves practically everywhere of interest to visitors. The only downsides: it doesn't stop at the airport (the last stop is about 0.75-miles short) and it doesn't run on weekends.

The green line does a loop around town. The blue line heads south via Whale Park to the Fortress of the Bear. The red line heads north to the cruise dock and the ferry terminal. Crescent Harbor serves as the terminus for all three lines.

TAXI

For a ride around Sitka, try **Hank's Taxi** (☎907-747-8888) or **Baranof Taxi** (☎907-738-4722).

JUNEAU

In This Chapter

Juneau at a Glance...

Juneau is a capital of contrasts and conflicts. It borders a waterway that never freezes but lies beneath an ice field that never melts. It's the state capital but since the 1980s Alaskans have been trying to have that changed. Welcome to America's strangest state capital, which draws more than a million cruise-ship passengers a year. Superb hiking starts barely 10 minutes from downtown, a massive glacier calves into a lake 12 miles up the road, and boats and seaplanes take off from the waterfront bound for nearby bear-viewing, ziplining and whale-watching.

With a Day in Port

○ Explore **South Franklin St** with its shops, bars and restaurants.

○ Reserve time for impressive art at the **Sealaska Heritage building** (p140) and freshly refurbished exhibits at the **Alaska State Museum** (p140).

○ In the afternoon, head to the **Last Chance Mining Museum** (p140); then scale Mt Roberts as far as the **Tramway** (p140) station and come back down on the gondola.

Best Places for...

Local life Pel'Meni (p143)

Coffee Heritage Coffee Co & Cafe (p145)

Cocktails Amalga Distillery (p145)

Local fish Tracy's King Crab Shack (p145)

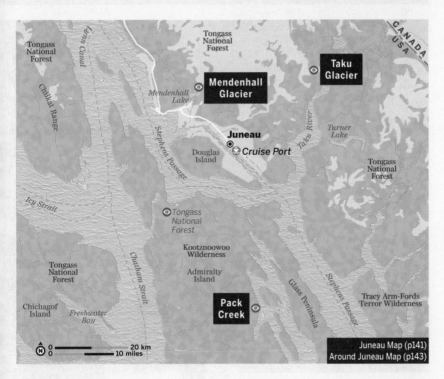

Tongass National Forest

Lynn Canal

CANADA USA

Tongass National Forest

Chilkat Range

Mendenhall Lake

Mendenhall Glacier

Taku Glacier

Taku River

Juneau

Juneau
⊙ *Cruise Port*

Stephens Passage

Douglas Island

Turner Lake

Tongass National Forest

Icy Strait

⊙ Tongass National Forest

Kootznoowoo Wilderness

Chatham Strait

Admiralty Island

Glass Peninsula

Stephens Passage

Tracy Arm-Fords Terror Wilderness

Tongass National Forest

Chichagof Island

Freshwater Bay

Pack Creek ⊙

Ⓝ 0 ——————— 20 km
0 ——————— 10 miles

Juneau Map (p141)
Around Juneau Map (p143)

Getting from the Port

Cruise ships get a far better deal than the state ferry, pulling into a line of docks that starts just south of the downtown core, next to the Mt Roberts Tramway base station. As many as six ships can dock at once, meaning if you're last in the queue, you'll have further to walk. Free shuttles provide wheels for those who would rather not.

Fast Facts

Money First Bank (605 Willoughby Ave) and Wells Fargo (123 Seward St) have ATMs.

Tourist Information Juneau Visitor Center is on the cruise-ship terminal right next to the Mt Roberts Tramway.

Best for Free Wi-fi Free internet access and wi-fi at Juneau Library.

Mt Roberts Trail

VW PICS/CONTRIBUTOR/GETTY IMAGES ©

Juneau Day Hikes

Few cities in Alaska have such a diversity of hiking trails as Juneau. A handful of these trails start near the city center, the rest are 'out the road.'

Great For...

☑ **Don't Miss**

The Last Chance Mining Museum (p140) at the start of the Perseverance Trail.

Mt Roberts Trail

The 5-mile climb up Mt Roberts starts a short way up Basin Rd on the edge of town and offers various options for hikers. Some just ascend fairly steeply through the trees for 2 miles to the top of the tramway with its restaurant and nature center, but it's worth pressing on to experience the flower-bedizened alpine meadows immediately above.

The next landmark, half-a-mile beyond the tramway, is a wooden cross with good views of Juneau and Douglas. Above the cross you enter high alpine terrain and

Mt Roberts Tramway

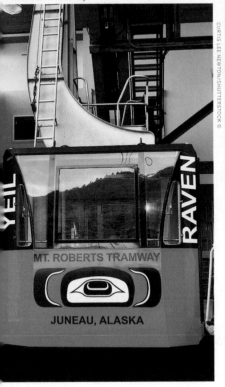

CURTIS LEE NEWTON/SHUTTERSTOCK ©

Explore Ashore

The trailhead for Mt Roberts is a 20- to 25-minute walk from the cruise terminal. The Perseverance trailhead is another 20 minutes further on. Allow one hour to ascend to the top station of the Mt Roberts Tramway and 3½ hours to do the Perseverance Trail (out and back).

❶ Need to Know

The Mt Roberts Tramway costs $33/16 per adult/child but you can hike up the Mt Roberts Trail, spend $10 in the restaurant and then take the tram down for free.

✖ Take a Break

Drink in the view at the top station of the Mt Roberts Tramway in the **Timberline Bar & Grill** (📞907-463-1338; mains $17-45; ⊙11am-8pm).

sometimes encounter snow as the path narrows, traversing a ridge that connects to Mt Gastineau (3666ft). Beyond Gastineau, the path drops into a saddle before ascending again to Mt Roberts (3818ft).

You can 'cheat' on the way down by riding the last segment on the Mt Roberts Tramway to S Franklin St for only $10.

Perseverance Trail

The Perseverance Trail, off Basin Rd, is Juneau's most popular. The trail is a path into Juneau's mining history.

To reach the Perseverance Trail, head north out of town on Basin Rd as it curves away from the city into the mountains following Gold Creek. The trailhead is at the road's end, at the parking lot for the Last Chance Mining Museum (p140). The trail leads into Silverbow Basin, an old mining area that still has many hidden and unmarked adits and mine shafts. From the Perseverance Trail, you can pick up Granite Creek Trail and follow it to the creek's headwaters basin, a beautiful spot.

Mendenhall Glacier

Mendenhall Glacier

Going to Juneau and not seeing the Mendenhall is like visiting Rome and skipping the Colosseum. The most famous of Juneau's ice floes grinds 13 miles from its source and has a half-mile-wide face.

Great For...

☑ Don't Miss

Ranger talks in the visitor center in front of its panoramic windows.

Naturalists estimate that within a few years the Mendenhall Glacier will retreat onto land, and within 25 years retreat out of view entirely from the observation area and visitor center. On a sunny day the glacier is beautiful, with blue skies and snowcapped mountains in the background. On a cloudy and drizzly afternoon it can be even more impressive, as the ice turns shades of deep blue. The river of ice is at the end of Glacier Spur Rd.

Visitor Center

This mini-museum holds ranger talks, shows an 11-minute film and displays exhibits relating to the glacier and its formation. There are huge panoramic windows that

Ice climber

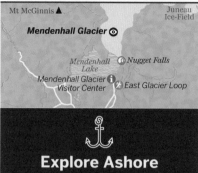

Mt McGinnis ▲   Juneau Ice-Field

Mendenhall Glacier ◉

Mendenhall   ◉ Nugget Falls
Lake
Mendenhall Glacier ❶
Visitor Center   East Glacier Loop

Explore Ashore

The easiest way to get to the glacier is via the 'blue bus' operated by **Mendenhall Glacier Transport/M & M Tours** (☎907-789-5460; www.mightygreat-trips.com; per person $35), **which picks up from the cruise-ship docks downtown every 30 minutes. The half-hourly Capital Transit bus is cheaper ($2), but drops you 1.5 miles short of the Mendenhall visitor center.**

❶ Need to Know

Mendenhall Glacier Visitor Center
(6000 Glacier Spur Rd; ◷8am-7:30pm) FREE

✗ Take a Break

There is no food at the glacier or the visitor center. Bring your own.

look out over the lake, the glacier and gushing Nugget Falls. Various trails lead out directly from the visitor center (pick up a free map).

East Glacier Loop

One of many trails near Mendenhall Glacier, this one is a 2.8-mile round-trip providing good views of the glacier from a lookout at the halfway point, where you can also look down on Nugget Falls. Pick up the loop along the Trail of Time, a half-mile nature walk that starts at the Mendenhall Glacier Visitor Center.

Nugget Falls

This spectacular waterfall is a mini-Niagara (in season) caused by Nugget Creek diving off a hanging valley into Mendenhall Lake. The easy half-mile walk to the falls from the Mendenhall Glacier Visitor Center is popular, meaning you're more likely to spot packs of selfie-taking tourists than salmon-hunting bears.

Taku Glacier

NENAD BASIC/SHUTTERSTOCK ©

Salmon Bake at Taku Glacier Lodge

The most popular tours in Juneau are flightseeing, glacier viewing and salmon bakes, and a trip to this historic off-the-grid lodge combines all three.

Great For...

☑ Don't Miss

Walking off your salmon lunch on a short trail in the vicinity of Taku Glacier Lodge.

Wings Airways (p111), a local floatplane company, has a monopoly on access to the lodge. Its trips include flying across a half-dozen glaciers to the lodge where an incredible meal of wild salmon awaits. The trip is a popular cruise-ship excursion. Sign up at the Wings Airways office behind Merchant's Wharf on Juneau's waterfront.

Flightseeing

The journey to and from the lodge allows for approximately 40 minutes of fightseeing. Flying over the expansive Juneau Icefield you will home in on five major glaciers including the enormous Taku Glacier which is over 1.5 miles thick and 36 miles long – and getting longer. It is one of the few advancing glaciers in Alaska.

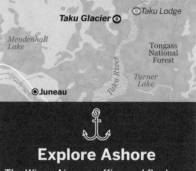

Explore Ashore

The Wings Airways office and float-plane dock is five minutes' walk from the cruise-ship terminal. The tour, including flights and a meal, lasts three hours.

ℹ Need to Know

☎907-586-6275; www.wingsairways.com; adult/child $315/270

✕ Take a Break

You are served a full salmon bake lunch at the Taku Glacier Lodge as part of the package.

The Lodge

The Taku Glacier Lodge – 25 miles, as the crow flies, northeast of Juneau – was built in 1923 in the very early days of Alaskan tourism. Nearly 100 years later it is still standing, yet remains unconnected to any road. Originally conceived as a hunting and fishing lodge it served briefly as a sled-dog breeding center and was reincarnated in its current format in 1979.

Salmon Bake

Fresh salmon is baked over a wood fire on an outdoor barbecue and served inside the lodge with bread, beans and coleslaw. Black bears are regular visitors on the adjacent lawn. A couple of short trails call for some after-lunch exploration.

Brown bear at Pack Creek

KERRY HARGROVE/SHUTTERSTOCK ©

Bear Viewing at Pack Creek

Just 15 miles south of Juneau is Admiralty Island National Monument. The monument's main attraction for visitors is its guided tours of Pack Creek, one of Southeast Alaska's chief bear-viewing sites.

Great For...

☑ Don't Miss

Watching bruins (from a safe distance) splashing playfully around in Pack Creek.

Pack Creek

Pack Creek flows from 4000ft mountains before spilling into Seymour Canal on Admiralty Island's east side. The extensive tide flats at the mouth of the creek draw a large number of bears in July and August to feed on salmon. This, and its proximity to Juneau, make it a favorite spot for observing and photographing the animals.

Seeing the Bears

Bear viewing at Pack Creek takes place at **Stan Price State Wildlife Sanctuary**, named for an Alaskan woodsman who lived on a float-house here for almost 40 years. The vast majority of visitors to the sanctuary are day-trippers who arrive and depart

⚓

Explore Ashore

This trip needs careful pre-planning as Pack Creek permits are limited (book ahead) and time is tight. From Juneau, it's best to organize a guided package. Trips take around six hours including return flights. Getting to and from the airport takes 15 minutes each way by taxi.

❶ Need to Know

permits adult $25-50, child $10-25

✕ Take a Break

Grab breakfast before you go, time permitting, in **Juneau's Rookery** (p145).

on floatplanes. Upon arrival, all visitors are met by a ranger who explains the rules and then each party hikes to an observation tower – reached by a mile-long trail – that overlooks the creek.

Seeing five or six bears would be a good viewing day at Pack Creek. You might see big boars during the mating season from May to mid-June; otherwise it's sows and cubs the rest of the summer.

Permits & Tours

From June to mid-September, the US Forest Service (USFS) and Alaska Department of Fish and Game operate a permit system for Pack Creek and only 24 people are allowed per day from July to the end of August. Guiding and tour companies receive half the permits, leaving 12 for individuals who want to visit Pack Creek on their own. The **National Recreation Reservation Service** (☎518-885-3639; www.recreation.gov) handles Pack Creek permits. Tours (including permits) can be booked through **Pack Creek Bear Tours** (☎907-789-3331; www.packcreekbeartours.com; 1873 Shell Simmons Dr; ◷9am-7pm) from $789 per person.

Capital History Stroll

One of the US's quieter, more unusual state capitals, Juneau sits on a steep hill with a backdrop of steep, green-hued mountains.

Start Cruise Dock
Distance 1 mile
Duration 1 hour

4 Head uphill to the **Wickersham State Historical Site**, a wooden mining-era museum to a bygone age.

Evergreen Bowl & Cope Park

Goldbelt Ave

Indian St

Dixon St

Main St

Distin St

Calhoun Ave

7th St

Seward St

5th St

4th St

5 Possibly Juneau's most handsome building, the **Governor's Mansion** mixes arts and crafts with neoclassical pillars.

7 Fill in the remaining gaps of the city's history at the **Juneau-Douglas City Museum** (p140).

6 There's no dome, but a replica of the liberty bell can be found outside the diminutive **Alaska State Capitol**.

N 0   200 m
  0   0.1 miles

3 Navigate toward the onion dome of the small, but old **St Nicholas Russian Orthodox Church** (p140).

2 Take a peek at the antique-heavy bar and reception area of the **Alaskan Hotel**, the oldest in Alaska.

7th St

6th St

Harris St

Gold St

5th St

4th St

N Franklin St

3rd St

2nd St

Seward St

1st St

Gastineau Ave

Front St

3

8

FINISH

P

Shattuck St

Ferry Way

Marine Way

S Franklin St

2

1 Follow the historic artery of **S Franklin St** from the cruise dock into downtown Juneau.

8 Investigate native masks and impressive Tsimshian carving at **Sealaska Heritage** (p140), a new cultural center.

START

Take a Break

Order a foccacia sandwich downtown in the **Rookery** (p145).

◎ SIGHTS

Alaska State Museum   Museum

(Map p141; ☑907-465-2901; www.museums.
state.ak.us; 395 Whittier St; adult/child $12/
free; ⊙9am-5pm; ☻) Demolished and rebuilt in a snazzy new $140-million complex
in 2016, the result is impressive. Sometimes called SLAM (State Library, Archives
and Museum), the museum shares digs
with the state archives along with a gift
store, the Raven Cafe, an auditorium, a
research room and a historical library. The
beautifully curated displays catalogue
the full historical and geographic breadth
of the state, from native canoes to the oil
industry.

**Last Chance
Mining Museum**   Museum

(Map p143; ☑907-586-5338; 1001 Basin Rd;
adult/child $5/free; ⊙9:30am-12:30pm & 3:30-
6:30pm) Amble out to the end of Basin Rd, a
beautiful 1-mile walk from the north end of
Gastineau Ave, to the former Alaska-Juneau
Gold Mining Company complex. It's now
a museum where you can view remains of
the compressor house and examine tools
of what was once the world's largest hard-
rock gold mine.

Mt Roberts Tramway   Cable Car

(Map p141; www.mountrobertstramway.com; 490
S Franklin St; adult/child $33/16; ⊙11am-9pm
Mon, 8am-9pm Tue-Sun; ☻) As far as cable
cars go, this tramway is rather expensive
for a five-minute ride. But from a marketing
point of view its location couldn't be better.
It whisks you right from the cruise-ship
dock up 1750ft to the timberline of Mt
Roberts, where you'll find a restaurant, gift
shops, a small raptor center and a theater
with a film on Tlingit culture.

**Treadwell Mine
Historical Trail**   Historic Site

(Map p143) It's hard to envisage today, but
the Treadwell mine on Douglas Island was
once the largest gold mine in the world, set
up like a mini-town with its own baseball di-
amond, stores, dormitories and blacksmith.
Reaching its zenith in the 1880s, the mine

was subsequently abandoned after part
of it slid into the sea in 1917. Today, spooky
reminders of Juneau's affluent mining past
poke through the forest on this well-
signposted historical trail with recently
installed interpretive boards.

**Juneau-Douglas
City Museum**   Museum

(Map p141; www.juneau.org; 114 W 4th St; adult/
child $6/free; ⊙9am-6pm Mon-Fri, 10am-
4:30pm Sat & Sun; ☻) This museum focuses
on gold with interesting mining displays
including 3D photo viewers, timelines,
interactive exhibits and the video *Juneau:
City Built on Gold*. If you love to hike in the
mountains, the museum's 7ft-long relief
map is the best overview of the area's
rugged terrain.

Sealaska Heritage   Cultural Centre

(Map p141; ☑907-463-4844; www.sealaska
heritage.org; 105 S Seward St; $5; ⊙9am-8pm)
The Sealaska Heritage Institute, founded
in 1980 to promote Native Alaskan culture,
opened this hugely impressive facility in
2015 in the downtown Walter Soboleff
building. The whole place is a work of art,
with much of the detail completed by
Tsimshian artist David Boxley. As well as
serving as headquarters for the institute,
the center contains a full-scale replica of a
clan house and a unique exhibit on native
masks.

**St Nicholas Russian
Orthodox Church**   Church

(Map p141; ☑907-586-1023; 326 5th St;
admission by donation; ⊙noon-5pm Mon-Fri, to
4pm Sat & Sun) Of 1893 vintage and etched
against the backdrop of Mt Juneau, this
diminutive onion-domed church is the
oldest Russian orthodox church in Alaska.
Through a small gift shop filled with
matryoshkas (nestling dolls) and other
handcrafted items from Russia, you enter
the church where, among the original vest-
ments and religious relics, a row of painted
saints stare down at you. Playing softly
in the background are the chants from a
service. It's a small but spiritual place.

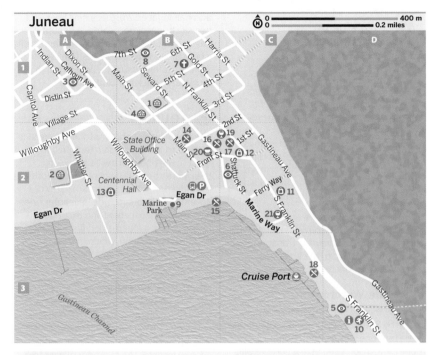

Juneau

◎ Sights
1 Alaska State Capitol B1
2 Alaska State Museum A2
3 Governor's Mansion A1
4 Juneau-Douglas City Museum B1
5 Mt Roberts Tramway D3
6 Sealaska Heritage C2
7 St Nicholas Russian Orthodox
    Church B1
8 Wickersham State Historical Site B1

⦿ Activities, Courses & Tours
9 Adventure Bound Alaska B2
10 Mendenhall Glacier
    Transport/M & M Tours D3

⦿ Shopping
11 Alaskan Brewing Co Depot C2
12 Hearthside Books C2
13 Juneau Arts and Culture Center A2

⊗ Eating
14 In Bocca Al Lupo B2
15 Pel'Meni B2
16 Rookery B2
17 Saffron C2
18 Tracy's King Crab Shack C3

⦿ Drinking & Nightlife
19 Amalga Distillery C2
20 Heritage Coffee Co & Café B2
21 Red Dog Saloon C2

✪ ACTIVITIES
⦿ Paddling

Day trips and extended paddles in sea kay-
aks are possible out from the Juneau area.
Alternatively, you can freshwater kayak on
Mendenhall Lake.

Alaska Boat & Kayak Center   Kayaking
(Map p143; ☏907-364-2333; www.juneaukayak.
com; 11521 Glacier Hwy; single/double kayaks
$55/75; ⊙9am-5pm) Based in Auke Bay Har-
bor, this places offers kayak rental, transportation services and multiday discounts.
The company has self-guided ($125) and

Walking on the Glacier

Above & Beyond Alaska (Map p143; www.beyondak.com) offers a couple of novel trips to the Mendenhall Glacier, both of which include a short trek on the crevasse-ridden surface of the icy behemoth. The 6½-hour 'Glacier Canoe Paddle & Trek' uses communal canoes to approach the glacier face. The eight-hour 'Mendehall Glacier Trek' accesses the ice via the 3.5-mile long West Glacier trail. Both are competently guided.

guided paddles ($169) on Mendenhall Lake. The former includes kayaks, transportation and a waterproof map that leads you on a route among the icebergs.

Whale-Watching

A Juneau tour de force! The whale-watching in nearby Stephens Passage is so good that some tour operators offer to refund your money if you don't see at least one whale. The boats depart from Auke Bay, and most tours last three to four hours.

Harv & Marv's Whale-Watching
(☏907-209-7288; www.harvandmarvs.com; per person $160) Small, personalized tours with no more than six passengers in the boat. They pick up from the cruise dock.

Gastineau Guiding Whale-Watching
(Map p143; ☏907-586-8231; www.stepintoalaska. com; 1330 Eastaugh Way; adult/child $230/185) Gastineau caters to small groups and spe-cializes in whale-watching, often including a little hiking on the side. Their five-hour 'whale-watching and glacier rainforest trail' tour includes a guided hike near the Mendenhall Glacier.

Ziplining

Alaska Zipline Adventures Adventure Sports
(Map p143; ☏907-321-0947; www.alaskazip.com; adult/child $149/99) Possibly Alaska's most

adrenaline-laced zip, these nine lines and two sky bridges are located at beautiful Eaglecrest Ski Area on Douglas Island, from where they zigzag across Fish Creek Valley. Transportation (usually a boat) from the cruise-ship dock is included.

ⓖ TOURS

The easiest way to book a tour in Juneau is to head to the cruise-ship terminal, where most of the operators will be hawking their wares from a line of outdoor booths, like sideshow barkers at a carnival. More adventurous tours include helicopter rides over the Juneau Icefield and excursions to Tracy Arm, a steep-sided fjord 45 miles southeast of Juneau, which has a pair of tidewater glaciers and a gallery of icebergs floating down its length.

NorthStar Trekking Hiking
(Map p143; ☏907-790-4530; www.northstar trekking.com; 1910 Renshaw Way) NorthStar offers several full-on glacier treks of varying levels that helicopter you directly out to the Juneau Icefield. The two-hour glacier trek ($399) crosses 2 miles of frozen landscape riddled with crevasses.

Adventure Bound Alaska Boating
(Map p141; ☏907-463-2509; www.adventure boundalaska.com; 76 Egan Dr; adult/child $160/95) This longtime tour operator uses a pair of boats that leave daily from the Juneau waterfront to explore Tracy Arm.

ⓐ SHOPPING

Juneau Arts & Culture Center Arts & Crafts
(JACC; Map p141; www.jahc.org; 350 Whittier St; ⊙9am-6pm) Inside the impressive JACC gallery is the work of a local artist every month, while the adjacent Lobby Shop is a place for Southeast Alaskans to sell their artworks.

Hearthside Books Books
(Map p141; www.hearthsidebooks.com; 254 Front St; ⊙10am-8pm Mon-Fri, to 6pm Sat, noon-5pm

Around Juneau

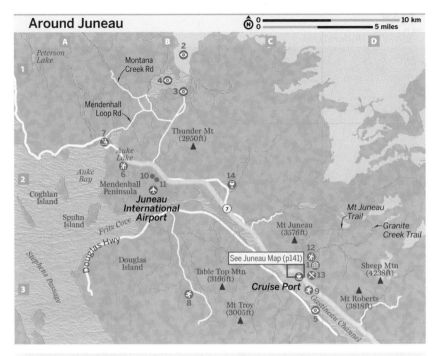

Around Juneau

Sun; 🍴) Juneau has fabulous bookshops for a town of its size. This well-loved nook has good travel and kids sections.

✖ EATING

Once a culinary desert in a rainforest setting, Juneau is finally beginning to serve up a restaurant scene worthy of a state capital. Several new bistros and bars are catering to an increasingly savvy crowd who want more than fried fish for dinner.

Pel'Meni — Dumplings $

(Map p141; Merchant's Wharf, Marine Way; dumplings $7; ⊙11:30am-1:30am Sun-Thu, to 3:30am Fri & Sat) Juneau was never part of Russia's Alaskan empire, but that hasn't stopped the city succumbing to a silent invasion of *pelmeni* (homemade Russian dumplings), filled with either potato or beef, spiced with hot sauce, curry and cilantro, with a little sour cream and rye bread on the side. They're served in what is a cross between

Understand

Tongass – A Forest the Size of Ireland

In many ways Southeast Alaska is the **Tongass National Forest** (☎907-586-8800; www.
fs.usda.gov/tongass). Welcome to the largest national forest in the US, a tract of land almost the size of Ireland and significantly larger than adjacent Wrangell-St Elias National Park (itself the second-biggest national park in the world).

Dedicated in 1907 by President Teddy Roosevelt, the forest encompasses most of the Alexander Archipelago's 1110 islands as well as some mainland areas. Around 75,000 people live in the forest in a series of small towns and villages, all of which, bar Haines, Hyder and Skagway, are cut off from the main continental road network. Notwithstanding, the protected area gets one million annual visitors, nearly 14 times its actual population, most of whom arrive on cruise ships. Despite being the largest temperate rainforest in the world, packed with Sitka spruce, western hemlock and red cedar, 40% of the Tongass isn't actually forest at all, but is comprised of wetlands, ice and high mountain terrain.

For adventurers, rustic off-the-grid accommodation is available in 150 scattered USFS cabins, most of them only accessible by boat or floatplane. There are also 13 campgrounds, four of them free of charge. Offering an extra level of protection in the forest are two national monuments, Misty Fjords and Admiralty Island.

As a national forest, the Tongass is notably different to national parks such as Glacier Bay, which it surrounds. National parks are all about preservation. National forests, while highlighting protective environmental measures, are designed for multiuse. In the Tongass you can hunt, fish and take your dog for a walk on a trail. Agriculture and controlled logging are also permitted, and the forest hosts a number of important towns including the Alaskan capital, Juneau, with a population of 33,850.

Rookery Cafe $$

(Map p141; ☑907-463-3013; www.therookery
cafe.com; 111 Seward St; lunch $9-14, dinner mains
$15-24; ⊙7am-9pm Mon-Fri, 9am-9pm Sat) A
brilliant combo of laid-back coffee shop by
day and hip bistro by night, the Rookery
serves Portland, OR's Stumptown coffee
and original breakfasts, lunch and dinners.

Saffron Indian $$

(Map p141; ☑907-586-1036; www.saffronalaska.
com; 112 N Franklin St; mains $8-19; ⊙11:30am-
9pm Mon-Fri, 5-9pm Sat & Sun; ☑) Juneau flirts
with *nuevo* Indian food at Saffron and the
results are commendable. There are plenty
of delicate breads to go with the aromatic
curries, with a strong bias toward vegetarian
dishes (including a good spinach paneer).

Tracy's King
Crab Shack Seafood $$

(Map p141; www.kingcrabshack.com; 406 S Franklin St; crab $13-45; ⊙10am-8pm) The best of
the food shacks along the cruise-ship berths
is Tracy's. On a boardwalk surrounded by a
beer shack and a gift shop, she serves up
outstanding crab bisque, mini crab cakes
and 3lb buckets of king-crab pieces ($110).
Grab a friend or six and share.

In Bocca Al Lupo Italian $$

(Map p141; ☑907-586-1409; 120 2nd St; pizza &
pasta $14-17; ⊙5-9pm Mon-Sat) Another step
on Juneau's stairway to culinary heaven
is this hip new Italian place whose dark
(surely temporary) facade hides a beautiful
streamlined woody interior where you can
sit at the bar and watch the chefs tuck
pizzas into a glowing wood-fire oven.

🍷 DRINKING & NIGHTLIFE
Red Dog Saloon Bar

(Map p141; www.reddogsaloon.com; 278 S Franklin
St; ⊙11am-10pm) A sign at the door says it all –
'Booze, Antiques, Sawdust Floor, Community Singing' – and the tourists love it! Most
don't realize, much less care, that this Red
Dog is but a replica of the original, a gold-
mining-era Alaskan pub that was across the
street until 1987. Now that was a bar.

Alaska Brewing Company

Established in 1986, Alaska's largest
brewery (Map p143; www.alaskanbeer.com;
5429 Shaune Dr; ⊙11am-6pm) has always
been a pioneer. Its amber ale is ubiquitous
across the state and rightly so. Note: this
is not a brewpub but a tasting room with
tours. It isn't located downtown, either,
but 5 miles to the northwest in Lemon
Creek. The brewery runs hourly guided
tours around its small facility, which include samples of up to six lagers and ales.
You can arrive by bus or taxi, but the best
way to get here is on a shuttle that runs
from its downtown retail store, **Alaskan
Brewing Co Depot** (Map p141; 219 S Franklin
St; ⊙9am-6pm Mon-Sat, 10am-6pm Sun).

Heritage Coffee Co & Café Coffee

(Map p141; ☑907-586-1087; www.heritagecoffee.
com; 130 Front St; ⊙6am-7:30pm; � 🛜) ☕ Owner
of seven perennially busy Juneau cafes,
Heritage was an early starter in the coffee
boom. It's been roasting beans for over 35
years in an old Starbucks roaster. Of the sev-
en cafes, this downtown favorite with huge
muffins is where you'll most likely end up.

Amalga Distillery Distillery

(Map p141; ☑907-209-2015; www.amalga
distillery.com; 134 N Franklin St; ⊙1-8pm) ☕
First Haines, now Juneau: microdistilling
has arrived in Southeast Alaska. At the
time of writing, the guys at Amalga were so
new that their whiskey was still maturing,
but you can taste their Juneauper gin, best
appreciated with homemade tonic.

ℹ️ GETTING AROUND
The most useful bus routes are buses 3 and 4
which head from downtown to the Mendenhall
Valley via Auke Bay Boat Harbor, and buses 1 and
11 that shuttle between downtown and Douglas
Island. Fares are $2/1 each way per adult/child,
and exact change is required. All buses stop at
the **Downtown Transit Center** (Egan Dr, cnr
Main St).

Aerial view of Glacier Bay National Park

Glacier Bay National Park

Glacier Bay, where seven tidewater glaciers spill out of the mountains and fill the sea with icebergs of all shapes, sizes and shades of blue, is the crowning jewel of Alaskan cruising.

Great For...

USA   CANADA   ⦿ Skagway

Haines

Glacier Bay National Park
❶

Glacier Bay

Gulf of Alaska

Juneau ⦿

❶ Need to Know

www.nps.gov/glba

Explore Ashore

Although two cruise ships a day enter Glacier Bay National Park, barely any of them stop to let passengers disembark. Instead, National Park rangers come on board the ships to give narrations and presentations, and answer any questions.

☑ Don't Miss

Scanning the shoreline and its many beaches for black and brown bears.

Glacier Bay is heavily protected as a national park. There is practically no infrastructure or any trails that are marked. The only settlement – tiny Gustavus – is situated just outside the park at the bay's southeastern entry. Beyond lie 3.3 million acres of top-drawer wilderness. Around 99% of the 450,000 annual visitors access the national park on cruise ships, private boat tours or kayaks and never put a foot on dry land.

Glaciers

The national park's obvious highlight is its profusion of landscape-altering glaciers. But, Glacier Bay National Park's ice, like glaciers all over Alaska, is rapidly melting.

Humpback whale breaching in Glacier Bay

This is particularly true in Muir Inlet, commonly known as the East Arm. Twenty years ago this sinuous channel was home to three active tidewater glaciers, but now McBride is the only one that is still present.

As a result, most cruise ships ply the bay's West Arm, an ice-encrusted fjord that is backed by the Fairweather range and adorned with an impressive array of glaciers that flow seaward off the Brady ice field. The most popularly viewed glaciers are the Lamplugh, the John Hopkins (which is now considered to be the park's only advancing glacier) and the Grand Pacific. The latter guards the West Arm's extreme northerly point and is located mostly in Canada.

✕ Take a Break

Cruise ships don't generally dock in Glacier Bay National Park, meaning you're confined to using the onboard refreshments.

Wildlife

Apart from its high concentration of tidewater glaciers, Glacier Bay is a dynamic habitat for humpback whales. Other wildlife seen at Glacier Bay includes porpoises, sea otters, brown and black bears, wolves, moose and mountain goats. Don't underestimate the avian show courtesy of eagles (golden and bald), osprey. loons, terns and kittiwakes. Park naturalists will be your eyes and ears. Bring binoculars!

BETTY WILEY/GETTY IMAGES/MOMENT RF ©

Hoonah Packing Company (p153)

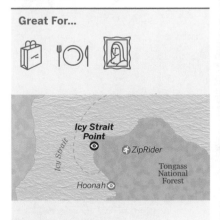

Icy Strait Point

Conceived in the early 2000s, Icy Strait Point, on Chichagof Island, is a purpose-built assemblage of shops, restaurants and tour companies offering adventurous activities. It is Alaska's only privately-owned cruise-ship destination.

Great For...

Icy Strait Point

Icy Strait

ZipRider

Tongass National Forest

Hoonah

ℹ️ Need to Know

📞 907-945-3141; www.icystraitpoint.com; 108 Cannery Rd, Hoonah

Explore Ashore

The Icy Strait Point tourist complex is right next to the cruise-ship dock. The village of Hoonah is a 20- to 30-minute stroll south along the coast. All organized activities are tailored to fit in with the cruise-ship schedule.

☑ Don't Miss

Catapulting off Hoonah Mountain on a ginormous zipline.

Icy Strait Point is owned and operated by the Huna Totem Corporation whose members are comprised mostly of Tlingit people with ties to the nearby village of Hoonah. While this modern 'tourist town' might feel a little contrived and artificial, it does a good job of displaying and promoting local Tlingit culture.

ZipRider

Despite being little-visited by wilderness explorers on the independent traveler circuit, Icy Strait Point parades what is, arguably, Alaska's most hair-raising adventure: North America's largest zipline. The 5330ft-long rappel starts at the top of Hoonah Mountain before dropping abruptly 1330ft down to the ferry dock

Icy Strait Point boardwalk

above a carpet of coniferous treetops. It's a 45-minute bus ride to the top and a 90-second zip coming down (adult/child $140/100).

Hoonah

First settled by the Huna Tlingit in the 1750s, the village of Hoonah is a grittier antidote to slick, pricey Icy Strait Point. Here you'll find a smattering of community shops and restaurants, some weather-beaten totems, a carving shed and a population of around 800 tough-minded Alaskans living on the edge of the 'Bush'. The off-the-grid community generates one-third of its own power through a local dam.

✖ Take a Break

Take a pew at the **Cookhouse Restaurant** (mains $17–20), where cannery workers once went for lunch.

The red wooden buildings of the erstwhile Hoonah Packing Company dating from 1912 have been refashioned to house the modern tourist-ville of Icy Strait Point. Inside the upgraded sheds you'll find shops, restaurants, a small theater, tour desks, and a museum relaying the history of the area and its one-time role as a salmon cannery and fishing facility.

RUBEN M RAMOS/SHUTTERSTOCK ©

Bojet Wikan Fishermen's Memorial Park (p156)

Petersburg

This proudly independent fishing community with strong Norwegian roots has a shallow port only suitable for small cruise ships, a factor that lends it a quiet, undisturbed, refreshingly local air.

Great For...

ⓘ Need to Know

www.petersburg.org

Explore Ashore

Petersburg only receives a limited number of small cruise ships. They pull up at the **Petro Marine Dock** south of town, an easy half-mile walk from the center. For 24-hour taxi service, there's **Midnight Rides Cab** (☎907-772-2222).

☑ Don't Miss

Petersburg's tiny downtown with its Norwegian flags, salty harbor and everyone-knows-everyone vibe.

The Town

If it's historic in Petersburg, you'll find it in **Sing Lee Alley**, an ensemble of geriatric wooden buildings dating from the 1910s. Much of the street is built on pilings over Hammer Slough, including the **Sons of Norway Hall**, a large white building with colorful rosemaling built in 1912 and the center for Petersburg's Norwegian culture.

At the southern end of Sing Lee Alley is **Bojet Wikan Fishermen's Memorial Park**. This deck-of-a-park sits suspended over Hammer Slough and features an impressive statue of a fisher honoring all his fellow crew members lost at sea. Also on display is the *Valhalla*, a replica of a Viking ship that was built in 1976 and purchased by Petersburg two years later.

Sing Lee Alley

Local Hikes

Within town, the 0.7-mile **Hungry Point Trail** begins at the ball field at the end of Excel St before cutting across muskeg. The gravel path keeps your feet dry, and surrounding you are stunted trees so short you have a clear view of Petersburg's mountainous skyline. The trail ends at Sandy Beach Rd. Head right a quarter-mile to reach **Outlook Park**, a marine wildlife observatory with free binoculars, to search Frederick Sound for humpbacks, orcas and sea lions.

Whale-Watching

Petersburg offers some of the best whale-watching in Southeast Alaska. From mid-May to mid-September humpback

✕ Take a Break

Salty Pantry (☏907-772-2665; 14 Harbor Way; sandwiches & snacks from $8; ⏱6:30am-2pm Mon-Fri, to 4pm Sat) Has quality coffee, home-baked cakes and creative sandwiches.

whales migrate through, and feed in, Frederick Sound, 45 miles northwest of Petersburg. Other wildlife that can be spotted includes Steller's sea lions, orcas and seals. Day- and half-day trips can be organized through **Whale Song Cruises** (☏907-772-9393; www.whalesongcruises.com; 207 N Nordic Dr; per person $371) and **Viking Travel** (☏907-772-3818; www.alaskaferry.com; 101 N Nordic Dr).

HAINES

Haines at a Glance...

The first thing you notice about Haines is that it isn't Skagway, the regional showpiece situated 33 nautical miles to the north. Instead, this is a quiet, independent, unassuming town of native artists, outdoor-adventure lovers and 100% Alaskans hooked on the tranquil life. People come here to see bald eagles in the wild, dissect 1000 years of Chilkat-Tlingit culture, ponder the remains of an old military barracks, and enjoy the best drinking scene in an American town of this size.

With a Day in Port

○ Wander around **Fort Seward** (p166) and enjoy the ambiance of Haines at the **Hammer Museum** (p166) and **Rusty Compass Coffeehouse** (p170).

○ Earmark plenty of time for a trip up to the **Chilkat Bald Eagle Preserve** and the nearby **Jilkaat Kwaan Heritage Center** (p109).

○ Don't leave town without tasting the suds at **Haines Brewing Company** (p171).

Best Places for...

Craft Beer Haines Brewing Company (p171)

Cocktails Port Chilkoot Distillery (p171)

Coffee Rusty Compass Coffeehouse (p170)

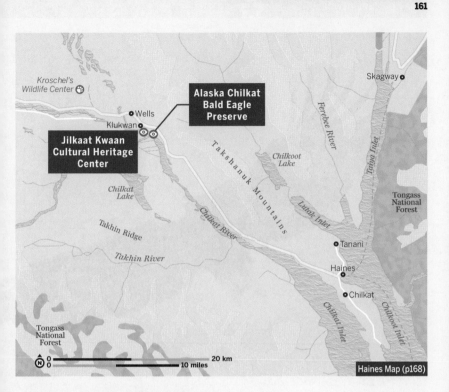

Haines Map (p168)

Getting from the Port

Cruise ships tie up at the **Port Chilkoot Dock**, adjacent to Fort Seward and quarter of a mile from Main St. A free shuttle loops around the town when ships are in.

Fast Facts

Money First National Bank Alaska (123 Main St)

Tourist Information Haines Convention & Visitors Bureau (www.visithaines.com)

Best for Free Wi-fi Rusty Compass Coffeehouse (p170)

Bald eagle

Alaska Chilkat Bald Eagle Preserve

The Alaska Chilkat Bald Eagle Preserve was created in 1982 when the state reserved 48,000 acres along the Chilkat, Klehini and Tsirku Rivers. It protects the largest known gathering of bald eagles in the world.

Great For...

☑ **Don't Miss**

A float trip on a raft down the Chilkat River.

Each year from October to February, more than 4000 eagles congregate in the preserve to feed on spawning salmon. They come because an upwelling of warm water prevents the river from freezing, thus encouraging the late salmon run. It's a remarkable sight – hundreds of birds sitting in the bare trees lining the river, often six or more birds to a branch.

The best time to see this wildlife phenomenon is during the Alaska Bald Eagle Festival in November. However, you can still see eagles during the summer from the Haines Hwy, where there are turnouts for motorists to park and look for birds. The best view is between Mile 18 and Mile 22, where you'll find spotting scopes, interpretive displays and viewing platforms along the river.

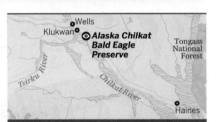

Explore Ashore

The preserve is situated 20-miles outside Haines and there is no regular public transportation. If you're on a limited schedule, it is easier to go on an organized tour with transport included. Most trips last four hours (six if you're coming from Skagway).

❶ Need to Know

http://dnr.alaska.gov/parks/units/eagleprv.htm

✕ Take a Break

Grab a snack to go from **Rusty Compass** Coffeehouse (p170) in Haines before heading out.

Boat & Land Tours

Several operators tour the area by boat and land.

Alaska Nature Tours (p169) Conducts four-hour tours (adult/child $78/63) daily in summer. The tours cover much of the scenery around the Haines area but concentrate on the river flats and river mouths, where you usually see up to 40 nesting eagles.

Chilkat River Adventures (☑907-766-2050; www.jetboatalaska.com; Haines Hwy) Uses jet boats for its Eagle Preserve River Adventure. The tour includes bus transportation 24 miles up the river to the jet boats and then a 1½-hour boat ride ($100 per person) to look for eagles and other wildlife.

American Bald Eagle Foundation

If you can't make it out to the preserve, this relatively new **museum** (www.baldeagles.org; 113 Haines Hwy; adult/child $10/5; ◷9am-5pm Mon-Fri, 11am-3pm Sat; 👪) is located right in town. There are two live American Bald Eagles, and a couple of other raptors with handlers giving regular demonstrations. The museum also focuses on Alaskan wildlife with numerous taxidermic exhibits.

Tlingit weaving in the Chilkat style

NATIONAL GEOGRAPHIC CREATIVE/ALAMY STOCK PHOTO ©

Jilkaat Kwaan Cultural Heritage Center

Part of a welcome renaissance in Tlingit art and culture in Alaska, this new heritage center near Haines includes some of the most prized heirlooms from the Alaska Native lexicon.

Great For...

☑ **Don't Miss**

Admiring the rarely photographed and (until recently) rarely seen whale house posts.

Located in the ancient native village of Klukwan 22 miles north of Haines, this impressive cultural center, which opened in 2016, includes a museum, clan house, carving studio, salmon drying room and shop. There are also regular dance performances (which usually coincide with cruise-ship visits) and even art classes.

Knowledge Camp

To get a full appreciation of the center, it's best to sign up for a guided tour. As well as taking you through the museum, local guides also bring you to the Knowledge Camp where you can observe the smoking and drying of salmon, see a traditional clan house and 37ft Tlingit canoe, and watch wood-carvers at work in the adze shed. Tours cost $35 for individuals, or $210 if

Explore Ashore

Guided tours last five hours dock-to-dock out of Haines. If you go it alone, you'll need to rent a car. Reserve 1¼ hours for a tour of the heritage center and 1 hour for the drive (round-trip).

❶ Need to Know

☏907-767-5485; www.jilkaatkwaanheritage center.org; Mile 22, Haines Hwy; $15; ⊘10am-4pm Mon-Fri, noon-3pm Sat, closed Oct-Apr

✕ Take a Break

Full tours include a picnic lunch. Otherwise load up in Haines before you go.

you book a group tour through **Chilkat Guides** (www.skagwayexcursions.com). Group tours include transport, a 1½-hour float on the Chilkat River and a Tlingit dancing show.

Whale House Collection

The highlight of the museum is four elaborate house posts and a rain screen – the legendary 'whale house collection' – carved by a Tlingit Michelangelo called Kadjisdu over 200 years ago and only recently made available for public viewing. The posts were spirited out of the village in 1984, supposedly bought by an art dealer in Seattle. When members of the Chilkat found out the artifacts were gone, they sued. The trial was long and divisive. The posts remained

locked in a Seattle warehouse for over a decade trapped in legal limbo before they were finally returned.

Klukwan

The ancient Chilkat Tlingit village of Klukwan (meaning 'eternal place') is just off the main Haines Hwy beside the Chilkat River. The Chilkat Tlingit are known for their complex weaving techniques used to fashion intricate wool blankets and robes. The village is currently home to around 100 people.

◉ SIGHTS

Sheldon Museum
Museum

(www.sheldonmuseum.org; 11 Main St; adult/child $7/free; ☺10am-5pm Mon, Tue, Thu & Fri, 9am-5pm Wed, 1-4pm Sat & Sun) The Sheldon Museum is known for its collection of indigenous artifacts, including a particularly interesting display on rare Chilkat blankets. The rest of the museum is devoted to Haines' pioneer and gold-rush days including such treasures as the sawed-off shotgun that trailblazer Jack Dalton used to convince travelers to pay his toll. There's a small gift shop in the entrance.

Hammer Museum
Museum

(www.hammermuseum.org; 108 Main St; adult/child $5/free; ☺10am-5pm Mon-Fri, to 2pm Sat) This extravagantly esoteric museum is an exercise in how to make hammers look interesting. And – get this – it largely succeeds. Plucked from the extensive collection of local tool restorer Dave Pahl, the small, well-utilized space displays over 2000 hammers, from a stone hammer used to build the pyramids at Giza, to the heavy-duty tools of erstwhile dentists, shoemakers and blacksmiths. There are even five mannequins donated by the Smithsonian Institute and a giant hammer sculpture outside fashioned by Pahl himself.

Fort Seward
Historic Site

Alaska's first permanent military post is reached by heading uphill (east) at the Front St–Haines Hwy junction. Built in 1903 and decommissioned after WWII, the fort is now a national historical site, with a handful of restaurants, lodges and art galleries in the original buildings. A walking-tour map of the fort is available at the visitor center, or you can just wander around and read the historical panels that have been erected there.

Alaska Indian Arts Center
Arts Center

(www.alaskaindianarts.com; 24 Fort Seward Dr; ☺9am-5pm Mon-Fri) Indigenous culture can be seen in Fort Seward in the former military post hospital, home of the Alaska Indian Arts Center. During the week you can watch artists carve totems, weave Chilkat blankets or produce other works of art. It's a friendly, congenial place. Check out the totems inlaid with glass pieces inspired by Seattle-based glass artist, Dale Chihuly.

Inquire within about Tlingit wood-carving workshops.

Kroschel's Wildlife Center
Wildlife Reserve

(☎907-767-5464; www.kroschelfilms.com; $50) Twenty-eight miles north of Haines is Kroschel's Wildlife Center, run by an ex-Hollywood animal trainer. There are 15 species of Alaskan wildlife here, including bears, lynx and wolves, and the feeling is definitely less zoo and more wild. Tours are by appointment only; you won't be able to enter if you simply show up. Add $25 extra for round-trip transport.

✪ ACTIVITIES

Cycling

You can discover some great road trips or what little single-track mountain biking there is in Haines by visiting one of two local bike shops, both of which rent bicycles at good day rates. The most popular road trip is the 22-mile ride out to Chilkoot Lake.

Sockeye Cycle
Cycling

(☎907-766-2869; www.cyclealaska.com; 24 Portage St; ☺9am-5:30pm Mon-Fri, to 4pm Sat) These guys have two stores – the other is in Skagway – and a good reputation for organizing both day and multiday tours, including the surprisingly synergistic bike-hike-brew tour ($175) which ends up at Haines Brewing Company (p171). They also rent bikes to DIYers for $45 per day.

Hiking

Two major trail systems are within walking distance of Haines. South of town are the Chilkat Peninsula trails, including Battery Point and the climb to Mt Riley. North of

Understand

Haines' History

Originally a stronghold of the wealthy Chilkat-Tlingit, whose village, Klukwan, dates back at least 1000 years, Haines was put on the map by a gun-toting entrepreneur named Jack Dalton. In 1897 Dalton turned an old tribal trade route into a toll road for miners seeking an easier way to reach the Klondike. The Dalton Trail quickly became a heavily used pack route to mining districts north of Whitehorse, a factor that led, in part, to the army arriving in 1903 to sort out mining conflicts, add muscle to a border dispute with Canada and keep an eye on occasionally fraught Native–settler relations. Fort William H Seward was established as Alaska's first permanent military post. For the next 20 years it was Alaska's only army post and was later used as a rest camp during WWII.

WWII led to the construction of a 159-mile link between the Southeast and the Alcan. Built in 1942 as a possible evacuation route in case of a Japanese invasion, the route followed the Dalton Trail and was so rugged it would be 20 years before US and Canadian crews even attempted to keep it open in winter. By the 1980s, the 'Haines Cut-off Rd' had become the paved Haines Hwy, and now more than 50,000 travelers in cars and RVs follow it annually.

Logging no longer sustains Haines and the last cannery closed in 1972. The town now survives on a mix of cruise traffic and independent tourists.

Alaska Indian Arts Center
RUBEN M RAMOS/SHUTTERSTOCK ©

Haines is the path to the summit of Mt Ripinsky. Stop at the visitors bureau and pick up the brochure *Haines is for Hikers,* which describes the trails in more detail. For outdoor gear or a guided hike, stop by **Alaska Backcountry Outfitter** (☑907-766-2876; www.alaskanaturetours.net; 111 2nd Ave; ⊙10am-5pm).

Battery Point Trail   Hiking
This 2-mile trail is a walk along the shore to Kelgaya Point; cut across to a pebble beach and follow it to Battery Point for views of Lynn Canal. The trail begins a mile beyond Portage Cove Recreation Site at the end of Beach Rd and has been extensively updated. Not surprisingly, it's a local favorite.

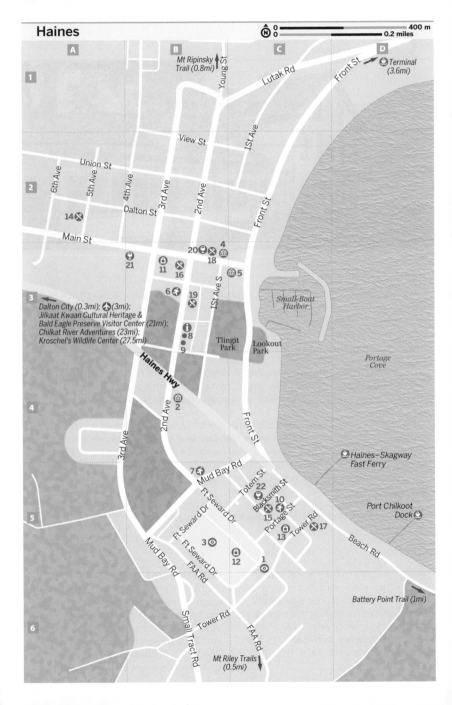

Haines

Dalton City (0.3mi); (3mi);
Jilkaat Kwaan Cultural Heritage &
Bald Eagle Preserve Visitor Center (21mi);
Chilkat River Adventures (23mi);
Kroschel's Wildlife Center (27.5mi)

Haines

Rafting

Chilkat Guides　　　　　　　Rafting
(☑907-766-2491; www.raftalaska.com; floats $133) Runs a four-hour Chilkat River raft float with a picnic lunch. Affiliated to the excellent **Alaska Mountain Guides & Climbing School** (☑800-766-3396; www.alaskamountainguides.com; 57 Mud Bay Rd).

☺ TOURS

Alaska Nature Tours　　　Outdoors
(☑907-766-2876; www.alaskanaturetours.net; 109 2nd Ave; ⚐) Offers environmentally focused tours with knowledgeable guides for activities that range from birding and bear watching to easy hikes to Battery Point. Its Twilight Wildlife Watch is a 2½-hour tour (adult/child $78/60) that departs at 6pm and heads up the Chilkat River, stopping along the way to look for eagles, mountain goats and brown bears who emerge at dusk.

Mountain Flying
Service　　　　　　　Scenic Flights
(☑907-766-3007; www.mountainflyingservice.com; 132 2nd Ave) Offers an hour-long tour of the Glacier Bay's East Arm for $170 per person and an 80-minute tour of the more dramatic West Arm for $199. The two-hour outer coast flight lands on beach; it costs $299. On a clear day, it's money well spent.

☺ SHOPPING

Despite a lack of cruise-ship traffic, or maybe because of it, Haines supports an impressive number of local artists and has enough galleries to fill an afternoon.

Wild Iris　　　　　　　Arts & Crafts
(22 Tower Rd) This art gallery is the most impressive of a growing number on the edge of Fort Seward. Outside the home is a beautiful Alaskan garden; inside, a fine selection of original jewelry, silk-screened prints, cards, pastels and other local art.

Sea Wolf Art Studio　　Arts & Crafts
(www.tresham.com; Fort Seward; ⊕hours vary, May-Sep) Housed in a log cabin in the middle of Fort Seward's old parade ground is Tresham Gregg's gallery. Gregg is one of Haines' best-known Alaska Native artists, and he combines the imagery of the spiritism, animism and shamanism of Northwest Coast Indians to create wood carvings, totems, masks, bronze sculpture and talismanic silver jewelry.

Babbling Book　　　　　　Books
(☑907-766-3356; 223 Main St; ⊕11am-5pm Mon-Sat, noon-5pm Sun) Small bookshop stuffed full of plenty of Alaska-themed books, cards and calendars, while its walls serve as the noticeboard for Haines' cultural scene.

✪ EATING

Haines backs up its progressive drinking scene with a couple of fine unfancy restaurants along with a handful of the usual suspects (fish and chips and burger joints).

For fresh vegetables, there's the Haines Farmer's Market held every other Saturday and some Wednesdays during the summer at the Southeast Alaska State Fairground from 10am to noon. **Howsers IGA** (211 Main St; ⊗8am-8pm Mon-Sat, 10am-7pm Sun) is the main supermarket.

Rusty Compass Coffeehouse
Cafe **$**

(116 Main St; panini $10-13; ⊗6:30am-4pm Mon-Sat, 9am-2pm Sun) Hands-on, mega-friendly coffee and sandwich bar that could hold its own in Seattle, let alone Haines. It backs up its expertly made coffee with fresh

Haines Festivals

Haines stages the **Great Alaskan Craftbeer & Home Brew Festival** (⊗May) in the third week of May when most of the state's microbrews compete for the honor of being named top suds.

Like every other Alaskan town, Haines has a festive celebration for **Fourth of July**, but the town's biggest event is the **Southeast Alaska State Fair** (www.seakfair.org; 196 Fair Dr). Staged at the end of July, the fair is five days of live music, an Ugliest Dog Contest, logging and livestock shows and the famous pig races that draw participants from all Southeast communities.

BLAINE HARRINGTON III/GETTY IMAGES ©

baked goods made on-site and substantial panini and soups. The small interior is a mix of buzzing conversation and flickering laptops.

Sarah J's
Cafe **$**

(132 2nd Ave; breakfast $6-9, sandwiches $9-10; ⊗6:30am-5pm Mon-Fri, 7am-3pm Sat & Sun; 🅟) 🌱 Sarah's has recently relocated from Fort Seward to the town center, but it still maintains its ephemeral roots in a food truck with a little awning tacked on the side. As with all Alaskan food trucks, the food is formidable with great breakfast burritos, homemade granola, organic smoothies, baked goods, perky coffee and more.

Fireweed Restaurant
Bistro **$$**

(37 Blacksmith St; salads $10-19, pizzas $14-30; ⊗4:30-9pm Tue-Sat; 🅟) This clean, bright and laid-back bistro is in an old Fort Seward building and its copious salads are an ideal antidote to the Southeast's penchant for grease. A quick scroll down the menu will reveal words like 'organic,' 'veggie' and 'grilled' as opposed to 'deep fried' and 'captain's special.'

Vegetarians and carnivores alike can indulge in sandwiches, burgers and the town's best pizza, all washed down with beer served in icy mugs. The locals love it.

Pilot Light
American **$$**

(☏907-766-2962; 31 Tower Rd; mains $19-27; ⊗5-9pm Wed-Mon) Johnny come lately, the new kid in town. Pilot Light occupies an unpretentious multilevel house on the cusp of Fort Seward. The food is top drawer, especially if you like fish. Locals rave about the salmon risotto and Alaskan fisherman's stew, but angels really take flight when you taste the home-baked sourdough bread.

It even serves its own house-blend coffee along with potent Haines-brewed beer. Heaven.

Chilkat Bakery & Restaurant
Thai, American **$$**

(☏907-766-3653; cnr 5th Ave & Dalton St; mains $12-20; ⊗7am-3pm & 5-8pm Thu-Tue, 7am-3pm Wed) Baked goods, Thai food, Mexican *comida* and American chow; the Chilkat is a peddler of numerous genres and the master of at least two of them – the Thai food and cakes and pastries are pretty good. It occupies a white clapboard house with a long front porch decorated with flower baskets, just off the main drag. Decor is mega-casual.

🍷 DRINKING & NIGHTLIFE

Possibly the best drinking scene for a town of its size in the whole of North America. Tiny Haines (population 1700-ish) has its own microbrewery and its own microdistillery, and they're both excellent.

Haines Brewing
Company   Brewery

(📞907-766-3823; www.hainesbrewing.com; Main St, cnr 4th Ave; ⊙noon-7pm Mon-Sat) Surely one of the finest small breweries in America, this Haines operation, founded in 1999, has a lovely tasting room in what passes for downtown Haines. The beautiful wood and glass structure serves all of the locally brewed favorites, including Spruce Tip Ale, Elder Rock Red and the potent Black Fang stout (8.2% alcohol content).

It's no small wonder that Haines hosts the Great Alaskan Craftbeer & Home Brew Festival.

Port Chilkoot
Distillery   Distillery

(📞907-766-3434; www.portchilkootdistillery. com; 34 Blacksmith St; ⊙2-8pm Mon-Sat) A fantastic resource in such a tiny town, this microdistillery is not just a token gesture; it's inventive enough to compete with anything in the Lower 48. Housed in Fort Seward's former bakery, and with a small on-site shop and tasting room, it serves a wide array of spirits, from recently matured bourbon to absinthe, gin and vodka.

A full menu of cocktails is available for those who like their poison mixed with fruitier flavors. Try a Bee's Knees made with lemon, honey and the homemade 50 fathoms gin.

Visiting Haines from Skagway

It's possible to visit Haines even if your cruise ship doesn't dock here. Skagway, which is on the itinerary of the vast majority of Alaskan cruise ships, is only 33 nautical miles away. **Haines-Skagway Fast Ferry** (📞907-766-2100; www.haines skagwayfastferry.com; round-trip adult/child $73/36.50; ⊙May-Sep) uses a speedy catamaran to zip up and down the Taiya Inlet between Skagway and Haines in 45 minutes. The 80ft cat arrives and departs from Haine's **Port Chilkoot Dock**, close to the town center, five to six times a day in peak season.

Haines Harbor
RUBEN M RAMOS/SHUTTERSTOCK ©

Fogcutter Bar   Bar

(Main St; ⊙10am-midnight) Haines is a hard-drinking town, and this is where a lot of locals belly up to the bar and spout off.

ℹ️ GETTING AROUND

BUS

Haines Shuttle (📞907-766-3768; www.haines shuttle.com) provides service to the state ferry terminal, airport and various local trailheads.

CAR

To visit Alaska Chilkat Bald Eagle Preserve or Jilkaat Kwaan Cultural Heritage Center on your own, you can rent a car at **Captain's Choice Motel** (📞907-766-3111; www.capchoice.com; 108 2nd Ave N; s/d $144/155), which has compacts for around $79 a day with unlimited mileage.

SKAGWAY

Skagway at a Glance...

At first sight, Skagway appears to be solely an amusement park with a million visitors treading its sunny boardwalks every summer. But, haunted by Klondike ghosts and beautified by a tight grid of handsome false-fronted buildings, this is no northern Vegas. Skagway's history is very real. During the 1898 gold rush, 40,000 stampeders passed through the nascent settlement. Today, most of the town's important buildings are managed by the National Park Service and this, along with Skagway's location on the cusp of a burly wilderness, has saved it from overt Disneyfication. Dive in and join the show.

With a Day in Port

● Take the morning train up to **White Pass** (p176). On your return go for lunch at the **Sweet Tooth Cafe** (p186).

● Call into the **Klondike Gold Rush Visitor Center** (p178) and sign up for an afternoon walking tour.

● Save time for a beer in the **Red Onion Saloon** (p189) and take advantage of the evening light to walk out to the **Gold Rush Cemetery & Reid Falls** (p182).

Best Places for...

Craft beer Skagway Brewing Company (p188)

Brunch Sweet Tooth Cafe (p186)

Historical atmosphere Red Onion Saloon (p189)

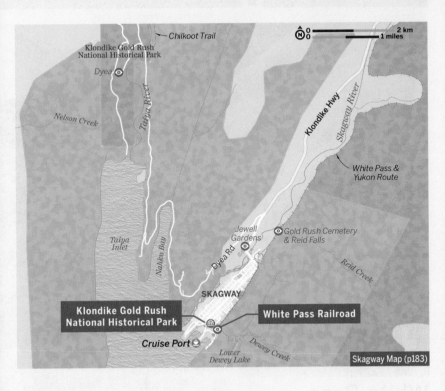

SKAGWAY

Klondike Gold Rush National Historical Park

White Pass Railroad

Cruise Port

Skagway Map (p183)

Getting from the Port

Cruise ships dock five-minutes' walk from the town center, either next to the small-boat harbor or in Taiya Inlet at the far end of Terminal Way.

The city operates the **SMART bus** (p189), which moves people (primarily cruise-ship passengers) from the docks up Broadway St and to Jewell Gardens and the Alaska 360 gold dredge on the edge of town.

Fast Facts

Money Wells Fargo (Broadway St at 6th Ave)

Tourist Information Klondike Gold Rush National Historical Park Museum & Visitor Center (p178)

Best for free Wi-fi Skagway Library

White Pass & Yukon Route railroad

White Pass Railroad

This epic railroad, which runs between Skagway, Alaska and Carcross in the Yukon, was built across White Pass between 1898 and 1900 just in time to catch the coattails of the Klondike Gold Rush.

Great For...

☑ Don't Miss

Enjoying the view from the open-air platforms at the end of each carriage.

The Railway

Built in a roller-coaster two years between 1898 and 1900, the 110-mile White Pass & Yukon Route (WP&YR) was an extraordinary engineering feat for its time. Precipitous terrain, 4% gradients and working temperatures that could plunge to -60°F made its construction a massive challenge. On completion, the line stretched from Skagway, AK to Whitehorse in the Yukon. After closing in 1982 the WP&YR was revived as a heritage railway and today pulls its elegant old-fashioned carriages as far as Carcross in Canada.

IZABELA23/SHUTTERSTOCK ©

⚓

Explore Ashore

Skagway's train station is a five-minute walk from the cruise terminal. There are three main train excursions ranging from three to eight hours. The most popular is the three-hour **Summit Tour**, which ascends to the top of White Pass and the border with Canada before returning.

❶ Need to Know

☑800-343-7373; www.wpyr.com; 231 2nd Ave; ☻May-Sep

✕ Take a Break

Grab a slice of pizza in the **Red Onion Saloon** (p189) next to the station.

White Pass

Trains start climbing almost immediately they leave Skagway on their 20-mile journey up to White Pass on a spectacular narrow-gauge line that incorporates two major switchbacks along with various bridges and tunnels. In summer, the steep green walls of the canyon and the gaping drop-offs directly beside the track make for a heart-in-your-mouth experience. The exposed summit of White Pass with its border flags and snaking highway is a harsh barren plateau open to the stormy elements.

Lake Bennett

Longer train excursions cross the Canadian border and press on to Lake Bennett and Carcross before returning to Skagway. Lake Bennett (not reachable by road) was where the two main gold rush trails once merged. In 1898 it sported a huge tent city full of gold prospectors. Today there is nothing but a campground, an old wooden church and a station that has been turned into a small railway museum.

Moore Homestead

RICHARD CUMMINS/GETTY IMAGES ©

Klondike Gold Rush National Historical Park

This fascinating homage to the rough and tumble of the Klondike Gold Rush is showcased in a selection of historic buildings in and around Skagway's town center, run by the National Park Service.

Great For...

☑ Don't Miss

The turbulent story of the rise and fall of gold-rush conman Jeff 'Soapy' Smith.

Visitor Center Museum

The recently improved **National Park Service center** (📞907-983-9200; www.nps.gov/klgo; Broadway St, at 2nd Ave; ⏲8:30am-5:30pm May-Sep) **FREE** is in the original 1898 White Pass & Yukon Route depot. The center is spread over two interconnecting buildings. One contains a small museum, explaining some of the Klondike background. The other space is a visitor center staffed by park rangers. At the visitor center you can sign up for free walking tours (displayed on a blackboard) and view a fabulous 25-minute film *Gold Fever: Race to the Klondike*.

Moore Homestead

The founder of Skagway was not a gold-hungry Klondike stampeder but the savvy Captain William Moore, who arrived

RICHARD CUMMINS/GETTY IMAGES ©

Explore Ashore

The main parts of the historical park are concentrated within a few blocks of each other in downtown Skagway, five minutes' walk from the cruise-ship dock. To browse them all should take around two hours – more if you sign up for a free walking tour.

ⓘ Need to Know

www.nps.gov/klgo

✕ Take a Break

Grab breakfast, brunch or lunch in the **Sweet Tooth Cafe** (p186).

in the area on a hunch in 1887 and built himself a small cabin in the then unin-habited woods. The log cabin (the oldest structure in town) still stands alongside Moore's newer **homestead** (5th Ave & Spring St; ⊘10am-5pm) FREE built on the eve of the gold rush in 1897.

Jeff Smith's Parlor

Soapy Smith's old den of iniquity has recently been renovated by the National Park Service to keep the rose-tinted legend of the erstwhile conman alive. Entry to the **parlor** (2nd Ave & Broadway St; tours $5) is by tour only (except on weekends when it's open house 9am to 5pm) with NPS rangers providing overviews of the small interior decorated in period style.

Mascot Saloon Museum

The only saloon in Alaska that doesn't serve booze – although it did during the gold rush, and plenty of it. Built in 1898, the Mascot was one of Skagway's 80 to 100 saloons during its heyday as 'the roughest place in the world.' The NPS has turned it into a small **museum** (Broadway St, at 3rd Ave; ⊘8:30am-5:30pm May-Sep) FREE, with a mock-up of the bar, complete with life-sized mannequins.

Gold Rush Skagway

All the most melodramatic elements of Alaska's history are lurking in the false-fronted wooden edifices of Skagway. Close your eyes and you can almost see the gold.

Start Visitor Center
Distance 2 miles
Duration 2 hours

3 Admire the bizarre driftwood facade of the **Arctic Brotherhood Hall**.

2 Take a brothel tour and/or order pizza at the still bawdy **Red Onion Saloon** (p189).

1 Receive a dramatic introduction to Skagway's golden history at the national park **visitor center** (p178).

5th Ave
3rd Ave
4th Ave
State St
Broadway St
2nd Ave
Spring St
1st Ave
START
Congress Way
White Pass & Yukon Route

Ⓝ 0 —————— 200 m
0 —————— 0.1 miles

6 Get the story of Soapy Smith, Dead Horse Gulch and Tlingit basketry at **Skagway Museum** (p182).

State St

8th Ave

Broadway St

7th Ave

6th Ave

Spring St

FINISH

6

5

5 Try to invoke the drunken days of yore in the **Mascot Saloon Museum** (p179).

4 Visit the humble abode of Skagway's founding father in the **Moore Homestead Museum** (p179).

Take a Break

Beer and burgers at **Skagway Brewing Company** (p188).

Skagway Museum

KUSHAL BOSE/SHUTTERSTOCK ©

⊙ SIGHTS

Skagway's best sights are managed by the National Park Service and are a stimulating diversion from the town's copious popcorn makers and jewelry stores.

Skagway Museum   Museum

(📞907-983-2420; cnr 7th Ave & Spring St; adult/child $2/1; 🕐9am-5pm Mon-Sat, 1-4pm Sun) Skagway Museum is not only one of the finest in a town filled with museums, but it's one of the finest in the Southeast. It occupies the entire 1st floor of the venerable century-old McCabe Building, a former college, and is devoted to various aspects of local history, including Alaska Native baskets, beadwork and carvings, and, of course, the Klondike Gold Rush.

Junior Ranger
Activity Center   Museum

(Broadway St, at 4th Ave; 🕐10am-3pm Mon-Fri; 👶) FREE At the Pantheon Saloon, built in 1903, kids are the customers. The historic bar is now home to the Klondike Gold Rush National Historical Park's Junior Ranger

Program, where children and their parents can touch and examine artifacts, dress up as stampeders and shoulder a miner's pack on their way to earning a Junior Ranger badge.

Gold Rush Cemetery
& Reid Falls   Cemetery

Visitors who become infatuated with 'Soapy' Smith and Frank Reid can walk out to this wooded cemetery, located a 1½-mile stroll northeast on State St, where they, and many others, are buried. Follow State until it curves into 23rd Ave and take the track on the right just before crossing the bridge over the Skagway River. Soapy's modest grave is close to the entrance. Reid's more extravagant stone monument is nearby. From Reid's gravestone, it's a short hike uphill to lovely **Reid Falls**, which cascades 300ft down the mountainside.

Jewell Gardens   Gardens

(📞907-983-2111; www.jewellgardens.com; Klondike Hwy; adult/child $12.50/6; 🕐9am-5pm May-Sep) If the crowds are overwhelming

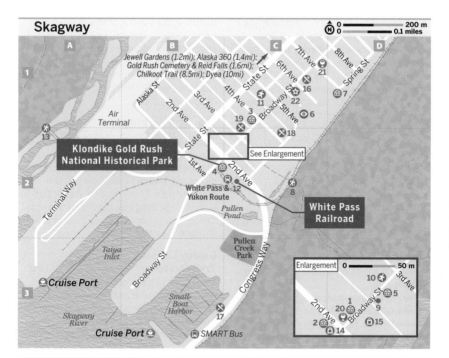

Skagway

◎ Sights
1 Arctic Brotherhood Hall	D3
2 Jeff Smith's Parlor	C3
3 Junior Ranger Activity Center	C1
4 Klondike Gold Rush National Historical Park Museum & Visitor Center	B2
5 Mascot Saloon Museum	D3
6 Moore Homestead Museum	C1
7 Skagway Museum	D1

⊕ Activities, Courses & Tours
8 Dewey Lakes Trail System	C2
9 Klondike Tours	D3
Red Onion Saloon Tours	(see 20)
10 Skagway Float Tours	D3
11 Sockeye Cycle	C1
12 White Pass & Yukon Route Railroad	C2
13 Yakutania Point & Smuggler's Cove	A2

⊕ Shopping
14 Alaska Geographic Museum Store	D3
15 Skaguay News Depot	D3

⊗ Eating
16 Bites on Broadway	C1
17 Skagway Fish Company	B3
18 Starfire	C2
19 Sweet Tooth Cafe	C1

⊜ Drinking & Nightlife
20 Red Onion Saloon	D3
21 Skagway Brewing Company	C1

⊛ Entertainment
22 Days of '98 Show	C1

you, cross the Skagway River and head over to Jewell Gardens. Located where Henry Clark started the first commercial vegetable farm in Alaska, the garden is a quiet spot of flower beds, ponds, giant vegetables and a miniature train. There is also a pair of glassblowing studios where artists give fascinating demonstrations while making beautiful glassware. Call for glassblowing times and then hop on a SMART bus that will drop you off at the entrance.

Dyea
Historic Site

In 1898 Skagway's rival city, Dyea (die-*ee*), was the trailhead for **Chilkoot Trail** (📞907-983-9234; www.nps.gov; Broadway St, Skagway), the shortest route to Lake Bennett, where stampeders began their float to Dawson City. After the White Pass & Yukon Route railroad was completed in 1900, Dyea quickly died. Today it's a few old crumbling cabins, the pilings of Dyea Wharf and Slide Cemetery, where 47 men and women were buried after perishing in an avalanche on the Chilkoot Trail in April 1898.

To explore the ghost town, pick up the Dyea Townsite *Self-Guided Walking Tour* brochure from the NPS center. The guide will lead you along a mile loop from the town-site parking area past what few ruins remain. Or join a ranger-led walk, which meets at the parking area at 3pm Monday to Thursday.

Dyea is a 9-mile drive along winding Dyea Rd, whose numerous hairpin turns are not for timid RVers. But it's a very attractive drive, especially at Skagway Overlook, a turnoff with a viewing platform 2.5 miles from Skagway. The overlook offers an excellent view of Skagway, its waterfront and the peaks above the town. Just before crossing the bridge over the Taiya River, you pass the Dyea Campground.

🟢 ACTIVITIES

The 33-mile Chilkoot Trail is Southeast Alaska's most popular hike. Less daunting are a couple of trail systems that originate downtown and two more that you can reach by train. There is no US Forest Service office in Skagway, but the NPS Visitor Center (p178) has a free brochure entitled *Skagway Trail Map*.

Dewey Lakes Trail System
Hiking

This series of trails leads east of Skagway to a handful of alpine and subalpine lakes, waterfalls and historic sites. From Broadway, follow 3rd Ave southeast to the railroad tracks. On the east side of the

Chilkoot Trail

Understand

Chilkoot Pass versus White Pass: Every Stampeder's Dilemma

Two rugged mountain barriers faced stampeders on their way to the Klondike gold fields in 1897–98: White Pass, between Skagway and Lake Bennett, and Chilkoot Pass, between Dyea and Lake Bennett. For many hopefuls, the decision about which one to cross came down to a coin toss. Neither route was easy. A feverish prospector who had tried both described one as 'hell' and the other as 'damnation.' Another proclaimed: 'Whichever way you go, you will wish you'd gone the other.'

White Pass, at 2864ft, is the lower of the two mountain crossings, though the 1897 route was significantly longer in mileage (44 miles). Furthermore, with a more gradual gradient than Chilkoot, it was accessible by horse. However, the pass was invariably muddy, narrow and treacherous. Indeed, so many packhorses died on the trail during the frigid winter of 1897–98, worked to death by their cruel, inexperienced owners, that it became known as Dead Horse Pass. Jack London, who summited White Pass on his way to Dawson in 1897, described the tragic scenes which saw over 3000 horse carcasses left abandoned in the snow.

The 33-mile Chilkoot Trail between Dyea and Lake Bennett is higher and steeper than White Pass, and merciless winds often greeted prospectors at the 3525ft summit. Since horses couldn't ascend, stampeders had to lug all their own gear up the steepest section, the so-called golden stairs, climbing in single file up narrow steps carved into the ice. However, thanks to a long history of Alaska Native use, the Chilkoot was, at least, an established trail and, as a result, was far more popular. Around 30,000 people crossed Chilkoot Pass during the gold rush (all carrying a mandatory 1 tonne of supplies) compared to around 5000 who tackled White Pass. Nevertheless, the Chilkoot quickly fell out of favor after an avalanche killed over 60 people in April 1898.

Today, the Chilkoot remains an established trail protected as part of the Klondike Gold Rush National Historical Park (p178). Up to 3000 people hike it in any given season. The railway line built through White Pass in 1900 caused the trail to be quickly abandoned. Nevertheless, you can still pick out parts of the erstwhile path – narrow and overgrown – from the train line close to the US–Canadian border crossing.

Chilkoot Trail

tracks are the trailheads to Lower Dewey Lake (0.7 miles), Icy Lake (2.5 miles), Upper Reid Falls (3.5 miles) and Sturgill's Landing (4.5 miles).

Yakutania Point & Smuggler's Cove — Hiking

The Skagway River footbridge, at the foot of the airport runway on 1st Ave, leads to a couple of easy strolls. To reach Yakutania Point, turn left at the far side of the bridge and follow the mile-long trail to picnic areas with lovely views. Sheltered Smuggler's Cove, with its fire pit, lies 0.25 miles further on.

🌀 TOURS

Skagway Float Tours — Rafting

(📞907-983-3688; www.skagwayfloat.com; 209 Broadway St; ⏰9am-6:30pm Mon-Sat, to 4pm Sun) Fancy some bliss on the river? Try the three-hour tour of Dyea that includes a 45-minute float down the placid Taiya River (adult/child $75/55); there are two per day at 9am and 1:30pm. The Hike & Float Tour ($95/75) is a four-hour outing that includes hiking 2 miles of the Chilkoot Trail then some floating back; there are several per day.

Klondike Tours — Tours

(📞907-983-2075; www.klondiketours.com; cnr Broadway St & 3nd Ave) Offers all number of reasonably priced tours from gold-panning to ziplining.

Alaska 360 — Tours

(📞907-983-3175; www.alaska3sixty.com; Mile 1.7, Klondike Hwy; 2hr tours $50) The recently renamed Klondike Gold Fields offers tours of a former working gold dredge, which was in Dawson before being moved to Skagway, where it has hit the mother lode. There is also a gold-panning show with a crack at finding dust yourself, a brewpub, and the inevitable snack shacks and gift shops on-site.

🔒 SHOPPING

Skagway is chock-a-block with shops for tourists, in particular souvenir and jewelry stores. Few of them are locally owned, so you're better to shop for mementos elsewhere.

Alaska Geographic Museum Store — Books

(Broadway St & 2nd Ave; ⏰8:30am-5:30pm May-Sep) NPS bookstore selling classic Klondike tomes and essential Chilkoot Trail maps ($8.50).

Skaguay News Depot — Books

(www.skagwaybooks.com; 264 Broadway St; ⏰8:30am-6:30pm Mon-Fri, 9am-5pm Sat & Sun) A small bookstore with an excellent selection on the Klondike Gold Rush.

✖ EATING

Skagway's small stash of restaurants is staffed by seasonal workers. There's nowhere particularly posh to choose from, though many places play off Skagway's erstwhile reputation as a center of debauchery (read: servers dressed in period costume).

Bites on Broadway — Cafe $

(📞907-983-2166; 648 Broadway St; sandwiches $11; ⏰6am-6pm Mon-Fri, to 4pm Sat, to 2pm Sun) Skagway's best bona fide coffee shop shares space with a gift store and sells some energy elongating sweet snacks to complement its cups of joe, apple crumb cake and rhubarb coffee cake among them.

Sweet Tooth Cafe — Cafe $$

(315 Broadway St; breakfast $10-17; ⏰6:30am-2:30pm) Skagway's quick-turnover, always busy diner plays heavy on the gold-rush theme. Expect to get your coffee refill poured by a lady dressed like Katherine Ross in *Butch Cassidy and the Sundance Kid*. Beyond the theatrics, the food is reliable diner fare. Breakfasts are best (porridge, eggs, pancakes, etc), but also make note of the cinnamon buns and eclairs.

Yakutania Point trail

Skagway Brewing Company

Starfire   Thai $$

(☏907-983-3663; 4th Ave, at Spring St; lunch
$12-15, dinner $14-19; ⊙11am-10pm; ✐) Skagway's token Thai restaurant is authentic
and good, with a small lunch menu and
a large, varied dinner menu. Order spicy
drunken noodles or curry dishes in five
colors (purple is Fire with Flavor!) and
enjoy it with a beer on the outdoor patio,
so pleasant and secluded you would never
know Skagway's largest hotel is across the
street.

Skagway Fish
Company   Seafood $$$

(☏907-983-3474; Congress Way; mains $18-52;
⊙11am-9pm) Overlooking the harbor, with
crab traps on the ceiling, this is a culinary
homage to fish. You can feast heartily on
halibut stuffed with king crab, shrimp and
veggies, or king-crab bisque, but surprisingly, what many locals rave about are its
baby back ribs. Its bar has the best view in
town.

🍷 DRINKING &
ENTERTAINMENT

In 1898 Skagway had 80 saloons. These
days there are significantly less, although
you will find a microbrewery and the still
rowdy Red Onion Saloon.

Skagway Brewing
Company   Microbrewery

(www.skagwaybrewing.com; cnr 7th Ave &
Broadway St; burgers $15; ⊙10am-10pm Mon-Fri,
11am-10pm Sat & Sun) Skagway's sole microbrewery offers stampeders such choices as
Prospector Pale Ale, Boomtown Brown and
Chilkoot Trail IPA. There's a full menu with
nightly dinner specials, and a quiet outdoor
deck in the back to escape the rowdiness at
the front. It lures tired hikers like Klondike
miners into a bordello.

Red Onion Saloon   Bar

(www.redonion1898.com; Broadway St, at 2nd
Ave; ⊙4-10pm Mon-Fri, noon-10pm Sat & Sun Apr-
Oct) Skagway's most beloved brothel at the

AMERICA/ALAMY STOCK PHOTO/ALAMY ©

turn of the century is now its most famous saloon. The 'RO' is done up as a gold-rush saloon, complete with mannequins leering down at you from the 2nd story to depict pioneer-era working girls. When bands are playing here, it'll be packed, noisy and rowdy – but always fun. It also has the best pizza in town.

Facetious **tours** (📞907-983-2222) of the upstairs brothel rooms run daily throughout the summer.

Days of '98 Show   Theater

(📞907-983-2545; www.thedaysof98show. com; 598 Broadway St, cnr 6th Ave; adult/child $25/12.50) This melodramatic show, held in the old Eagle's fraternity hall, is almost as longstanding as the events it portrays (it's been running since 1923). The evening show begins with 'mock gambling,' then moves on to a show focusing on Soapy and his gang. Up to four shows are offered daily.

ℹ GETTING AROUND

BUS

The city operates the **Smart bus** (📞907-983-2743; single rides/day passes $2/5; ⏱7am-9pm May-Oct), which moves people from the docks up Broadway St and to Jewell Gardens and the Alaska 360 gold dredge on the edge of town.

SCOOTER

Skagway Scooters (📞907-612-0127; www. skagwayscooters.com; Broadway St & 4th Ave; ⏱6am-7pm) rents scooters for $45 per hour. Handy for getting out to Dyea and Jewell Gardens.

TAXI

Chilkoot Trail Dyea Transport (📞907-617-7551; trumooreservices@outlook.com) Very reliable taxi service to Dyea and the Chilkoot trailhead.

Whittier's cruise-ship port

WHITTIER

Whittier at a Glance...

Whittier is a wonderfully weird Cold War anachronism set on the edge of some sublime coastal wilderness where rugged fjords dispatch tumbling glaciers into Prince William Sound. Even by Alaskan standards, this is a bizarre outpost. The 'town' is dominated by two Cold War military installations: the hopelessly ruined Buckner building and the equally incongruous Begich Towers, a 14-story skyscraper that houses most of Whittier's population. Abandoned as a military base in the 1960s, Whittier avoided ghost-town status to become a popular cruise-ship port and day-trip destination from Anchorage. Outdoor enthusiasts revere it for its kayaking and glacier viewing.

With a Day in Port

● Imbibe coffee at **Cafe Orca** (p204) before embarking on Whittier's self-guided **Historical Walking Tour** (p201), being sure to take in the **Buckner Building** (p200), **Begich Towers** (p200) and the **Prince William Sound Museum** (p200).

● Stop for fish and chips in **Swiftwater Seafood Cafe** (p204).

● Reserve the afternoon for a spirited hike up to **Portage Pass** (p194).

Best Places for...

Coffee Cafe Orca (p204)

Ice cream Vardy's Ice Cream & Pizza Parlor (p204)

Fish and chips Swiftwater Seafood Cafe (p204)

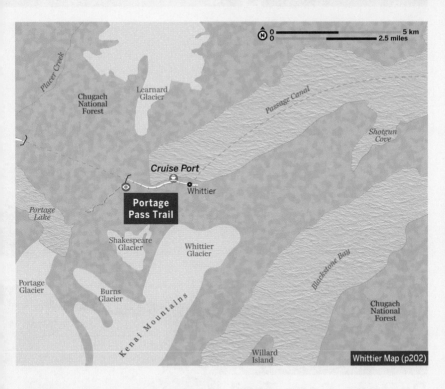

Whittier Map (p202)

Getting from the Port

Whittier is tiny. The cruise-ship dock is right opposite the train station and five minutes' walk from the harbor where you'll find most of the town's restaurants and tour companies.

Fast Facts

Money There's an ATM at the Anchor Inn (100 Whittier St).

Tourist Information There's no official tourist office. Most of the tour companies overlooking the harbor can offer basic information.

Best for Free Wi-fi Anchor Inn is a multipurpose venue with a hotel, grocery store and wi-fi access.

Portage Glacier

NELSON SIRLIN/SHUTTERSTOCK ©

Portage Pass Trail

Before the opening of the Anton Anderson Memorial Tunnel, the Portage Pass trail was the only route into what is now Whittier. Historically, it was utilized by Alaska Natives and early settlers.

Great For...

☑ Don't Miss

The fabulous two-way view at the top of Portage Pass of glacier and inlet.

Whittier's sole US Forest Service-maintained trail is a superb afternoon hike, providing good views of Portage Glacier, Passage Canal and the surrounding mountains and glaciers. Clearly marked in its early stages, the trail proceeds along an old roadbed and is easily reachable on foot from town.

To reach the trailhead, head west out of town toward the road-rail tunnel on a paved path that parallels the main road. Just before the tunnel a road branches left over the railroad tracks and dead-ends at a small parking area where a signpost marks the start of the trail.

Explore Ashore

The trailhead is a 15- to 20-minute walk from the cruise-ship terminal. From the trailhead it takes roughly one hour to ascend to the pass. Those with more time can press on to Portage Lake.

❶ Need to Know

www.fs.usda.gov/activity/chugach/recreation/hiking

✕ Take a Break

Load up with a pre-hike sandwich in **Whittier's Cafe Orca** (p204).

The Pass

The trail follows an old walking route where Alaska Natives once portaged goods between Turnagain Arm and Prince William Sound. The good path climbs steadily along the flank of a mountain for around a mile, finishing at a promontory (elevation 750ft) that offers views ahead toward Portage Glacier and back over Passage Canal.

The trail then descends for a half-mile to Divide Lake and Portage Pass. At this point the trail ends, and a route through alder trees continues to descend to a beach on Portage Lake.

Portage Lake & Glacier

At Divide Lake the trail ends, and a route through alders drops quickly to Portage Lake. It's a 2-mile hike one-way from the trailhead to the lake, and it's well worth bashing some brush at the end. There are great views from the shores of Portage Lake and plenty of places to set up camp on the alluvial flats.

The Portage Glacier disgorges icebergs into the south end of the lake, which only came into being around 100 years ago as the glacier began to retreat.

Blackstone Bay

RUSS HEINL/SHUTTERSTOCK ©

Glacier Boat Trips

A profusion of tidal glaciers inhabit the waters of Prince William Sound around Whittier. Well-equipped tour agencies with offices on the cruise-ship dock offer half-day boat tours.

Great For...

☑ Don't Miss

The sight and sound of icebergs falling off glaciers in Blackstone Bay.

Two main boat touring companies, **Major Marine Tours** (☑800-764-7300, 907-274-7300; www.majormarine.com; Harbor Loop Rd) and **Phillips Cruises & Tours** (☑907-276-8023, 800-544-0529; www.26glaciers.com; Harbor View Rd) offer five-hour boat tours that cruise around the magnificent glaciers located in the western fjords of Prince William Sound, most of which lie within the Chugach National Forest. Tours are run in comfortable high-speed catamarans with food available on board the boat. Expert tour guides provide commentary about the physical geography of the icy behemoths and the abundant wildlife they support.

Explore Ashore

Whittier's glacier tours are strongly geared toward cruise-ship passengers with trips timed to coincide with the ship schedules. Both glacier tour companies have offices and departure points right next to the cruise-ship dock. Tours last around five hours.

❶ Need to Know

Tours depart between noon and 1pm (May to September).

✖ Take a Break

Both of the main tour companies offer a full meal on their boats.

You can shop around for smaller companies such as **Epic Charters** (☑907-242-4339; www.epicchartersalaska.com; Harbor Loop Rd; single/double kayak per day $65/75; ⊗8am-6pm), offering less crowded tours on smaller boats.

Surprise Glacier

Slipping like a slow-moving landslide into Harriman fjord 20 miles northeast of Whittier, the Surprise is one of the Sound's most active glaciers, an eerie mass of creaking, groaning ice that regularly disgorges giant bergs into the narrow seawater channel. Seals hitch rides on ice floes and sea otters splash around in the vicinity.

Blackstone Bay

Only 20 nautical miles south of Whittier, sheltered Blackstone Bay protects seven glaciers, two of which kiss the ocean where they calve their mansion-sized icebergs into the sea. Other loftier ice flows jettison waterfalls over steep cliffs into the sound, while wildlife – both marine mammals and birds (and sometimes bears) – fly, splash and prowl in the vicinity. The bay is a favorite spot for kayakers, some of whom paddle all the way from Whittier to get here.

Kayakers in Blackstone Bay

RAY BULSON/GETTY IMAGES ©

Kayaking Around Whittier

Secluded at the head of sheltered Passage Canal and enveloped in a glacial landscape that supports a plethora of wildlife, Whittier is an ideal push-off point for kayakers.

Great For...

☑ Don't Miss

The noisy, crowded kittiwake colony on the uninhabited side of Passage Canal.

Due to time constraints, most cruise passengers partake in kayaking tours – Lazy Otter Charters (p203), Alaska Sea Kayakers (p203) and Sound Paddler (p203) all offer good day trips. For experienced paddlers, it's perfectly feasible to rent your own kayak and go it alone.

Blackstone Bay

One of the kayaking highlights of Alaska, Blackstone Bay is named, somewhat ominously, for a visiting 19th-century miner who froze to death in a snowstorm. There are seven glaciers in the bay, two of which

Explore Ashore

Whittier's kayaking companies are located next to the harbor, five minutes' walk from the cruise-ship dock. Day trips range from three-hour paddles in Passage Canal to eight-hour excursions to Blackstone Bay. The latter includes a water-taxi transfer.

❶ Need to Know

Kayaking excursions cost from $89/325 for three/eight hours.

✕ Take a Break

You're in the wilderness. Fill up before you go in **Whittier's Wild Catch Cafe** (p204).

touch the salt water, including the giant Blackstone. Other glaciers jettison foaming cascades of fresh water into the bay's icy depths.

Wildlife is a common sight as you negotiate the moving sea of ice and there are beaches for camping on the north and south shores.

Boat and kayaking trips that travel out to the bay are two-a-dime in Whittier. Experienced kayakers sometimes paddle here all the way from Whittier. For those travelers who are on a tight cruise-ship schedule,

day trips (eight hours) can be arranged with water-taxi transfers included.

Passage Canal

Passage Canal is the westernmost fjord in Prince William Sound. Its south shore (whereupon lies Whittier) is relatively sheltered and speckled with hidden coves and views of the Billings Glacier hanging high above the water. The north shore is more precipitous and decorated with waterfalls and a large black-legged kittiwake colony, a favored destination for paddlers.

⊙ SIGHTS

Prince William Sound Museum
Museum

(100 Whittier St; $5; ⊗10am-8pm) Whittier's history goes back to – well – 1941, so you might be surprised to hear that it has a museum. Bivouacked next to a grocery store beneath the Anchor Inn, it does a good, if modest, job of chronicling 75 years of Whittier's pioneer settlement, WWII military activity and subsequent Cold War building 'spree.'

After a few opening salvos, the story (told mainly with photos and extended captions) strays away from Whittier to cover the War in the Pacific – more specifically the American-Japanese battles in the Aleutian Islands during WWII.

Begich Towers
Landmark

(100 Kenai St) Part of Whittier's bizarreness stems from the fact that most of its inhabitants live in the same building, the 14-story Begich Towers. The Begich started life as the Hodge building in 1956 when it was constructed to house newly arrived military personnel living temporarily in a trailer park.

Abandoned by the military in 1960, it was subsequently purchased by the City of Whittier in 1972 and has since housed up to 150 people, along with a grocery store, post office and community center. An underground tunnel links it to the local elementary school.

You can wander into the main lobby where there's a photo display tracking Whittier's history.

Buckner Building
Ruins

(Blackstone Rd) You can't miss this ugly Cold War creation that melds into the surrounding landscape like a moose on a catwalk. Hailing from an architectural school best described as 'brutalist,' the ginormous Buckner was constructed in 1953 to act as a kind of mini-city for Whittier's military personnel – a function that it fulfilled for less than a decade. When the military pulled out of Whittier in 1960 the building was abandoned.

It has since fallen into disrepair, a victim of vandalism, asbestos and a lack of

Buckner Building

KEVIN SMITH/GETTY IMAGES ©

Understand

Born in World War II

Understanding how Whittier was born is key to unraveling the complexities of this odd non sequitur.

Shortly after the Japanese attack on the Aleutian Islands during WWII, the US began looking for a spot to build a secret military installation. The proposed base needed to be not only an ice-free port, but also as inaccessible as possible, lost in visibility-reducing cloud cover and surrounded by impassable mountains. They found it all right here.

And so, in this place that would be considered uninhabitable by almost any standard, surrounded by 3500ft peaks and hung with sloppy gray clouds most of the year, Whittier was built. A supply tunnel was blasted out of solid granite, one of Alaska's true engineering marvels, and more than 1000 people were housed in a single tower, the Buckner Building. It wasn't picturesque, but it was efficient.

The army maintained Whittier until 1968, leaving behind not only the Buckner Building, now abandoned, but also the 14-story Begich Towers.

A labyrinth of underground tunnels connects the apartment complex with schools and businesses, which certainly cuts down on snow-shoveling time. The structure has also given rise to a unique society, where 150-odd people, though virtually isolated from the outside world, live only a few feet from one another – high-rise living in the middle of the wilderness. It's a must-see attraction for cultural anthropologists.

For years Whittier was accessible only by train or boat, despite being only 11 miles from the most traveled highway in Alaska. But in 2000, the Anton Anderson Memorial Tunnel was overhauled for auto traffic and, since then, one of the most abnormal places imaginable has been easily accessible – though normalization seems yet to happen.

sufficient funds to do it up. Today it remains in limbo, too expensive to renovate but apparently too 'historic' to pull down.

❸ ACTIVITIES

Historical Walking Tour   History
Pick up a map at the **Anchor Inn** (☏907-472-2354; www.anchorinnwhittier.com; 100 Whittier St; s/d $120/140; 🛜) or the **Inn at Whittier** (☏907-472-3200; www.innatwhittier.com; Harbor Loop Rd; r $169-299; P🛜) and follow the self-guided seven-stop tour through the Whittier Army Port Historical District. You'll find information signs on the walls of each building, including the Buckner Building and Begich Towers. The walk will deposit you at the Prince William Sound Museum, which rounds off the story nicely.

Horsetail Falls Trail   Hiking
One in a trio of lovely trails accessible from town, the Horsetail Falls Trail starts at the end of the Reservoir Rd behind the Buckner Building and winds up the mountainside on a series of boardwalks through a mixture of forest and muskeg to a wooden platform high above Whittier. It's just over a mile in length, and delivers a priceless view.

The Horsetail Falls are only visible in the distance.

Shotgun Cove Trail   Hiking
The Shotgun is more of a dirt road than a trail in its initial stages tracking along a delightful stretch of coast with waterfalls, a kittiwake colony and the Billings Glacier visible on the opposite side of Passage Inlet.

From the northeast corner of the Buckner Building, follow Salmon Run Rd for half a mile to the Lu Young Park Picnic

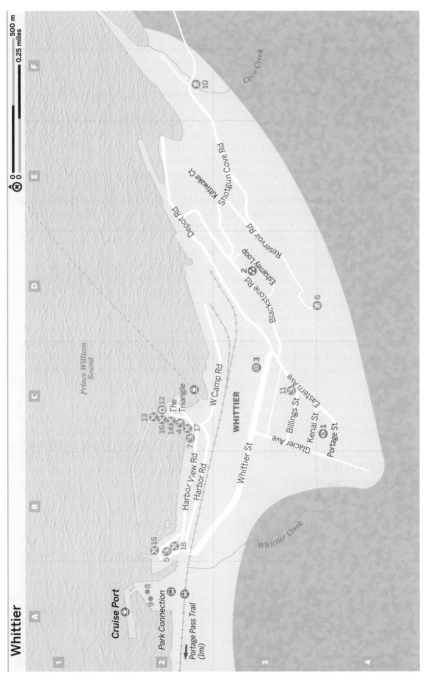

Whittier

Cruise Port

Prince William Sound

Park Connection

Portage Pass Trail
(1mi)

Harbor View Rd

Harbor Rd

Depot Rd

Shotgun Cove Rd

Kittiwake Ct

Reservoir Rd

Eshamey Loop

Blackstone Rd

W Camp Rd

Whittier St

WHITTIER

Glacier Ave

Billings St

Eastern Ave

Kenai St

Portage St

The
Triangle

Cove Creek

Whittier Creek

500 m
0.25 miles

Whittier

Area, where king and silver salmon run during June and late August. Beyond here an undulating dirt road continues along the coast. It's 1½ miles to Second Salmon Run where a trail alongside the creek leads up to a waterfall. The dirt road ends just past the creek, whereupon the rough-and-ready **Emerald Cove Trail** continues for several more miles, partly on boardwalks through a mixture of forest and muskeg. About a mile in, a side trail leads down to a beach.

⊙ TOURS

Alaska Sea Kayakers
Kayaking

(☎877-472-2534, 907-472-2534; www.alaska seakayakers.com; The Triangle; ⊙7am-7pm) Rents out kayaks (single/double $65/80 per day), arranges water taxis and multiday tours to places like Harriman Fjord, Nellie Juan Glacier and Whale Bay. It has booking offices at the harbor and the Triangle. Guided sea-kayaking trips include three-hour tours to the kittiwake colony across the passage ($89), half-day trips ($145 to $235) and a Blackstone Bay full-day trip ($345).

Lazy Otter Charters
Kayaking

(☎907-694-6887, 800-587-6887; www.lazyotter. com; Harbor View Rd; ⊙6:30am-7pm) Lazy Otter operates out of a very pleasant cafe on the harbor and offers all the adventurous water activities you could hope for, including a guided kayaking trip (with water-taxi transfer) to Blackstone Bay ($325 per person). It also runs a water taxi for experienced indie kayakers and rents out fiberglass kayaks (single/double $55/95 per day).

Sound Paddler
Kayaking

(Prince William Sound Kayak Center; ☎907-472-2452; www.pwskayakcenter.com; 101 Billings St; ⊙7am-8pm) This well-run operation has been outfitting kayakers since 1981. Perry and Lois Solmonson rent kayaks including outer rain gear (single/double/triple $70/120/150, discounted for multiple days) and run guided tours. The day-long excursions to Blackstone Bay ($625 for two people; hefty discount if you can rustle up six people) are top flight.

⊙ SHOPPING

Log Cabin Gifts
Arts & Crafts

(☎907-472-2501; The Triangle; ⊙11am-6pm) Looking like a museum to Alaskan eccentricities, this genuine log cabin is adorned with reindeer antlers and Alaska Native art. The knickknacks, including lots of high-quality leatherwork, are handmade by owner Brenda Tolman.

H MARK WEIDMAN PHOTOGRAPHY/ALAMY ©

Swiftwater Seafood Cafe

🍴 EATING

Whittier's half-dozen eating joints hug the harbor and aim their fish dishes at hungry cruisers or day-trippers from Anchorage.

The town is too small for a bar scene. Most people grab a drink with their food overlooking the harbor.

Cafe Orca Cafe $
(The Triangle; light meals $8-12; ⊙11am-7pm) Gourmet sandwiches, some of the best chowder on the Sound, and a great little waterfront deck are the perfect combination for the best lunch in town. If it's raining, sit inside with a hot espresso.

Vardy's Ice Cream & Pizza Parlor Ice Cream, Pizza $
(The Triangle; ice cream $3-6; ⊙11am-9pm) Under the same ownership as Swiftwater Seafood Cafe, this newer place is sheltered two doors away in a white clapboard bungalow and serves a casual assortment of ice cream, pizzas and various sweet treats. It's a welcome addition to this tiny community.

Swiftwater Seafood Cafe Seafood $$
(www.swiftwaterseafoodcafe.com; The Triangle; mains $10-18; ⊙11:30am-9pm Sun-Thu, to 10pm Fri & Sat) This tiny hole in the wall has a walk-up counter where you order your food and pay before eating. Halibut and chips and red seafood chowder are the signature dishes, but there's also crab cakes, fried zucchini, burgers, calamari, and bread pudding for dessert. Service is exceedingly friendly.

Peruse the photos of famous Alaskan shipwrecks as you wait or head to the outside patio to watch weighty clouds amass over the harbor.

Wild Catch Cafe Seafood $$
(☎907-472-2252; 12 Harbor Loop Rd; burgers $14-16; ⊙6am-7pm) This place is relatively new in Whittier's small restaurant universe, and its 'wild catch' appears primarily in its salmon burgers, and halibut and chips. The menu is inscribed on a big blackboard and there are two eating options – take-out from a cafe window, or sit-down indoors. It also does Whittier's best breakfast, stuffed

into a burrito and washed down with Alaska-roasted Kaladi Brothers coffee.

Ask about the boxed lunches – great for fishing trips.

China Sea   Chinese $$

(☑907-472-3663; The Triangle; lunch buffet $13, dinner $13-25; ☺11am-10pm) This red clapboard building overlooking the harbor serves up Chinese and Korean food with a sideline in fish and chips. There's a generous lunch buffet featuring sweet-and-sour halibut, plus boring old chow mein and fried rice.

Inn at Whittier
Restaurant   Seafood $$$

(☑907-472-3200; Harbor Loop Rd; breakfast & lunch $9-20, dinner $23-36; ☺7am-9pm) This hotel dining room with glorious views of the Sound (cloudy or not) cooks up steaks, seafood and a spicy cajun shrimp alfredo that's out of this world. Have a martini at the posh lounge attached to the restaurant.

❶ GETTING THERE & AWAY

Whittier is the start and/or finish point for numerous cruises. As a result, many people travel overland to the port from Anchorage. There are three main types of direct transportation.

BUS

Buses to Whittier are limited and normally only operate around the once- or twice-weekly cruise ship visits.

Park Connection (☑800-266-8625; www.alaskacoach.com) has plush coaches that whisk people between Anchorage and Whittier when there's a ship in dock (usually Saturdays). One-way tickets for the two-hour journey cost $65; book online.

CAR

Whittier Access Rd, also known as Portage Glacier Access Rd, leaves the Seward Hwy at Mile 79, continuing to Whittier through the claustrophobic Anton Anderson Memorial Tunnel, which at 2.7 miles long is the longest 'railroad-highway' tunnel in North America. Negotiating the damp one-lane shaft as you skid across the train tracks is almost worth the steep price of admission (per car/RV $13/22), which is charged only if you're entering Whittier; if you bring your car into town on the Alaska Marine Hwy you can exit through the tunnel for free. Eastbound and westbound traffic alternate every 30 minutes, with interruptions for the Alaska Railroad. Bring a magazine.

Whittier has car rentals with **Avis** (☑907-440-2847; www.avis.com; Lot 8, Small-boat Harbor; ☺8am-8pm).

TRAIN

The **Alaska Railroad** (☑907-265-2494, 800-544-0552; www.akrr.com) *Glacier Discovery* train runs daily to and from Anchorage (2½ hours, $83) from late May to mid-September from Whittier's train station, little more than a platform and an awning next to the cruise dock.

❶ GETTING AROUND

Everywhere in Whittier is easily walkable.

SEWARD

Seward at a Glance...

Perched on the edge of Resurrection Bay, Seward offers out-of-this-world views of water, sky, mountain and forest. Because of its size (and its history as a railroad port), there is plenty of nightlife and lots of good restaurants in the picturesque old-time downtown area.

Just a jump from town, you have access to Kenai Fjords National Park, superb sea kayaking, birding and whale-watching, and hikes that can take you to the top of the Harding Icefield or across the whole Kenai Peninsula. The body of the city is divided into two centers: the newer, touristy harbor and the historic downtown area.

With a Day in Port

○ Catch the Exit Glacier shuttle to **Kenai Fjords National Park** (p210). View the glacier from the local trail network.

○ Return to Seward, enjoy coffee, snacks and art at **Resurrect Art Coffee House Gallery** (p217), before visiting the **Alaska Sealife Center** (p212).

○ In the afternoon, stroll the **Small-Boat Harbor** (p212) in order to work up enthusiasm for a fish dinner at **Chinooks** (p216).

Best Places for...

Craft Beer Seward Brewing Company (p217)

Coffee & Art Resurrect Art Coffee House Gallery (p217)

Beer & Live Music Yukon Bar (p217)

Seafood Chinooks (p216)

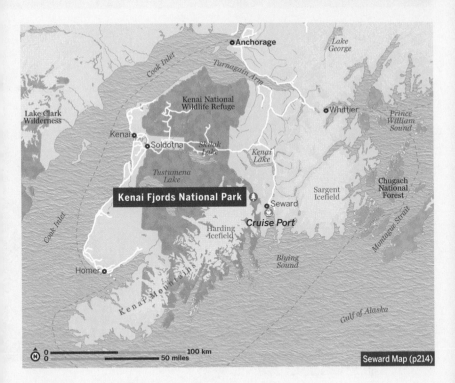

Seward Map (p214)

Getting from the Port

When cruise ships are in town, the free **Seward Shuttle** runs between the ferry terminal and downtown every 30 minutes.

Fast Facts

Money First National Bank of Anchorage (303 4th Ave) is one of two banks in town. There are ATMs in Safeway and the Yukon Bar.

Tourist Information Chamber of Commerce is at the entrance to town.

Best for Free Wi-Fi Seward Community Library & Museum (p212)

Hiking Exit Glacier

Kenai Fjords National Park

Kenai Fjords protects 587,000 acres of Alaska's most awesome, impenetrable wilderness. Crowning the park is the massive Harding Icefield; from it, countless tidewater glaciers pour down, carving the coast into dizzying fjords.

Great For...

☑ Don't Miss

The free ranger-led hikes from the Exit Glacier Nature Center.

Exit Glacier

The marquee attraction of Kenai Fjords National Park is Exit Glacier, named by explorers crossing the Harding Icefield who found the glacier a suitable way to 'exit' the ice and mountains.

From the **Exit Glacier Nature Center** (☺9am-8pm), the **Outwash Plain Trail** is an easy 0.75-mile walk to the glacier's alluvial plain – a flat expanse of pulverized silt and gravel, cut through by braids of gray meltwater. The **Edge of the Glacier Trail** leaves the first loop and climbs steeply to an overlook at the side of the glacier before returning. Both trails make for a short hike that will take one or two hours; you can return along the half-mile nature trail to the ranger station.

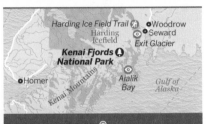

Harding Ice Field Trail •Woodrow
Harding ●Seward
Icefield Exit Glacier
Kenai Fjords ⚓
National Park
•Homer Aialik Gulf of
Bay Alaska
Kenai Mountains

⚓

Explore Ashore

Exit Glacier Guides run a **shuttle**
(☏907-224-5569; www.exitglaciershuttle.
com; round trip $15; ⊙9:30am-5pm Mon-Thu,
from 8:30am Fri-Sun) from downtown
Seward and the boat harbor to Exit
Glacier and back every hour. It's best to
reserve a minimum half-day to see the
glacier, more if partaking in an organized activity.

❶ Need to Know

☏907-224-2125; www.nps.gov/kefj

✖ Take a Break

The park is close to Seward, and your
best eating options are there. Otherwise, bring your own grub.

Aialik Bay

Aialik Bay is a popular arm for kayakers.
The high point of the trip is Holgate Glacier,
an active tidewater glacier that's the main
feature of all the boat tours. **Kayak Adventures Worldwide** (☏907-224-3960; www.
kayakak.com) 🚣 guides educational half- and
full-day trips out of Seward. Trips to Aialik
Bay start at $399 and include a water taxi
and a guided paddle to Aialik Glacier.

Harding Icefield Trail

This strenuous and yet extremely popular
4-mile trail (a six- to eight-hour round-trip)
follows Exit Glacier up to Harding Icefield.

The 700-sq-mile expanse remained
undiscovered until the early 1900s, when
a map-surveying team discovered that
eight coastal glaciers flowed from the exact
same system. Today you can rediscover
it via a steep, roughly cut and sometimes
slippery ascent to 3500ft. Beware of bears;
they're common here.

Seward Community Library & Museum

⊙ SIGHTS

Alaska Sealife Center   Aquarium

(📞800-224-2525; www.alaskasealife.org; 301 Railway Ave; adult/child $25/13; ☺9am-9pm Mon-Thu, 8am-9pm Fri-Sun; 🚼) A fitting legacy of the *Exxon Valdez* oil-spill settlement, this $56-million marine research center is more than just one of Alaska's finest attractions. As the only cold-water marine-science facility in the Western Hemisphere, it serves as a research and educational center and provides rehabilitation for injured marine animals. Plan to spend the better part of a great afternoon here.

Kids will love the tidepool touch tank, where they can hold sea anemones and starfish, as well as the ship's helm and the massive two-story tanks where you can see seals, birds and more both above and below the water. An outdoor observation platform offers a fabulous view of the mountains ringing Resurrection Bay where you can watch salmon thrash their way up a fish ladder.

It's worth including an Encounter tour ($75 per person): you'll get face-to-face with the creatures you normally only see behind the glass with deeper dives into the lives of octopus, puffins or marine mammals.

Small-Boat Harbor   Harbor

At the northern end of 4th Ave this harbour hums during the summer with fishing boats, charter vessels, cruise ships and a number of sailboats. At its heart is the **Harbormaster's Office** (📞907-224-3138; 4th Ave; ☺8am-5pm). Look for the huge anchors outside. Radiating outward from the docks are seasonal restaurants, espresso bars and tourist services.

Seward Community Library & Museum   Museum

(www.cityofseward.us; 239 6th Ave; museum adult/child $4/free; ☺10am-5pm Tue-Sat, 1-5pm Sun) This eclectic museum has an excellent Iditarod exhibit, a rare 49-star

US flag, and relics of Seward's Russian era, the 1964 Good Friday Earthquake and the 1989 oil spill. There are also lots of amusing antiques, including an ancient electric hair-curling machine, plus movies and a children's section.

The staff are enthusiastic and knowledgeable, and worth engaging. The library is a good place to relax on a rainy day (and entry is free).

Benny Benson Memorial
Monument

This humble monument at the corner of the Seward Hwy and Dairy Hill Lane honors Seward's favorite son, Benny Benson. In 1926 the orphaned 13-year-old Alaska Native boy submitted his design for the Alaska state flag, arguably the loveliest in the Union.

His stellar design (you can see one of his first at the library) includes the North Star, symbolizing the northernmost state, the Great Bear constellation for strength, and a blue background representing the sky and the forget-me-not, Alaska's state flower.

⊙ ACTIVITIES

There are excellent hikes in town and nearby Kenai Fjords National Park. The park offers the best blue-water paddling you could imagine.

⊙ Cycling

Popular with hikers, the **Lost Lake Trail** is single-track riding that is sometimes steep and technical but highly rewarding nonetheless. Local cyclists say the Iditarod National Historic Trail and the Resurrection River Trail are also good rides.

Seward Bike Shop
Cycling

(411 Port Ave; cruisers full/half-day $28/18, mountain bikes $38/25; ⊙10am-6pm) Rents out bikes and has the latest details on local biking trails.

Alaska's Mural Capital

Seward is the undeniable mural capital of Alaska. There are more than two dozen public paintings in town – mostly on buildings in the downtown area. Enjoy historic treatments of Exit Glacier (it really was that big), tributes to the Mt Marathon Race and more politically charged pieces. See www.sewardmural society.com for details or sign up for an excellent 1½-hour tour with the **Painted Whale** (☑907-521-0311; www.sewardmurals .com; per adult/child $18/free).

Downtown Seward
JOSEPH SOHM/SHUTTERSTOCK ©

⊙ Hiking

Exit Glacier Guides
Hiking

(☑907-224-5569; www.exitglacierguides.com; 405 4th Ave; ⊙8am-5:30pm) ✔ Exit Glacier Guides gives you the chance to tread upon Seward's backyard glacier. Its six-hour ice-hiking trip costs $130 per person, gears you up with crampons and ropes, ascends partway up the Harding Ice Field Trail and then heads out onto the glacier for crevasse exploration and interpretive glaciology.

It also offers helicopter tours, hiking tours and a historic downtown tour as well as overnight journeys.

Mt Marathon Trail
Hiking

(www.mmr.seward.com) This steep, punishing trail is the scene of a grueling race every Fourth of July. Don't take the Racer's Trail, at the west end of Jefferson St, without

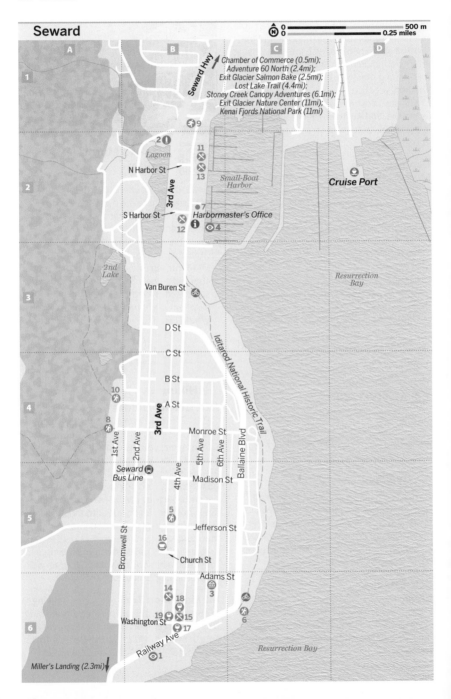

Seward

0 500 m
0 0.25 miles

Seward Hwy

Chamber of Commerce (0.5mi);
Adventure 60 North (2.4mi);
Exit Glacier Salmon Bake (2.5mi);
Lost Lake Trail (4.4mi);
Stoney Creek Canopy Adventures (6.1mi);
Exit Glacier Nature Center (11mi);
Kenai Fjords National Park (11mi)

Lagoon

N Harbor St

3rd Ave

S Harbor St

Small-Boat
Harbor

Cruise Port

Harbormaster's Office

2nd
Lake

Van Buren St

Resurrection
Bay

D St

C St

B St

Iditarod National Historic Trail

A St

3rd Ave

Monroe St

1st Ave
2nd Ave
4th Ave
5th Ave
6th Ave
Ballaine Blvd

Seward
Bus Line

Madison St

Jefferson St

Bromwell St

Church St

Adams St

Washington St

Railway Ave

Miller's Landing (2.3mi)

Resurrection Bay

Seward

someone who's been up before. Instead, take the so-called Jeep Trail at the end of Monroe St, where you'll still have access to the peak and a heavenly bowl behind the mountain.

According to local legend, grocer Gus Borgan wagered $100 in 1909 that no one could run Mt Marathon in an hour, and the race was on. Winner James Walters clocked in at 62 minutes, losing the bet but becoming a legend. The 3.1-mile suffer-fest quickly became a celebrated Fourth of July event and today is Alaska's most famous footrace. It pits runners from all over the world against the 3022ft-high peak. Be careful: the runner's trail is painful – think Stairmaster with a view – and every summer several tourists who didn't know what they were in for are rescued.

Iditarod National Historic Trail
Hiking

This legendary trail to Nome begins at the foot of Ballaine Blvd. Here, a memorial marks Mile 0 and a paved bike path heads 2 miles north along the beach. A more interesting segment of the trail for hikers, however, can be reached by heading east 2 miles on Nash Rd, which intersects the Seward Hwy at Mile 3.2.

From here you can follow the Iditarod National Historic Trail through woods and thick brush for a 4-mile hike to Bear Lake. Nearby is the unmarked trailhead for the **Mt Alice Trail**, a fairly difficult and highly recommended 2.5-mile climb to the alpine

summit. Bald eagles, blueberries and stunning views can be had elsewhere, but it's the solitude – this trail is relatively unused – and afternoon light that make Mt Alice great. Back at Bear Lake, you can either backtrack to town or forge on another 11 miles to rejoin the Seward Hwy.

Two Lakes Trail
Hiking

(cnr 1st Ave & A St) This easy 1-mile loop circumnavigates pleasant Two Lakes Park, through woods and picnic grounds, across a creek and around the two promised lakes at the base of Mt Marathon. Unsatisfied hikers can access the Jeep Trail nearby, which climbs Mt Marathon, for a much more intense climb.

◎ Kayaking

Miller's Landing
Kayaking

(☏907-331-3113; www.millerslandingak.com; cnr Lowell Rd & Beach Dr; ◷5:30am-11pm) Offers kayak rentals for experienced kayakers (single/double $45/55 per day), which include all necessary gear. It also provides lessons, custom tours and guided day-trips to Aialik Bay ($450 for a group of one to three; if you're solo, call and ask if you can slot into an existing group to save money).

◎ Ziplining

Stoney Creek Canopy Adventures
Zipline

(☏907-224-3662; www.stoneycreekca.com; 13037 Knotwood St; adult/child $149/119)

Accessed from Mile 6.5 of the Seward Hwy, this three-hour canopy zipline takes you whizzing past giant Sitka spruce and mirror ponds. There are eight zip runs in all, plus three suspension bridges and two rappels.

TOURS

Major Marine Tours   Boating

(☎907-274-7300; www.majormarine.com; small-boat harbor, Seward; ⊗7am-9pm) Major Marine Tours includes a national-park ranger on every boat. It has a half-day Resurrection Bay tour (adult/child $79/39.50), a full-day Northwestern Fjords ($224 per person), and an assortment of semicustomized trips for birders, whale-watchers and more. With most tours, you can also have a prime rib and salmon buffet feast for $19.

Adventure 60 North   Kayaking

(☎907-224-2600; www.adventure60.com; 31872 Herman Leirer Rd) This is a reputable kayaking and adventure outfitter, with guided kayak tours of Resurrection Bay (half-/full day $68/130), stand-up paddleboard tours as well as guided hikes.

Kenai Fjords Tours   Boating

(☎888-749-1016; www.kenaifjords.com; small-boat harbor) This long-running operation offers a wide variety of options, including a six-hour national-park tour (adult/child $159/80). Instead of having a naturalist on board, the captain rocks the mic. A few options offer a lunchtime salmon bake on Fox Island.

Prices range from $79 to $198 for four- to nine-hour tours. Children are half price. Smaller vessels are available for more intimate tours, often adapted to the interests of the group.

EATING

Lighthouse Cafe & Bakery   Bakery $

(☎907-224-6091; 1210 4th Ave; breakfast & lunch $3-8, dinner $5-12; ⊗6am-2pm Mon-Thu, 5am-2pm & 5-8pm Fri-Sun) This busy joint has plenty of warm, fresh-baked goods to start your day. On weekends there's an Indian buffet dinner for $15.

Sea Bean Cafe   Cafe $

(www.seabeancafe.com; 225 4th Ave; light meals $7-12; ⊗7am-9pm; 🛜) Serves hot paninis, wraps, Belgian waffles, ice-cream, smoothies and espressos.

The Cookery   Bistro $$

(☎907-422-7459; www.cookeryseward.com; 209 5th Ave; mains $16-25; ⊗5-10pm Tue-Sun) Seward's best restaurant serves excellent land-based cuisine, but local seafood is where it really shines. Start off with local oysters and bubbly, and then delight in whatever fresh seafood is on the menu.

Chinooks   Seafood $$

(☎907-224-2207; 1404 4th Ave; mains $14-35; ⊗11:30am-10pm) Seward's best waterfront eatery, this airy, steel-walled spot features a good selection of creative plates featuring local seafood such as smoked scallop, mac 'n' cheese and puttanesca. The cocktails (and mocktails) are delicious and creative.

Exit Glacier Salmon Bake   Seafood $$

(Herman Leirer Rd; mains $13-28; ⊗5-10pm) Its motto – 'cheap beer and lousy food' – is wrong on the second count. Locals like the salmon sandwich, which you can adorn with pickles from a barrel. It's a quarter-mile from the Seward Hwy turnoff.

Ray's Waterfront   Seafood $$$

(☎907-224-5606; www.rayswaterfrontak.com; small-boat harbor; lunch $16-25, dinner $17-45; ⊗11am-10pm) Ray's has amazing views, popular seafood dishes and attentive service in a fine-dining atmosphere that retains its Alaskan vibe. The bar is a friendly place to rehydrate.

DRINKING & NIGHTLIFE

Seward has no shortage of welcoming watering holes, most featuring a mix of young and old, locals and tourists. Almost all the bars are downtown.

Resurrect Art Coffee House Gallery
Cafe

(320 3rd Ave; ⊙7am-7pm; 🛜) Located in an old high-ceilinged church, this place serves espressos and snacks next to a massive soapstone wood stove. It also carries a great collection of local art and often hosts live music and performances. The best place to read the paper and check out the view is from the airy choir loft.

Stop by here for First Friday art walks – local art shows held on the first Friday of each month at galleries around town.

Seward Brewing Company
Brewery

(☑907-422-0337; www.sewardbrewery.com; 139 4th Ave; ⊙11:30am-10pm) You'll find home-crafted brew at this expansive restaurant and taphouse. The food ($12 to $21) is just as good as the beer; it's a departure from standard pub grub and includes Alaskan faves such as salmon poke, halibut curry and fried rockfish.

Thorn's Showcase Lounge
Lounge

(208 4th Ave; ⊙10am-midnight Mon-Thu, to 1am Sat & Sun) This curio-bedecked plush leather lounge serves the strongest drinks in town – try its white Russians – and is said to have the best halibut around (mains $14 to $18). The Jim Beam collection is valued at thousands of dollars; can you spot the pipeline bottle?

Yukon Bar
Bar

(☑907-224-3063; 201 4th Ave; ⊙noon-2am) There are hundreds of dollars pinned to this bar's ceiling and almost nightly live music in the summer. It's festive.

🛈 GETTING THERE & AROUND

Seward is a popular embarkation point for cruise passengers, with good transport connections to Anchorage.

BUS

Park Connection (☑800-266-8625; www. alaskacoach.com) Has a daily service from Seward to Denali National Park (one-way $155) via Anchorage (one-way $65).

Seward Bus Line (☑907-224-3608; www. sewardbuslines.net; 539 3rd Ave) Departs at 9:30am and 2pm daily en route to Anchorage ($40). It also offers service at 9:30am to Whittier ($60, minimum two passengers).

Seward Shuttle When cruise ships are in town, the free shuttle runs between the ferry terminal and downtown every 30 minutes.

TRAIN

Alaska Railroad (☑907-265-2494; www.akrr. com; 408 Port Ave; one-way/round-trip $105/168) Offers a daily run to Anchorage from May to September. It's more than just public transportation: it's one of the most famous rides in Alaska, complete with glaciers, steep gorges and rugged mountain scenery.

ANCHORAGE

Anchorage at a Glance...

Wedged between 5000ft peaks and an inlet filled with salmon and whales, the Big Apple of the north is unlike any other city.

This is a place where bears are seen wandering bike paths, moose munch on neighborhood gardens, and locals pull salmon from a creek within blocks of hotels and office buildings.

Dive into this city of parks, museums and restaurants and you'll see why almost half the state's population calls it home.

With a Day in Port

○ Caffeine-load and order a crab omelet at **Snow City Cafe** (p231). Prioritize the **Anchorage Museum** (p107) before eyeballing the shops on W 5th Ave.

○ In the afternoon hire a bike for a ride on the **Tony Knowles Coastal Trail** (p227), popping into the **Oscar Anderson House** (p226) before you rev up.

○ The bike miles should be enough to earn you a beer and quesadilla in **49th State Brewing** (p232).

Best Places for...

Coffee Side Street Espresso (p232)

Breakfast Snow City Café (p231)

Beer Midnight Sun Brewing Company (p232)

Fine-dining Marx Bros Cafe (p232)

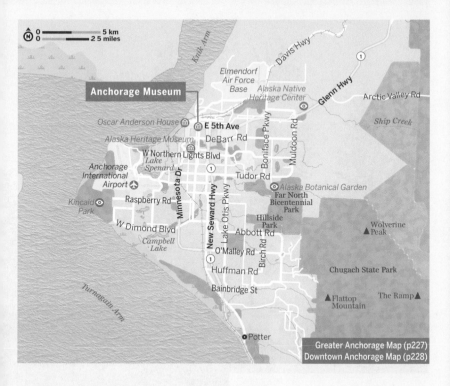

Getting from the Port

Very few cruise ships dock in Anchorage itself. Instead most ships depart from either Seward or Whittier to the south. Transfers, usually organized through the cruise line, are available by either bus or the **Alaska Railroad** (p233).

Fast Facts

Money Key Bank (601 W 5th Ave) is downtown and Wells Fargo (301 W Northern Lights Blvd) is the main bank in midtown.

Tourist Information Anchorage Convention & Visitors Bureau (www. anchorage.net)

Best for Free Wi-Fi Internet access and wi-fi are widely available all over Anchorage at hotels, restaurants, bars and even gift shops.

CHRIS AREND ©

Anchorage Museum

This world-class facility is Anchorage's cultural jewel. The new Rasmuson wing, home to the museum's prestigious art collection, has added 31,000 sq ft to what was already the largest museum in the state.

Great For...

☑ Don't Miss

Perusing the art in the new Rasmuson wing, which opened in September 2017.

Smithsonian Arctic Studies Center

The museum's flagship exhibit is the Smithsonian Arctic Studies Center, with more than 600 Alaska Native objects, such as art, tools, masks and household implements. Located on level 2 of the museum, it was previously housed in Washington, DC.

It's the largest Alaska Native collection in the state and it's surrounded by large video screens showing contemporary Alaska Native life. Nearby is the Listening Space, where you can listen to storytellers and natural sounds from Arctic Alaska.

Art of the North Gallery

Rehoused in the slick new Rasmuson wing which opened in 2017, the Art of the North Gallery on level 3 has increased the museum's art presentation space five-fold.

Explore Ashore

The recently extended museum justifies between one and two hours of your time. The train station (departure point for Whittier and Seward) is a 15-minute walk.

❶ Need to Know

www.anchoragemuseum.org; 625 C St; adult/child $18/9; ⊘9am-6pm summer; 👪

✕ Take a Break

The museum has its own cafe and restaurant called Muse.

Beautifully curated rooms display more than 200 works from Alaskan masters such as Eustace Ziegler and Sydney Laurence. Both contemporary and indigenous works are displayed side by side.

Alaska Exhibition

The level 2 Alaska Exhibition has also been upgraded. Using multimedia exhibits, visitors are sent on a circuitous thematic journey that traces 10,000 years of human settlement, from early subsistence villages to modern oil dependency.

Imaginarium Discovery Center

The museum also contains the Imaginarium Discovery Center, a hands-on science center for children that was previously housed in a separate downtown location.

There are also galleries devoted to traveling art exhibits, a planetarium and the KidSpace Gallery, which is designed for young children (and their parents) to explore the worlds of art, history and science through hands-on play. Clearly, this is a place where you can spend an entire afternoon.

Anchorage Amble

While the wider metropolis sprawls, downtown Anchorage is a relatively compact district with views of snow-capped mountains and the watery expanse of Cook Inlet lending it a tangible edge-of-the-wilderness feel.

Start Anchorage Museum
Distance 3 miles
Duration 3 hours

5 Embrace history in the **Oscar Anderson House** (p226), the only building in Anchorage over 100 years old.

6 Turn your stroll into a marathon on the **Tony Knowles Coastal Trail** (p227), which parallels Cook Inlet for 11 beautiful miles.

Classic Photo
If you're lucky, you might snap a moose on the Tony Knowles Coastal Trail.

Take a Break …
Dip into one of the food booths at **Anchorage Market & Festival** (p230).

FINISH **5**
6
Elderberry Park

Resolution Park

W 2nd Ave
W 3rd Ave
W 4th Ave
W 5th Ave
W 6th Ave
W 7th Ave

M St
L St
K St
I St
H St
G St
L St
I St

Christensen Dr

City Hall

0   500 m
0   0.25 miles
N

4 If you're here on the weekend, divert two blocks northeast to **Anchorage Market & Festival** (p230) and its food booths.

Alaska Railroad
Train Station

4 W 3rd Ave

3 Stop at the **information center**, housed in a typical Alaskan Log Cabin with a sod roof.

W 4th Ave

3 F St / D St

W 5th Ave

2 Town Square Park

E St / C St / B St / A St

W 6th Ave

D St

W 7th Ave

START **1**

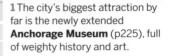

1 The city's biggest attraction by far is the newly extended **Anchorage Museum** (p225), full of weighty history and art.

2 Gravitate west for a cinematic northern lights display at the **Alaska Center for the Performing Arts** (p231).

◎ SIGHTS

Alaska Native
Heritage Center   Cultural Center

(Map p227; ☑907-330-8000; www.alaskanative.
net; 8800 Heritage Center Dr; adult/child $25/17;
☺9am-5pm) If you can't travel to the Bush
region to experience Alaska Native culture
firsthand, visit this 26-acre center and
see how humans survived – and thrived
– before central heating. This is much
more than just a museum: it represents a
knowledge bank of language, art and culture that will survive no matter how many
sitcoms are crackling through the Alaskan
stratosphere. It's a labor of love, and of
incalculable value.

Oscar Anderson
House   Historic Building

(Map p228; www.aahp-online.net; 420 M St;
adult/child $10/5; ☺noon-4pm Tue-Sun Jun-Aug)
Housed in the city's oldest wooden-framed
home, this little museum overlooks the delightful Elderberry Park. Anderson was the
18th American settler to set foot in Anchorage, and he built his house in 1915. Today

it's the only home museum in Anchorage,
and despite past budget problems, it's
open as a reminder that until fairly recently
there wasn't a single building in this city
that was a century old.

Alaska Heritage
Museum   Museum

(Map p227; ☑907-265-2834; www.wellsfargo
history.com/museums/anchorage; 301 W
Northern Lights Blvd; ☺noon-4pm Mon-Fri) **FREE**
Inside the midtown Wells Fargo bank, this
museum is home to the largest private
collection of Alaska Native artifacts in the
state and includes costumes, baskets and
hunting weapons. There are also original
paintings covering the walls, including
several by Sydney Laurence, and lots of
scrimshaw. The museum's collection is so
large that there are displays in the elevator
lobbies throughout the bank. You can call to
book a guided tour.

Alaska Botanical
Garden   Gardens

(Map p227; ☑907-770-3692; www.alaskabg.
org; 4601 Campbell Airstrip Rd; adult/child

Flattop Mountain Trail (p229)

PARKER EVERETT/SHUTTERSTOCK ©

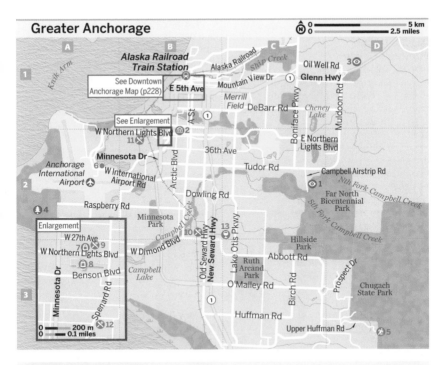

Greater Anchorage

$12/8; ☺daylight) The garden is a colorful showcase for native species, where gentle paths lead you through groomed herb, rock and perennial gardens in a wooded setting. The mile-long Lowenfels-Hoersting Family Nature Trail – built for tanks during WWII – is a great place to learn your basic Alaskan botany or just to stroll and watch the bald eagles pluck salmon from Campbell Creek. Guided tours are offered by appointment.

🏃 ACTIVITIES

Tony Knowles Coastal Trail

Cycling

(Map p228) Anchorage's favorite trail is the scenic 11-mile Tony Knowles Coastal Trail. It begins at the west end of 2nd Ave downtown and passes Elderberry Park before winding through Earthquake Park, around Point Woronzof and finally to Point Campbell in **Kincaid Park**. There are good views

Downtown Anchorage

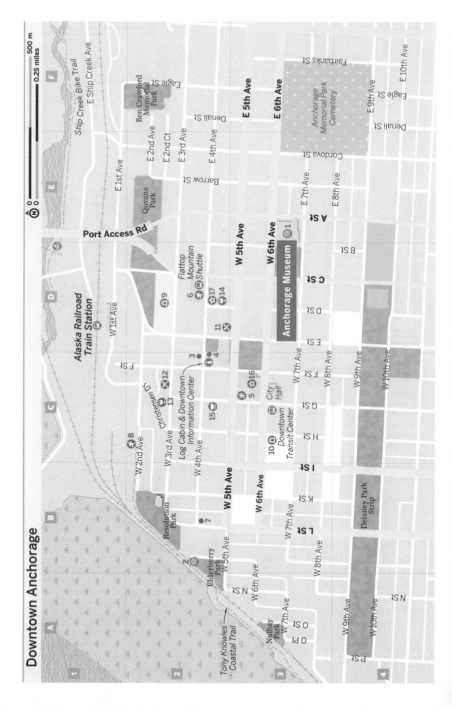

0 0
N

0 500 m
0 0.25 miles

Ship Creek Bike Trail
E Ship Creek Ave

Alaska Railroad
Train Station

Port Access Rd

Ben Crawford
Memorial
Park

Quvana
Park

E 1st Ave
E 2nd Ave
E 2nd Ct
E 3rd Ave
E 4th Ave

Eagle St
Denali St
Barrow St

E 5th Ave

E 6th Ave

Anchorage
Memorial Park
Cemetery

Fairbanks St
Eagle St
Denali St
Cordova St

E 7th Ave
E 8th Ave
E 9th Ave
E 10th Ave

W 1st Ave

Flattop
Mountain
Shuttle

6

9

17
14

11

Anchorage Museum

1

A St
B St
C St
D St
E St

W 5th Ave

W 6th Ave

3

12
13

4

f

Log Cabin & Downtown
Information Center

Christensen Dr

F St

8

W 2nd Ave
W 3rd Ave
W 4th Ave

15

5
16

City
Hall

F St
G St
H St
I St

W 7th Ave
W 8th Ave
W 9th Ave
W 10th Ave

10
Downtown
Transit Center

Resolution
Park

7

Elderberry
Park

2

W 5th Ave

W 6th Ave

J St
K St
L St

W 5th Ave
W 6th Ave
W 7th Ave
W 8th Ave

Delaney Park
Strip

Nulbay
Park

Tony Knowles
Coastal Trail

O St
O Pl

N St

W 9th Ave
W 10th Ave

P St

Downtown Anchorage

of Knik Arm and the Alaska Range, and the **Anchorage Lightspeed Planet Walk** `FREE`.

Flattop Mountain Trail `Hiking`
(Map p227) This very popular 3-mile round-trip hike to the 3550ft peak is easy to follow, though you'll scramble at the summit. It begins at Glen Alps and climbs steeply from there. Another trail continues along the ridgeline, and the 2-mile Blueberry Loop at the base is great for kids. For transportation there's Flattop Mountain Shuttle (p233).

🄶 TOURS
Rust's Flying Service `Scenic Flights`
(Map p227; ☎907-243-1595; www.flyrusts.com; 4525 Enstrom Circle) Offers a three-hour Denali flight that includes flying the length of the magnificent Ruth Glacier ($425), a Denali glacier landing ($495) and a three-hour Prince William Sound tour ($365 to $395). Also offers bear watching and fly-in fishing. All flights have a 3% transportation fee.

Alaska Photo Trek `Photography`
(Map p228; ☎907-350-0251; www.alaskaphototreks.com; 531 W 4th Ave) Unleash your wildlife paparazzo with year-round tours that cater specifically to shutter snappers. Led by professional photographers, tours range from the 2½-hour Anchorage PhotoWalk ($50) to a one-day brown bear flightseeing

tour ($1504), to a glacier helicopter tour ($1990). Optimum light and wildlife-sighting probability are taken into account. The twilight photo tour is especially nice in Alaska's long evenings.

Big Swig Tours `Food & Drink`
(☎907-268-0872; www.bigswigtours.com) Anchorage has nearly a dozen breweries, and this is one way to see several of them. There are three tours on offer: Anchorage Brews ($99), Anchorage Bike and Brew ($199) and Hops on the Rails ($299). The first two take you around the city for tastings and local insight while the third sends you on an excursion with the railroad.

Ghost Tours of Anchorage `History`
(Map p228; ☎907-274-4678; www.ghosttoursof anchorage.com; per person $15; ⊘7:30pm Tue-Sun) This excellent and quirky 90-minute downtown walk takes place nightly (rain or shine) in summer. To join, just show up in front of Snow City Café at 4th Ave and L St – site of perhaps the most notorious murder in Anchorage's history.

Among the stops is the Gaslight Lounge with its unexplained noises, seismic activity and a jukebox that kicks on by itself; the Historic Anchorage Hotel, which is said to have at least 28 'entities' as permanent guests. and a haunted women's restroom in an unexpected place.

Alaska Center for the Performing Arts (p232)

Anchorage City
Trolley Tours
Bus

(☏907-775-5603; www.alaskatrolley.com; 546 W 4th Ave; adult/child $20/10; ☺tours 9am-8:15pm) One-hour rides in a bright-red trolley past Lake Hood, Earthquake Park and Cook Inlet, among other sights. Tours depart on the hour (adult/child $20/10).

Arctic Bicycle Club
Bicycle

(☏907-566-0177; www.arcticbike.org) Alaska's largest bicycle club. It sponsors a wide variety of road- and mountain-bike tours during the summer. Its website includes a list of Alaska cycle shops.

🔘 SHOPPING

Dos Manos　Arts & Crafts

(Map p227; 1317 W Northern Lights Blvd; ☺11am-6pm Mon-Sat, to 5pm Sun) Billing itself as a 'funktional' art gallery, Dos Manos sells locally crafted art and jewelry, and very cool Alaska-themed T-shirts. A recent expansion allows room for large works of fine art. A great place to get a locally made souvenir.

Anchorage Market
& Festival
Arts & Crafts

(Map p228; www.anchoragemarkets.com; cnr W 3rd Ave & E St; ☺10am-6pm Sat, to 5pm Sun; 👪) This was called the 'Saturday Market' until it became so popular it opened on Sundays. It's an open market with live music and more than 300 booths stocked with hot food, Mat-Su Valley veggies, and souvenirs ranging from birch steins to birch syrup and T-shirts that proclaim your love of Alaska.

Title Wave Books
Books

(Map p227; www.wavebooks.com; 1360 W Northern Lights Blvd; ☺10am-8pm Mon-Sat, 11am-7pm Sun; 📶) A fabulous bookstore, with 25,000 sq ft of used books, including many on Alaska.

Oomingmak Musk
Ox Producers Co-op
Clothing

(Map p228; www.qiviut.com; 604 H St; ☺8am-8pm Mon-Fri, 10am-6pm Sat & Sun) Handles a variety of very soft, very warm and very expensive garments made of arctic musk-ox wool, hand-knitted in Inupiaq villages.

Alaska Native Heritage Center
Arts & Crafts

(Map p227; www.alaskanative.net; 8800 Heritage Center Dr; ⊙9am-5pm) This gift shop stocks jewelry, carvings and other 'artifacts'. There are booths where craftspeople make fresh knickknacks while you watch.

✖ EATING

The Anchorage dining scene ranges from fast food and espresso stands to farm fresh and superhip. Even the fanciest restaurants are generally low-key, so you can enjoy your salmon in your sandals.

The bustling city also boasts a variety of international cuisines, from Polynesian to Mexican to Vietnamese. Best of all, Anchorage restaurants and bars are smoke-free.

Snow City Café
Cafe $

(Map p228; ☎907-272-2489; www.snowcitycafe. com; 1034 W 4th Ave; breakfast $8-15, lunch $10-15; ⊙6:30am-3pm Mon-Fri, to 4pm Sat & Sun; 🛜) Consistently voted best breakfast by *Anchorage Press* readers, this busy cafe serves healthy grub to a clientele that ranges from the tattooed to the up-and-coming. For breakfast, skip the usual eggs and toast and try a 'crabby' omelet or a sockeye smoked salmon Benedict.

Yak & Yeti
Tibetan $

(Map p227; www.yakandyetialaska.com; 3301 Spenard Rd; mains $9-13; ⊙11am-2:30pm Mon-Fri, 5-9pm Wed-Sat) Billing itself as 'Himalayan' cuisine, Yak & Yeti serves delicious Indian, Nepalese and Tibetan dishes, including *momos* (Tibetan dumplings), curries and spiced meats. No alcohol is served, but you can bring your own. The homemade chai is perfect on a rainy day. The owners also run a **cafe** (1360 W Northern Lights Blvd; mains $8-13; ⊙10am-8pm Mon-Thu, to 9pm Fri & Sat, 11am-7pm Sun; 🖋) in the Northern Lights mall.

PHOnatik
Vietnamese $

(Map p227; 901 E Dimond Blvd; mains $8-12; ⊙11am-11pm Mon-Sat, noon-8pm Sun) This busy southside joint serves up Alaska-sized bowls of excellent pho, great for warming up after a chilly Hillside hike. Options range from vegetarian to oxtail pho, spring rolls and banh mi.

Rustic Goat
Bistro $$

(Map p227; ☎907-334-8100; www.rusticgoatak. com; 2800 Turnagain St; pizzas $14-16, mains $18-32; ⊙6am-10pm Mon-Thu, to 11pm Fri, 7am-11pm Sat, to 10pm Sun) This sweet little bistro is in the suburban Turnagain neighborhood, but it feels like a city loft. Old-growth timbers support two stories of windows that look out to the Chugach Mountains. The assorted menu includes wood-fired pizzas, steaks and salads. In the morning it's a casual coffee shop.

Ginger
Fusion $$

(Map p228; ☎907-929-3680; www.gingeralaska. com; 425 W 5th Ave; lunch $11-18, dinner $19-32; ⊙11:30am-2pm Mon-Fri, & 11am-2:30pm Sat & Sun, 5-10pm daily) Sleek and trendy, Ginger's menu is a fusion of Pacific Rim cuisine and classic Asian dishes. The end result is an artistic endeavor like banana and lemongrass soup or spicy tuna tower, served in surroundings that are elegant but still Alaska casual. The bar stocks fine wines and locally brewed beer, as well as a wide selection of sake.

Bear Tooth Grill
Tex-Mex $$

(Map p227; www.beartoothgrill.net; 1230 W 27th St; burgers $13-17, mains $11-22; ⊙11am-11:30pm Mon-Fri, 9:30am-11:30pm Sat & Sun) A popular hangout with an adjacent theater. It serves excellent burgers and Alaska seafood as well as Mexican and Asian fusion dishes. The microbrews are fresh and the cocktails are the best in town – if you're up for a splurge, lash out on *el Cielo* (the sky) margarita. It has an excellent Mexican-leaning brunch menu (with matching cocktails).

Marx Bros Café
Modern American $$$

(Map p228; ☎907-278-2133; www.marxcafe.com; 627 W 3rd Ave; dinner $38-46; ⊙5:30-10pm Tue-Sat) Old-school Anchorage fine dining with innovative cooking and a 500-bottle wine list are the reasons this 14-table restaurant (located in a historic home built in 1916) is so popular. The menu changes nightly, but the beloved halibut macadamia always stays put. In summer, book your table a week in advance.

🍸 DRINKING & NIGHTLIFE

With its young and lively population, Anchorage has a lot to do after the midnight sun finally sets. The city has nearly a dozen breweries, a distillery and a micro-cidery – more than enough for everyone. The free *Anchorage Press* has events listings.

Bubbly Mermaid
Wine Bar

(Map p228; 417 D St; ⊙11am-late Mon-Fri, from 10am Sat & Sun) Perch like a mermaid (or mer-man) at the prow of the boat that the Bubbly Mermaid uses for a bar as you pour champagne and local oysters down your throat. It's small, intimate and unique. Bubbly is $8 to $12; oysters $3 a pop.

Midnight Sun Brewing Company
Brewery

(Map p227; www.midnightsunbrewing.com; 8111 Dimond Hook Dr; ⊙11am-8pm) One of a growing handful of brewpubs in Anchorage, Midnight Sun sits in a loft in an industrial/suburban neighborhood on the south side of the city. Besides its excellent brews, it has a tasty menu that includes creative bruschetta and Taco Tuesdays. Refuel on the sunny little deck after a hike or mountain-bike ride in the Chugach.

49th State Brewing
Brewery

(Map p228; www.49statebrewing.com; 717 W 3rd Ave; lunch $15-19, dinner $13-30; ⊙11am-1am) The two-level rooftop deck overlooks Cook Inlet, Sleeping Lady, and Denali in the distance, and it's the place to throw back a cold one on a sunny evening. Inside has a sports-bar feel, but the menu is a bit more creative with specialties such as a yak quesadilla and crab-stuffed jalapeños. There's often live music in the adjacent theater.

Side Street Espresso
Coffee

(Map p228; 412 G St; light fare $4-7; ⊙7am-3pm Mon-Sat; 🛜) A long-standing shop that serves espresso, bagels and muffins between its art-covered walls.

🎭 ENTERTAINMENT

Cyrano's Theatre Company
Theater

(Map p228; 📞907-274-2599; www.cyranos.org; 413 D St) This small off-center playhouse is the best live theater in town, staging everything from *Hamlet* to *Archy and Mehitabel* (comic cockroach and a cat characters), Mel Brooks' jazz musical based on the poetry of Don Marquis and an ever-changing lineup of original shows, which typically run Thursday to Sunday.

Alaska Center for the Performing Arts
Performing Arts

(Map p228; 📞tickets 907-263-2787; www.myalaskacenter.com; 621 W 6th Ave) Impresses tourists with the 40-minute film *Aurora: Alaska's Great Northern Lights* (adult/child $13/7), screened on the hour from 9am to 9pm during summer in its Sydney Laurence Theatre. It's also home to the **Anchorage Opera** (📞907-279-2557; www.anchorageopera.org), **Anchorage Symphony Orchestra** (📞907-274-8668; www.anchoragesymphony.org), **Anchorage Concert Association** (📞907-272-1471; www.anchorageconcerts.org) and **Alaska Dance Theatre** (📞907-277-9591; www.alaskadancetheatre.org).

ℹ️ GETTING THERE & AWAY

AIR

Alaska Airlines (📞800-252-7522; www.alaskaair.com) Provides the most intrastate routes to travelers, generally through its contract carrier, Ravn Air, which operates services to Valdez, Homer, Cordova, Kenai and Kodiak.

Pen Air (📞800-448-4226; www.penair.com) Flies smaller planes to eight destinations in Southwest Alaska, including Cold Bay, Dillingham and Dutch Harbor.

BUS

Seward Bus Line (☎907-563-0800; www.sewardbuslines.net) Runs between Anchorage and Seward ($40, three hours) twice daily in summer. For an extra $5, you can arrange an airport pickup and drop-off.

TRAIN

From its downtown depot, the **Alaska Railroad** sends its *Denali Star* north daily to Talkeetna (adult/child $101/51), Denali National Park ($167/84) and Fairbanks ($239/120). The *Coastal Classic* stops in Girdwood ($80/40) and Seward ($89/45), while the *Glacial Discovery* connects to Whittier ($105/53). You can save 20% to 30% traveling in May and September.

❶ GETTING AROUND

BUS

People Mover (☎907-343-6543; www.peoplemover.org; 1-way adult/child $2/1;

⊙6am-midnight Mon-Fri, 8am-8pm Sat, to 7pm Sun) Anchorage's excellent bus system. Get a schedule at the **Downtown Transit Center** (www.muni.org; cnr W 6th Ave & G St) or call to obtain specific route and service information. An unlimited day pass ($5) is available at the transit center.

Flattop Mountain Shuttle (☎907-279-3334; www.hike-anchorage-alaska.com; 333 W 4th Ave; round-trip $23) Takes you to the trailhead for Anchorage's most climbed peak: Flattop. It departs Downtown Bicycle Rental at 12:30pm daily, returning at 4:30pm.

Valley Mover (☎907-892-8800; www.valleymover.org; 1-way/day pass $7/10) Offers about a dozen round-trip bus services a day that run between Eagle River, the Mat-Su Valley and Anchorage.

TAXI

Alaska Yellow Dispatch (☎907-222-2222)
Anchorage Checker Cab (☎907-276-1234)

Denali National Park

Denali National Park & Preserve

Denali National Park's six-million acres are both primeval and easily accessible. Here, you can peer at grizzly bears, moose, caribou, and North America's highest peak, all from the comfort of a bus.

Great For...

☑ Don't Miss

The network of short trails that criss-crosses the park entrance area close to the train station.

Denali

What makes 20,310ft Denali (formerly Mt McKinley) one of the world's great scenic mountains is the sheer independent rise of its bulk. Denali begins at a base of just 2000ft, which means that on a clear day you will be transfixed by over 18,000ft of ascending rock, ice and snow. By contrast, Mt Everest, no slouch itself when it comes to memorable vistas, only rises 12,000ft from its base on the Tibetan Plateau. Your first glimpse of the mountain comes between Mile 9 and Mile 11 on Park Rd – if you're blessed with a clear day.

Park Rd

Park Rd begins at George Parks Hwy and winds 92 miles through the heart of the park, ending at Kantishna, the site of several wilderness lodges.

Grizzly bear

Denali National Park & Preserve | Park Road | Healy | McKinley Park | Cantwell
Alaska Range
Denali (Mt McKinley)
George Parks Hwy
Talkeetna

⚓ Explore Ashore

Cruise-ship passengers generally get transported to Denali from Seward or Anchorage on 'cruisetours'. Trains and buses stop at Canyon by the park entrance. Shuttle trips into the park take between six and 13 hours (round-trip), depending where you turn around.

❶ Need to Know

www.nps.gov/dena; park entry $10

✕ Take a Break

Services in the park are limited. Load up with snacks at **Riley Creek Mercantile** (Mile 0.2, Park Rd; sandwiches $5-8; ⊘7am-11pm; 🛜).

With most of the road closed to private cars, the majority of visitors opt to enter the park via a shuttle or tour bus, and with good reason: the landscape is simply one of the great wilderness spaces of North America. If you're planning on spending the day riding the buses (it's an eight-hour round-trip to the popular **Eielson Visitor Center** (📞907-683-9532; www.nps.gov/dena/planyourvisit/the-eielson-visitor-center.htm; Mile 66, Park Rd; ⊘9am-7pm Jun–mid-Sep) **FREE** at Mile 66), pack plenty of food and drink.

The transport hub is the **Wilderness Access Center** (WAC; 📞907-683-9532; Mile 0.5, Park Rd; ⊘5am-7pm late May–mid-Sep) where you can buy shuttle tickets and pick up timetables.

Wildlife-Watching

Because hunting has never been allowed in the park, professional photographers refer to animals in Denali as 'approachable wildlife.' That means bear, moose, Dall sheep, wolves and caribou aren't as skittish here as in other regions of the state. This, along with the lack of trees on the high taiga landscape, makes the park an excellent place to view a variety of animals.

In Focus

Totem Bight State Park (p101), Ketchikan

DSHUMNY/SHUTTERSTOCK ©

Alaska Today

Alaska encompasses many realities, from immigrant-packed neighborhoods in Anchorage to miners, military and drillers in the Interior to indigenous villages where there are no connecting roads to the outside world but the kids are all active on social media. There are dozens of issues specific to the state's many isolated communities, but questions of personal freedom, natural resource extraction and environmental obligations – or lack thereof – often top the list.

Climate Change

According to the US Environmental Protection Agency, Alaska's average temperature has increased by approximately 3°F over the last six decades – roughly twice the warming level seen in the rest of the nation. In other words, parts of geographic Arctic Alaska are not technically Arctic environments anymore.

You might think Alaska could use some warmth, but that would be an ecological catastrophe. Warmer months bring more drought, wildfire and deforestation. In the past decade wildfires have consumed more boreal forest in Alaska than in any other decade recorded, and the area burned annually is projected to double by 2050. As if gripped in a double-ended pincer, Arctic Alaska is literally shrinking year by year: warmer summer

USA in land area (% of land area)

16 Alaska
7 Texas
4 California
1 New York
0.03 Rhode Island

if Alaska were 100 people

67 would be Caucasian
15 would be Alaska Native
6 would be Hispanic
3 would be African American
5 would be Asian
2 would be Pacific Island Origin
2 would be other

population per sq mile

Alaska   USA   Texas

♦ ≈ 1 person

months creep ever northwards, even as the ice pack that freezes off the northern coast of the state melts at an increased rate.

Alaska Native communities are commonly the first to experience the negative fallout of climate change, as their economies are often tied to sustenance-level hunting and trapping. In towns like Utqiaġvik (Barrow), climate change is not a thing to be debated on the internet – it is an immediate and pressing phenomenon that leaves, for example, polar bears wandering through town because the ice pack is melting so quickly.

Efforts to address all of the above are uphill battles, given a general attitude of human-made climate change denial at both the state and federal levels.

Economic Debates

Since the early 1980s, Alaska's economy has been fueled by oil. Close to 90% of the state's general fund revenue comes from taxes on oil and gas production, and as a result, residents do not pay state taxes on income, sales or inheritance, though you will often find local city and bed taxes, and larger cities levy a small property tax.

But the problem with such a narrow economy based largely on mineral extraction is that the minerals run out. Alaskan oil production has been in decline for the past two decades, from its peak of 2 million barrels a day in 1988 to just around 600,000 today.

Even if oil does not run out, its price changes. The fluctuating cost of oil has enormous impact on the Alaskan economy, and has provoked a series of state fiscal crises. Worries about budget deficits have forced major cuts to the Alaska Permanent Fund Dividend, a sum of money every Alaskan resident receives on an annual basis. With the Alaskan economy exposed to the variations of petroleum prices, public institutions like schools and hospitals have taken massive funding cuts.

Alaska's other major industries similarly rely on the state's natural resources. Logging and mining play a large part in the state's economic portfolio, and commercial fishing, rebuilt on expanding markets for wild salmon, brings in around $5.8 billion annually.

But Alaska's beauty is arguably the state's greatest natural resource. With some two million visitors per year, tourism is growing, and it's now the second-largest employer in the state.

JOHN ELK/GETTY IMAGES ©

History

The Aleuts called it Alaxsxag – where the sea breaks its back. The Russians christened it Bolshaya Zemlya, or the Great Land. Today, it's simply known as Alaska. The history of this subcontinent – the largest of the US' 50 states – has all the trappings of an epic: massive migrations, cultural annihilation, oil and gold rushes. From European settlement on, the history of this state is largely linked to the acquisition of the vast natural resources of this great frontier.

28,000–13,000 BC
The first Alaskans arrive, migrating across a 900-mile land bridge from Asia to North America – or perhaps by boat.

2000–1500 BC
Permanent settlements in high Arctic areas start to form, first in Siberia, then spreading across Alaska and Canada and into Greenland.

AD 1741
Danish explorer Vitus Bering, employed by Peter the Great of Russia, becomes the first European to set foot in Alaska.

Early Alaskans

Many parts of Alaska's early history are still debated; at the heart of this is how North America was first populated. Some say the first Alaskans migrated from Asia to America between 15,000 and 30,000 years ago, during an ice age that lowered the sea level and created a 900-mile land bridge linking Siberia and Alaska. The nomadic groups who crossed the bridge were not bent on exploration but on following the animal herds that provided them with food and clothing. Others posit that there was more continued contact between the Old and New Worlds, with continual migrations and commerce by boat.

The first major migration, which came across the land bridge from Asia, was by the Tlingits and the Haidas, who settled throughout the Southeast and British Columbia, and the Athabascans, a nomadic tribe that settled in the Interior. The other two major groups were the Iñupiat, who settled the north coast of Alaska and Canada (where they are known as Inuit), and the Yupik, who settled Southwest Alaska. The smallest group of Alaska Natives to arrive was the Aleuts of the Aleutian Islands.

1778	1784	1804
British explorer Captain James Cook looks for the Northwest Passage, but is eventually turned back by 12ft ice walls.	Russian Grigorii Shelikhov establishes the first permanent European settlement at Kodiak Island.	With four warships, Aleksandr Baranov defeats the Tlingit at Sitka and then establishes New Archangel (Sitka's former name).

The matrilineal Tlingit and Haida cultures were quite advanced. The tribes had permanent settlements and a class system that included chiefs, nobles, commoners and slaves – though upward (and downward) mobility were still possible. These tribes were noted for their excellent wood carving, especially carved poles, called totems, which can still be seen in Ketchikan, Sitka and many other places in the Southeast. The Tlingits were spread across the Southeast in large numbers and occasionally went as far south as Seattle in their huge dugout canoes. Both groups had few problems gathering food, as fish and game were plentiful in the Southeast.

Many tribes of the Pacific Northwest, including the Tlingit and Haida, celebrated 'potlatches.' These unique gatherings were in many ways designed to redistribute goods. Nobles would host the feasts, give gifts, free (or sometimes kill) slaves, and occasionally throw large copper shield-like objects into the ocean as a sign of their wealth. The practice was suppressed by Western interests (and even made illegal for a time) but remains today in some forms. Recent evidence indicates that Athabascan tribes also celebrated a version of the potlatch, possibly indicating a continual exchange of ideas and technologies between the numerous tribes.

Life was not so easy for the Aleuts, Iñupiat and Yupik. With much colder winters and cooler summers, these people had to develop a highly effective sea-hunting culture to sustain life in the harsh regions of Alaska. This was especially true for the Iñupiat, who could not have survived the winters without their skilled ice-hunting techniques. In spring, armed only with jade-tipped harpoons, the Iñupiat, in skin-covered kayaks called *bidarkas* and *umiaks,* stalked and killed 60-ton bowhead whales. Though motorized boats replaced the kayaks and modern harpoons the jade-tipped spears, the whaling tradition lives on in places such as Utqiaġvik (Barrow).

Age of Exploration

Due to the cold and stormy North Pacific, Alaska was one of the last places in the world to be mapped by Europeans.

Spanish Admiral Bartholomé de Fonte is credited by many with making the first European trip into Alaskan waters in 1640, but the first written record of the area was made by Vitus Bering, a Danish navigator sailing for the Russian tsar. In 1728 Bering's explorations demonstrated that America and Asia were two separate continents. Thirteen years later, Bering became the first European to set foot in Alaska, near Cordova. Bering and many of his crew died from scurvy during that journey, but his lieutenant returned to Europe with fur pelts and tales of fabulous seal and otter colonies, and Alaska's first boom was underway. The Aleutian Islands were quickly overtaken, with settlements at Unalaska and Kodiak Island. Chaos followed, as bands of Russian hunters robbed and murdered each other for furs, while the Aleuts, living near the hunting grounds, were almost annihilated through massacres, disease and forced labor. By the 1790s Russia had organized the Russian-American Company to regulate the fur trade and ease the violent competition.

1867	**1878**	**1880**
Secretary of State William H Seward negotiates the US purchase of Alaska from Russia for $7.2 million.	Ten years after a salmon saltery is opened on Prince of Wales Island, the first salmon cannery is built in Alaska.	Led by Tlingit Chief Kowee, Richard Harris and Joe Juneau discover gold in Silver Bow Basin.

 **Understand**

Fur Traders & Whalers Arrive

While Alaska lacks the great wars between indigenous peoples and settlers that occurred in other parts of the US, the settlement by Russian fur traders, whalers and other outside forces had a lasting impact on Alaska Native tribes. Before European contact, there were an estimated 80,000 people living in Alaska – a figure the state would not reach again until WWII.

Diseases introduced by Europeans were the biggest killers, but there were also limited violent clashes, especially between Russian fur traders and the Aleut. Slavery and the introduction of alcohol were other primary factors in the reduction of Alaska Native populations; some estimates indicate that during the Russian-American period the Aleut lost 80% of its tribe, and the Chugach, Tlingit, Haida and Dena'ina each lost 50%. The whalers that arrived at Iñupiat villages in the mid-19th century were similarly destructive, introducing alcohol, which devastated the lifestyles of entire villages. When the 50th anniversary of the Alaska Hwy was celebrated in 1992, many Alaska Natives and Canadians called the event a 'commemoration' not a 'celebration,' due to the destructive forces that the link to Canada and the rest of the USA brought.

The British arrived when Captain James Cook began searching the area for the Northwest Passage. On his third and final voyage, Cook sailed north from Vancouver Island to Southcentral Alaska in 1778, anchoring at what is now Cook Inlet before continuing on to the Aleutian Islands, Bering Sea and Arctic Ocean. The French sent Jean-François de Galaup, comte de La Pérouse, who in 1786 made it as far as Lituya Bay, now part of Glacier Bay National Park. The wicked tides within the long, narrow bay caught the exploration party off guard, killing 21 sailors and discouraging the French from colonizing the area.

Having depleted the fur colonies in the Aleutians, Aleksandr Baranov, who headed the Russian-American Company, moved his territorial capital from Kodiak to Sitka, where he built a stunning city, dubbed 'an American Paris in Alaska.' But Russian control of Alaska remained limited, and at the height of their residency, only 800 full-time Russian inhabitants lived here.

Seward's Folly

By the 1860s the Russians found themselves badly overextended: their involvement in Napoleon's European wars, a declining fur industry and the long lines of shipping between Sitka and the heartland of Russia were draining their national treasury. The

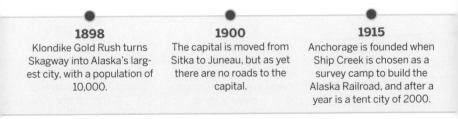

1898
Klondike Gold Rush turns Skagway into Alaska's largest city, with a population of 10,000.

1900
The capital is moved from Sitka to Juneau, but as yet there are no roads to the capital.

1915
Anchorage is founded when Ship Creek is chosen as a survey camp to build the Alaska Railroad, and after a year is a tent city of 2000.

country made several overtures to the US to sell Alaska, but it wasn't until 1867 that Secretary of State William H Seward signed a treaty to purchase the region for $7.2 million – less than 2¢ an acre.

By then the US public was in an uproar over the purchase of 'Seward's Ice Box' or 'Walrussia,' and on the Senate floor, the battle to ratify the treaty lasted six months. On October 18, 1867, the formal transfer of Alaska to the Americans took place in Sitka. In post–Civil War America, Alaska remained a lawless, unorganized territory for another 20 years.

This great land, remote and inaccessible to all but a few hardy settlers, stayed a dark, frozen mystery to most people, but eventually its riches were uncovered. First it was through whaling, then the phenomenal salmon runs, with the first canneries built in 1878 on Prince of Wales Island.

The Alaskan Gold Rush

What truly brought Alaska to the world's attention was gold. The promise of quick riches and frontier adventures was the most effective lure Alaska has ever had and, to some degree, still has today. Gold was discovered in the Gastineau Channel in the 1880s, and the towns of Juneau and Douglas sprang up overnight. In 1896, one of the world's most colorful gold rushes took place in the Klondike region of Canada's Yukon Territory, just across the border.

Often called 'the last grand adventure,' the Klondike Gold Rush occurred when the country and much of the world was suffering a severe recession. When the banner headline of the *Seattle Post-Intelligencer* bellowed 'GOLD! GOLD! GOLD! GOLD!' on July 17, 1897, thousands of people quit their jobs and sold their homes to finance a trip to the newly created boomtown of Skagway. From this tent city almost 30,000 prospectors tackled the steep Chilkoot Trail to Lake Bennett, where they built crude rafts to float the rest of the way to the goldfields. Nearly as many people returned home along the same route, broke and disillusioned.

The number of miners who made fortunes was small, but the tales and legends that emerged were endless. The Klondike stampede, though it only lasted from 1896 to the early 1900s, was Alaska's most colorful era and earned the state the reputation of being the country's last frontier.

Within three years of the Klondike stampede Alaska's population doubled to 63,592, including more than 30,000 non-Native people. Nome, another gold boomtown, was the largest city in the territory, with 12,000 residents, while gold prompted the capital to be moved from Sitka to Juneau. Politically, this was also the beginning of true Alaskan 'state building' – railroads were built, governing bodies were created, support industries were established, and a non-voting Alaskan delegate was sent to Congress in 1906. Nevertheless, it was still largely a transient state, with men outnumbering women five to one, and few people building their life-long homes here.

1923	1935	1942
President Warren G Harding comes to Alaska to celebrate the completion of the Alaska Railroad.	The first of 200 Depression-era families from Minnesota, Wisconsin and Michigan arrive in the Matanuska Valley to begin farming.	Japan bombs Dutch Harbor for two days during WWII and then invades the remote Aleutian Islands of Attu and Kiska.

Understand

Building the Alcan

A land link between Alaska and the rest of the US was envisioned as early as 1930, but it took WWII to turn the nation's attention north to embark on one of the greatest engineering feats of the 20th century: constructing a 1390-mile road through remote wilderness.

Deemed a military necessity and authorized by President Franklin Roosevelt only two months after the attack on Pearl Harbor, the Alcan was designed to be an overland route far enough inland to be out of range of airplanes transported on Japanese aircraft carriers. The exact route followed old winter roads, trap lines and pack trails, and by March 9, 1942, construction had begun. Within three months, more than 10,000 troops, most of them from the US Army Corps of Engineers, were in the Canadian wilderness. They endured temperatures of -30°F (-34.4°C) in April, snowfalls in June and swarms of mosquitoes and gnats for most of the summer.

When a final link was completed near Kluane Lake in late October, the Alcan was open, having been built in only eight months and 12 days.

World War II

In June 1942, only six months after their attack on Pearl Harbor, the Japanese opened their Aleutian Islands campaign by bombing Dutch Harbor for two days and then taking Attu and Kiska Islands. Other than Guam, it was the only foreign invasion of US soil during WWII and is often dubbed 'the Forgotten War' because most Americans are unaware of what happened in Alaska. The battle to retake Attu Island was a bloody one. After 19 days and landing more than 15,000 troops, US forces recaptured the plot of barren land, but only after suffering 3929 casualties, including 549 deaths. Of the more than 2300 Japanese on Attu, fewer than 30 surrendered, with many taking their own lives.

The Alcan & Statehood

Following the Japanese attack on the Aleutian Islands in 1942, Congress panicked and rushed to protect the rest of Alaska. Army and air force bases were set up at Anchorage, Fairbanks, Sitka and Whittier, and thousands of military personnel were stationed in Alaska. But it was the famous Alcan (the Alaska Hwy) that was the single most important project of the military expansion. The road was built by the military, but Alaska's residents benefited, as the Alcan helped them access and make use of Alaska's natural resources.

1959	**1964**	**1968**
Alaska officially becomes the 49th state when President Dwight Eisenhower signs the statehood declaration on January 3.	North America's worst earthquake, 9.2 on the Richter scale devastates Anchorage and South-central Alaska.	Oil and natural gas are discovered at Prudhoe Bay on the North Slope. The next year Alaska stages a $900 million oil-lease sale.

Understand

Uncle Ted

Ted Stevens was already a decorated WWII pilot and Harvard Law School graduate when in 1953, after accepting a position in Fairbanks, he moved to Alaska with his wife by driving the Alaska Hwy in the dead of winter. A mere six months later, Stevens was appointed the US Attorney for Fairbanks and was eventually elected as a state representative. In 1968 Stevens was appointed US senator for Alaska and held that position until 2009, never receiving less than 66% of the vote after his first election in 1970.

Such longevity allowed Stevens to break Strom Thurmond's record as the longest-serving Republican senator in 2007, with 38 years and three months of continual service. For the majority of Alaskans, Stevens had always been their senator – the reason many dubbed him 'senator for life.'

The senator was duly noted for his ability to bring home the 'pork': in 2008 the Feds returned $295 per Alaskan citizen in local projects (other states average only $34 per person). In 2005 Stevens was ridiculed by the national media when, in a speech from the Senate floor, he angrily opposed diverting the Bridge to Nowhere funds to help New Orleans recover from Hurricane Katrina. Congress dropped the specific allocation for the bridge, but Alaska still received the money and simply spent it elsewhere.

Stevens' legendary Senate tenure came to an end in 2009. The previous year, a jury found him guilty of federal corruption – failing to report tens of thousands of dollars in gifts and services he had received from friends – and convicted him of seven felony charges. Stevens vowed to appeal the decision, but in November Alaskans had had enough and narrowly voted him out of office in his bid for an eighth term. The indictment was dismissed after a federal probe found evidence of prosecutorial misconduct.

In 2010 Stevens was killed in a not-unusual Alaskan accident: a small-plane crash (outside Dillingham in Southwest Alaska).

In 1916 Alaska's territorial legislature submitted its first statehood bill. The effort was first quashed by the Seattle-based canned-salmon industry, which wanted to prevent local control of Alaska's resources; then the stock market crash of 1929 and WWII kept Congress occupied with more-demanding issues. But the growth that came with the Alcan, and to a lesser degree the new military bases, pushed Alaska firmly into the American culture and renewed its drive for statehood. When the US Senate passed the Alaska statehood bill on June 30, 1958, Alaska had made it into the Union and was officially proclaimed the country's 49th state by President Dwight Eisenhower the following January.

1971	**1980**	**1989**
President Richard Nixon signs the Alaska Native Claims Settlement Act to pave the way for the Trans-Alaska Pipeline.	President Carter signs the Alaska National Interests Lands Conservation Act (ANILCA), preserving 79.54 million acres of wilderness.	The *Exxon Valdez* runs aground on Bligh Reef and spills almost 11 million gallons of oil into Prince William Sound.

Alaska entered the 1960s full of promise, but then disaster struck: the most powerful earthquake ever recorded in North America (registering 9.2 on the Richter scale) hit Southcentral Alaska on Good Friday morning in 1964. More than 100 lives were lost, and damage was estimated at $500 million. In Anchorage, office buildings sank 10ft into the ground, and houses slid more than 1200ft off a bluff into Knik Arm. A tidal wave virtually obliterated the community of Valdez. In Kodiak and Seward, 32ft of the coastline slipped into the Gulf of Alaska, and Cordova lost its entire harbor as the sea rose 16ft.

The Alaskan Black-Gold Rush

The devastating 1964 earthquake left the newborn state in a shambles, but a more pleasant gift from nature soon rushed Alaska to recovery and beyond. In 1968 Atlantic Richfield discovered massive oil deposits underneath Prudhoe Bay in the Arctic Ocean. The value of the oil doubled after the Arab oil embargo of 1973. However, it couldn't be tapped until there was a pipeline to transport it to the warm-water port of Valdez. And the pipeline couldn't be built until the US Congress, which still administered most of the land, settled the intense controversy among industry, environmentalists and Alaska Natives over historical claims to the land.

The Alaska Native Claims Settlement Act of 1971 was an unprecedented piece of legislation that opened the way for a consortium of oil companies to undertake the construction of the 789-mile pipeline. The act allocated $962.5 million and 44 million acres (including mineral rights) to Alaska Natives. Half of the money went directly to the Native villages, while the other half funded the creation of 12 Native corporations. There are now 13 Native corporations in Alaska; they manage land, invest in diverse endeavors and provide dividends to Native peoples.

The Trans-Alaska Pipeline took three years to build, cost more than $8 billion – in 1977 dollars – and, at the time, was the most expensive private construction project ever undertaken.

The oil began to flow on June 20, 1977, and for a decade oil gave Alaska an economic base that was the envy of every other state, accounting for as much as 90% of state government revenue. With oil proceeds, the state created the Alaska Permanent Fund – which has grown from just $700,000 to more than $44 billion today. Full-time residents still receive annual dividend checks, although due to ongoing budget crises, the returns on those checks have been drastically slashed in recent years.

In the explosive growth period of the mid-1980s, Alaskans enjoyed the highest per-capita income in the country. The state's budget was in the billions. Legislators in Juneau transformed Anchorage into a stunning city, with sports arenas, libraries and performing-arts centers, and provided virtually every Bush town with a million-dollar school. From 1980 to 1986 this state of only half a million residents generated revenue of $26 billion.

2006	**2014**	**2015**
Sarah Palin, former mayor of Wasilla, beats the incumbent governor to become Alaska's first female governor.	The Environmental Protection Agency blocks the massive, controversial Pebble Mine project near Bristol Bay in the Southwest.	Alaska becomes the third state in the country to legalize marijuana use.

Downtown Skagway (p173)

DSHUMNYS/SHUTTERSTOCK ©

Alaskan Way of Life

Cut off from the rest of the United States, this great northern oasis has been attracting renegades, free thinkers, roughneck profiteers and nature lovers from the very beginning. Alaska is about independence, individualism and taking care of business. It's a state of transient workers, rugged frontiersmen and -women, and down-home sensibilities, and a place that attracts the eccentric in all of us. And that's what makes the Alaskan way of life so fascinating.

Regional Identity

Most of Alaska may be rural, roadless areas collectively known as the Bush, but most Alaskans are urban. Almost 70% of the residents live in the three largest cities: Anchorage, Fairbanks and Juneau.

The vast majority of households in rural Alaska participate in subsistence living. Studies show that 86% use game and 95% use fish. There are also Alaskans who gather and hunt the majority of their food and live in small villages that can only be reached by boat, plane or, in the winter, snowmobile. But the majority live in urban neighborhoods, work a nine-to-five job and shop at the supermarket.

And most Alaskans are newcomers. Only about a third of the state's population was born in Alaska; the rest moved there. Such a transient population creates a melting pot of ideas, philosophies and priorities. What they usually have in common is an interest in the great outdoors: they were lured here to either exploit it or enjoy it, and many residents do a little of both.

Thus debates in Alaska usually center on access to land, resources, and, in particular, the wilderness. There are some liberal bastions of environmentalism, Juneau and Homer being the best known, but over the years Alaskans have moved to the right, voting for Republican presidents, fighting tax increases and becoming one of the first states to pass a constitutional amendment banning same-sex marriages (which was later struck down within the court system). Alaska also became the third state in the USA to legalize cannabis use, in 2015.

Alaska is a firearms-friendly state, and travelers should know that opinions that favor gun control will likely not be appreciated, especially in rural areas. To be fair, many Alaskans live in places where the nearest law enforcement is hundreds of miles away, while the nearest bear is sometimes right outside their door. Even the most hardcore environmentalist may keep a rifle on hand for protection from wildlife if they live in an isolated enough area. Drive past any street sign in rural Alaska, and you'll likely notice it's been used as target practice.

Travelers come to visit and marvel at the grand scenery. But Alaskans are here to stay, so they need to make a living in their chosen home, a land where there is little industry or farming. They regard trees, oil and fish as an opportunity to do that.

Lifestyle

In Anchorage, residents can shop at enclosed malls, spend an afternoon at one of 162 parks, go in-line skating along paved bike paths, or get in their car and drive to another town. By contrast, in Nunapitchuk, 400 miles west of Anchorage on the swampy tundra of the Yukon–Kuskokwim Delta, the population is 526, there are no roads to or within town, homes and buildings are connected by a network of boardwalks, and there is just one store and a health clinic.

Rural or urban, Alaskans tend to be individualistic, following few outside trends and, instead, adhering to what their harsh environment dictates. Mother Nature and those -30°F (-34.4°C) winter days are responsible for the Alaskan dress code, even in Anchorage's finest restaurants. Alaskans also like to take care of things on their own, and many seek out spartan and tough living conditions. In the Bush, most homes feature a pile of old airplane parts, broken-down cars and construction materials in the front yard – you never know when a hard-to-find part may come in handy.

With that said, American visitors will find that most of the locals they meet in towns and cities have lifestyles similar to their own. They work, they love their weekends, they live in a variety of homes big and small, and they participate in double-coupon days at supermarkets. They may well have a hunting or fishing camp set up in an isolated area, but this is a place of retreat, as opposed to a place of residence.

Still, it is difficult to overstate the gap between urban and rural Alaska. In the deep Bush and Interior, communities are often entirely cut off from overland infrastructure, including groceries, and have limited (if any) access to law enforcement, medical care and public education. In indigenous communities, English may be a second language. The logistics of governing and

Anchorage Coffee Shops

According to a marketing research firm, Anchorage has three coffee shops per 10,000 residents, beating even Seattle, and making it, per capita, the country's mocha mecca.

Reindeer Games

At the turn of the 20th century, numerous Sami people, from northern Scandinavia and Russia, were brought to Alaska to teach reindeer husbandry to the Iñupiat. Domesticated reindeer aren't native to these lands, though their wild cousins, the caribou, are. Franklin Roosevelt's *Reindeer Act* prohibited the ownership of reindeer herds by non-Natives in Alaska.

managing a state of both concentrated urban areas and such extreme far-flung localities are akin to the challenges facing developing-world economies.

Even in remote villages, satellite-TV dishes and internet access provide connections to the rest of the world, which can both reduce or exacerbate a feeling of isolation. Internet access can make it easier to take online classes or remotely fill out employment or college applications, but it can also yield tragic consequences. In 2017, for example, a 16-year-old indigenous hunter from Gambell Island brought down a bowhead whale – a source of enormous respect and honor in a village where a whale is often the main source of winter protein in a sustenance diet. The hunter posted pictures of his kill online and was then inundated with social-media hate messages, including death threats, from animal-rights activists. He suffered through subsequent depression, although the local indigenous community rallied around him.

Alaska has social ills, exacerbated in large measure by the environment. The isolation of small towns and the darkness of winter have contributed to Alaska being one of the top 10 states for binge and heavy drinking, and, depending on the year, fifth or sixth overall for the amount of alcohol sold per capita. Since the 1980s, Alaska has seen some of the highest per-capita use of controlled drugs in the country, and its suicide rate is twice the national average. Alcohol abuse and suicide rates are higher for Alaska Natives than other populations. In rural areas, methamphetamine abuse is becoming widespread.

To survive this climate and to avoid such demons, you have to possess a passion for the land and an individualistic approach to a lifestyle that few, other than Alaskans, would choose.

Sports

The state sport of Alaska, officially adopted in 1972, is dog mushing, and the biggest spectator event is the Iditarod. But there are other spectator sports in Alaska that you don't have to bundle up to watch, including baseball. The Alaska Baseball League (www.alaska baseballleague.org) features six semipro teams of good college players eyeing the major leagues. Teams include Fairbanks' Alaska Goldpanners (www.goldpanners.pointstreak sites.com) and the Anchorage Bucs (www.anchoragebucs.com). Major leaguers who have played in Alaska include sluggers Barry Bonds and Mark McGwire.

When it comes to following professional sports, transplants tend to have loyalties to wherever they originally hail from, but most Alaska-born residents root for Seattle teams like the Seahawks and Mariners.

The state's most unusual sporting event is the World Eskimo-Indian Olympics (www. weio.org) held in July, when several hundred athletes converge on Fairbanks. For four days Alaska Natives compete in greased-pole walking, seal skinning, blanket tosses and other events that display the skills traditionally needed for survival in a harsh environment.

Alaska in the Popular Imagination

Alaska has a role in the collective imagination as a mysterious, often frozen, dramatically scenic land. Not surprisingly, the state's portrayal in popular media often reflects this idea.

Literature

Two of the best-known writers identified with Alaska were not native to the land nor did they spend much time there, but Jack London and Robert Service turned their Alaskan adventures into literary careers.

The first print run of Jack London's *Call of the Wild* – 10,000 books – sold out in 24 hours. London, an American, departed for the Klondike Gold Rush in 1897, hoping to get rich panning gold. Instead he produced 50 books of fiction and nonfiction in just 17 years, and became the country's highest-paid writer of the day.

Service, a Canadian bank teller, was transferred to Dawson City in 1902 and then wrote his first book of verse, *The Spell of the Yukon*. The work was an immediate success and contained his best-known ballads, 'The Shooting of Dan McGrew' and 'The Cremation of Sam McGee.' Both portray the hardship and violence of life during the gold rush.

Alaska's contemporary luminaries of literature are no less elegant in capturing the spirit of the Far North. Kotzebue author Seth Kantner followed his critically acclaimed first novel, *Ordinary Wolves,* with the equally intriguing *Shopping for Porcupine,* a series of short stories about growing up in the Alaska wilderness. *The Raven's Gift* by Don Rearden is a harrowing tale of village isolation and tundra survival, while *The Snow Child* is a standout debut from Pulitzer Prize–finalist Eowyn Ivey. One of the best Alaska Native novels is *Two Old Women* by Velma Wallis, an Athabascan born in Fort Yukon. This moving tale covers the saga of two elderly women abandoned by their migrating tribe during a harsh winter.

Other Alaskans who have captured the soul of the Far North include Nick Jans, whose *The Last Light Breaking* is considered a classic on life among the Iñupiat, and Sherry Simpson, who chronicles living in Fairbanks in the series of wonderful stories, *The Way Winter Comes.* For entertaining fiction using Alaska's commercial fishing as a stage, there's Bill McCloskey, whose three novels have characters ranging from the greenhorn fisherman to the hard-nosed cannery manager, with the plotline leaping from one to the next. His first, *Highliners,* is still his best.

Small cabins and long winter nights filled with sinister thoughts have also given rise to Alaska's share of mystery writers. Dean of the Alaskan whodunit is *New York Times* best-seller Dana Stabenow, whose ex-DA investigator Kate Shugak has appeared in around 20 novels, some of which are free as ebooks. Sue Henry is equally prolific, with musher-turned-crime-solver Jessie Arnold in novels such as *Murder on the Iditarod Trail* and *Cold Company.*

Alaska is also popular ground for nonfiction. Jon Krakauer's *Into the Wild* explores the lost journeyer Christopher McCandless and humanity's desire to seek isolation and connection with the earth. John McPhee's 1991 classic *Coming into the Country* explores the personalities of Alaska's fringe.

The Iditarod

The Iditarod is one of the most iconic races in the world, and dog mushing is one of Alaska's most beloved pastimes. Supporters say sled dogs are born and bred to run, and if you've ever been tethered to a team flying across the frozen tundra, you'd probably agree. But a growing number of opponents say races like the Iditarod are cruel. Numerous reports of underfed, beaten and culled sled dogs at operations in Canada, Colorado and Alaska beg the question: should you support a race that has seen the death of 140-plus dogs since 1973? Should you even take a tourist trip on a dogsled?

 **Understand**

Northern Overexposure: Reality TV in Alaska

There are a *lot* of reality TV shows filmed in Alaska these days, playing to a centuries-long American obsession with life on the frontier. It doesn't hurt that in the past, state film incentives would refund a third (sometimes more) of a show's production costs. It's fair to say the 'reality' on these shows was anything but. Those grizzled, bearded survivalists who pontificated on how close they were to frostbite and starvation? A lot of the time, they actually lived in villages with decent road access and well-stocked supermarkets.

Hollywood producers aren't the first folks to exaggerate the Alaska frontier narrative for the sake of making money, and they won't be the last. So take those breathless images of magnificent isolation and whispered monologues about the thin line between survival and death with a grain of salt.

Here are a few Alaska reality shows that, despite some corny moments, are worth your time:

Deadliest Catch (Discovery Channel) Crab fishing in the Bering Sea.

Ice Road Truckers (History) Long-haul truckers deliver goods to remote communities.

Ultimate Survival Alaska (National Geographic) Survival in the woods.

Cinema & TV

Hollywood and Alaska occasionally mix, especially in Hyder. This tiny, isolated town (population 83) has been the setting for numerous films, such as *Insomnia* (2002), in which Al Pacino plays a cop sent to a small Alaskan town to investigate a killer played by Robin Williams. There's also *Bear Island* (1978), loaded with stars, and *Ice Man* (1984), about scientists who find a frozen prehistoric man and bring him back to life. The 2007 movie *Into the Wild* featured many Alaska locations, including Anchorage, Healy, Denali National Park, Cantwell and the Copper River. Recent Hollywood tax breaks have also led to more films being shot in the 49th state.

A state with an entire season of nighttime has no shortage of noir and horror, and *30 Days of Night*, about vampires devouring a town during the sunless winter, is an excellent example of the genre.

Alaska has also been the backdrop for TV, including the Emmy Award–winning series *Northern Exposure,* but reality TV is where it's hit the mother lode. The Discovery Channel has basically staked its lineup on Alaska, with shows like *Alaskan Bush People* and the ever-popular crab-fight-fest, *Deadliest Catch*. Everywhere in-between you have spin-offs about gold mining, ice-trucking, survival and logging.

Music

Alaskan composer John Luther Adams won a Pulitzer Prize for Music in 2014 for his *Become Ocean* composition, which is inspired by the waterways and rhythms of Alaska. Singer-songwriter Jewel was raised in Homer and got her start playing local bars with her father. Hip-hop has become the preferred sonic expression for many Alaska Natives; if you get a chance, check out Samuel Johns, an Athabascan rapper who hails from Anchorage.

Wrangell-St Elias National Park

LONEROCK/SHUTTERSTOCK ©

Landscapes of Alaska

It's one thing to be told Denali is the tallest mountain in North America; it's another to see it crowning the sky in Denali National Park. It's a mountain so tall, so massive and so overwhelming it has visitors stumbling off the park buses. As a state, Alaska is the same, a place so huge, so wild and so unpopulated it's incomprehensible to most people until they arrive.

The Land

Dramatic mountain ranges arch across the landmass of Alaska. The Pacific Mountain System, which includes the Alaska, Aleutian and St Elias Ranges, as well as the Chugach and Kenai Mountains, sweeps along the south before dipping into the sea southwest of Kodiak Island. Further north looms the imposing and little-visited Brooks Range, skirting the Arctic Circle.

In between the Alaska and Brooks Ranges is Interior Alaska, an immense plateau rippled by foothills, low mountains and magnificent rivers, among them the third-longest in the USA, the mighty Yukon River, which runs for 2300 miles. North of the Brooks Range is the North Slope, a coastal plain of scrubby tundra that gently descends to the Arctic Ocean.

 **Understand**

Alaska's Glaciers

Alaska is one of the few places in the world where active glaciation occurs on a grand scale. There are an estimated 100,000 glaciers in Alaska, covering 28,000 sq miles, or 3% of the state, and containing three-quarters of all Alaska's fresh water. The effects of glaciation, both from current and ice-age glaciers, are visible everywhere and include wide U-shaped valleys, kettle ponds, fjords and heavily silted rivers.

Glaciers are formed when the snowfall exceeds the rate of melting and the solid cap of ice that forms begins to flow like a frozen river. The rate of flow, or retreat, can be anything but 'glacial,' and sometimes reaches tens of yards per day. While most of Alaska's glaciers are in rapid retreat, roughly 2% of them are advancing – actually growing in size. With that said, climate change is exacerbating the melt rates of some glaciers; guides working at the Matanuska Glacier, for example, report that local ice is retreating at unprecedented levels.

Glaciers are impressive-looking formations, and because ice absorbs all the colors of the spectrum except blue, they often give off a distinct blue tinge. The more overcast the day, the bluer the glacial ice appears. The exceptions are glaciers that are covered with layers of rock and silt (the glacier's moraine) and appear more like mounds of dirt. For example, the Kennicott Glacier in Wrangell-St Elias National Park is often mistaken for a vast dump of old mine tailings. Wrangell-St Elias is one of the best places in the world to see rock glaciers. Rather than an ice glacier covered with rock, a rock glacier reverses the composition ratio; they're 90% moving rock and silt held together by ice, and advance more slowly than normal ice glaciers.

The largest glacier in Alaska is the Malaspina, which sits at the southern base of Mt St Elias and blankets 850 sq miles.

One of the most spectacular sights is watching – and hearing – tidewater glaciers 'calve' icebergs (the act of releasing small to massive chunks of glacier). Tidewater glaciers extend from a land base into the sea (or a lake) and calve icebergs in massive explosions of water. Active tidewater glaciers can be viewed from tour boats in Glacier Bay National Park, Kenai Fjords National Park and Prince William Sound, which has the largest collection in Alaska.

In geological terms Alaska is relatively young and still very active. The state represents the northern boundary of the chain of Pacific Ocean volcanoes known as the 'Ring of Fire' and is the most seismically active region of North America. In fact, Alaska claims 52% of the earthquakes that occur in the country and averages more than 13 each day. Most are mild shakes, but some are deadly. Three of the six largest earthquakes in the world – and seven of the 10 largest in the USA – have occurred in Alaska.

Most of the state's volcanoes lie in a 1550-mile arc from the Alaska Peninsula to the tip of the Aleutian Islands. This area contains more than 65 volcanoes, 46 of which have been active in the last 200 years. Even in the past four decades Alaska has averaged more than two eruptions per year. If you spend any time in this state, or read about its history, you will quickly recognize that belching volcanoes and trembling earthquakes (as much as glaciers and towering peaks) are defining characteristics of the last frontier.

Southeast Alaska

Southeast Alaska is a 500-mile coastal strip extending from north of Prince Rupert right across to the Gulf of Alaska. In between are the hundreds of islands of the Alexander Archipelago, and a narrow strip of coast, separated from Canada's mainland by the glacier-filled Coast Mountains. Winding through the middle of the region is the Inside Passage waterway; it's the lifeline for isolated communities, as the rugged terrain prohibits road-building. High annual rainfall and mild temperatures have turned the Southeast into rainforest, broken up by majestic mountain ranges, glaciers and fjords.

Prince William Sound & Kenai Peninsula

Like the Southeast, much of this region (also known as Southcentral Alaska) is a jumble of rugged mountains, glaciers, steep fjords and lush forests. This mix of terrain makes Kenai Peninsula a superb recreational area for backpacking, fishing and boating, while Prince William Sound, home of Columbia Glacier, is a mecca for kayakers and other adventurers.

Geographically, the Kenai Peninsula is a grab-bag. The Chugach Range receives the most attention, but in fact mountains only cover around two-thirds of the peninsula. On the east side of the peninsula is glorious Kenai Fjords National Park, encompassing tidewater glaciers that pour down from one of the continent's largest ice fields, as well as the steep-sided fjords those glaciers have carved. Abutting the park in places, and taking in much of the most southerly part of the Kenai Peninsula, is Kachemak Bay State Park, a wondrous land of mountains, forests and fjords.

Covering much of the interior of the peninsula, the Kenai National Wildlife Refuge offers excellent canoeing and hiking routes, plus some of the world's best salmon fishing. On the west side, the land flattens out into a marshy, lake-pocked region excellent for canoeing and trout fishing.

Prince William Sound is completely enveloped by the vast Chugach National Forest, the second-largest national forest in the US.

Southwest Alaska

Stretching 1500 miles from Kodiak Island to the international date line, the Southwest is spread out over four areas: the Kodiak Archipelago including Kodiak Island; the Alaska Peninsula; the Aleutian Islands; and Bristol Bay. For the most part it is an island-studded region with stormy weather and violent volcanoes. This is the northern rim of the Ring of Fire, and along the Alaska Peninsula and the Aleutian Islands is the greatest concentration of volcanoes in North America.

Southwest Alaska is home to some of the state's largest and most intriguing national parks and refuges. Katmai National Park & Preserve, on the Alaska Peninsula, and Kodiak National Wildlife Refuge are renowned for bear-watching. Lake Clark National Park & Preserve, across Cook Inlet from Anchorage, is a wilderness playground for rafters, anglers and hikers.

Most of the Aleutian Islands and part of the Alaska Peninsula form the huge Alaska Maritime National Wildlife Refuge, headquartered in Homer. The refuge encompasses 3.5 million acres and more than 2500 islands, and is home to 80% of the 50 million seabirds that nest in Alaska.

Denali & the Interior

Mountains are everywhere. The formidable Alaska Range creates a jagged spine through the Interior's midsection, while the smaller ranges – the Chugach, Talkeetna and Wrangell to the south and the White Mountains to the north – sit on the flanks. From each of these mountain ranges run major river systems. Spruce and birch predominate in the lowland valleys with their tidy lakes. Higher up on the broad tundra meadows, spectacular wildflowers show their colors during summer months. Wildfire also plays its role here, wiping out vast swaths of forest nearly every summer.

The big name here, of course, is Denali National Park, blessed with the continent's mightiest mountain and abundant wildlife. Wrangell-St Elias National Park, located in the region's southeast corner, is the largest national park in the US and a treasure house of glaciers and untouched wilderness. Up in the Interior's northeast is Yukon-Charley Rivers National Preserve, located at the nexus of two of the state's legendary waterways.

The Bush

This is the largest slice of Alaska and includes the Brooks Range, Arctic Alaska and western Alaska on the Bering Sea. The remote, hard-to-reach Bush is separated from the rest of the state by mountains, rivers and vast roadless distances.

The mighty Brooks Range slices this region in two. To the north, a vast plain of tundra sweeps down to the frozen wasteland of the Arctic Ocean. In the western reaches, near towns such as Nome and Kotzebue, you'll find more tundra, as well as a flat landscape of lakes and slow-moving rivers closer to the Bering Sea, and rolling coastal hills and larger mountains heading toward the interior. In the far north, the Arctic Coastal Plain is a flat series of wetlands, lakes, rivers and tundra that extends all the way to the Arctic Ocean.

The Bush has several national parks and preserves. Gates of the Arctic National Park & Preserve spans the spires of the Brooks Range and offers spectacular hiking and paddling. Near Kotzebue is Kobuk Valley National Park, known for the Great Kobuk Sand Dunes and the oft-paddled Kobuk River, with the mountain-ringed Noatak National Preserve just to the north.

Climate

Oceans surround 75% of Alaska, the terrain is mountainous and the sun shines at a low angle. All this gives the state an extremely variable climate, and daily weather that is infamous for its unpredictability.

For visitors, the most spectacular part of Alaska's climate is its long days. At Point Barrow, Alaska's northernmost point, the sun doesn't set for 2½ months from May to August. In other Alaskan regions, the longest day is on June 21 (the summer solstice), when the sun sets for only two hours in Fairbanks and for five hours in the Southeast. Even after sunset in late June, however, there is still no real darkness, just a long twilight.

Southeast Alaska

The Southeast has a temperate maritime climate; like Seattle, but wetter. Juneau averages 57in of precipitation (rain or snow) annually, and Ketchikan gets 154in, most of which is rain as winter temperatures are mild.

Prince William Sound & Kenai Peninsula

Precipitation is the norm in Prince William Sound. In summer, Valdez is the driest of the towns; Whittier is by far the wettest. In all communities, average July daytime temperatures are barely above 60°F (15.6°C). So no matter what your travel plans are, pack your fleece and some bombproof wet-weather gear.

Weather-wise, the Kenai Peninsula is a compromise: drier than Prince William Sound, warmer than the Bush, wetter and cooler (in summer) than the Interior. Especially on the coast, extremes of heat and cold are unusual. Seward's normal daily high in July is 62°F

Understand

Climate Change & Alaska

Alaska's temperatures are rising, causing permafrost to melt, coastlines to erode, forests to die (or push north into new territory), and Arctic sea ice and glaciers to melt at alarming rates (90% of Southeast glaciers are retreating rapidly). Some scientists now predict the Arctic Ocean will be entirely ice-free in summer by 2040, or even sooner. Meanwhile, Portage Glacier can no longer be viewed from its visitor center, and Mendenhall Glacier is expected to retreat totally onto land and cease being a tidewater glacier within a few years.

Northern Alaska is ground zero when it comes to global warming, and with the vast majority of the land sitting on permafrost – and aboriginal traditions and whole ecosystems inextricably tied to the frozen earth and sea – the very balance of nature has been thrown into disaccord. At Shishmaref, a barrier island village on the Seward Peninsula, residents have watched with horror as homes have literally slipped into the Bering Sea due to the loss of protective sea ice that buffers them against storms. And Shishmaref is just one of 160 rural communities the US Army Corps of Engineers has identified as being threatened by erosion. Relocation plans have already begun for several of these.

Paradoxically, in Juneau sea levels are dropping as billions of tons of ice have melted away, literally springing the land to new heights. In some areas the land is rising 3 inches a year, the highest rate in North America. As a result, water tables are dropping, wetlands are drying up and property lines are having to be redrawn.

Beyond the disaster for humans, the changes to the Alaskan landscape and climate will have dramatic effects on the highly adapted organisms that call this place home. In Juneau, the rising land has already caused channels that once facilitated salmon runs to silt up and grass over. In the Far North, melting summer sea ice is expected to put such pressure on the polar bear that it has been listed as a 'threatened' species.

(16.7°C). Rainfall is quite high on the eastern coasts of the peninsula around Seward and Kenai Fjords National Park; moderate in the south near Homer and Seldovia; and somewhat less frequent on the west coast and inland around Soldotna and Cooper Landing.

Anchorage

Shielded from the dark fury of Southcentral Alaska's worst weather by the Kenai Mountains, the Anchorage Bowl receives only 14in of rain annually and enjoys a relatively mild climate: January averages 13°F (-10.6°C) and July about 58°F (14.4°C). Technically a sub-Arctic desert, Anchorage does have more than its fair share of overcast days, however, especially in early and late summer.

Southwest Alaska

With little to protect it from the high winds and storms that sweep across the North Pacific, the Southwest is home to the very worst weather in Alaska. Kodiak is greatly affected by the turbulent Gulf of Alaska and receives 80in of rain per year, along with regular blankets of pea-soup fog and occasional blustery winds. On the northern edge of the Pacific, Unalaska and the Alaskan Peninsula receive less rain (annual precipitation ranges from

60in to 70in), but are renowned for unpredictable and stormy bouts of weather. Southwest summer temperatures range from 45°F to 65°F (7°C to 18°C). For the clearest weather, try visiting in early summer or fall.

Denali & the Interior

In this region of mountains and spacious valleys, the climate varies greatly and the weather can change on a dime. In January temperatures can sink to -60°F (-51°C) for days at a time, while in July they often soar to above 90°F (32°C). The norm for the summer is long days with temperatures of 60°F to 70°F (15.6°C to 21.1°C). However, it is common for Denali National Park to experience at least one dump of snowfall in the lowlands between June and August.

Here, more than anywhere else in the state, it's important to have warm clothes while still being able to strip down to a T-shirt and hiking shorts. Most of the area's 10in to 15in of annual precipitation comes in the form of summer showers, with cloudy conditions common, especially north of Denali. The mountain, in Denali National Park, tends to be hidden by clouds more often than not.

In the Interior and up around Fairbanks, precipitation is light, but temperatures can fluctuate by more than 100°F during the year. Fort Yukon holds the record for the state's highest temperature, at 100°F (37.8°C) in June 1915, yet it once recorded a temperature of -78°F (-61.1°C) in winter. Fairbanks has the odd summer's day that hits 90°F (32°C) and always has nights during winter that drop below -60°F (-51.1°C).

The Bush

Due to its geographical diversity, the Bush is a land of many climates. In inland areas, winter holds sway from mid-September to early May, with ceaseless weeks of clear skies, negligible humidity and temperatures colder than anywhere else in America. Alaska's all-time low, -80°F (-62°C), was recorded at Prospect Creek Camp, just off the Dalton Hwy. Closer to the ocean winter lingers even longer than inland, but it is incrementally less chilly.

During the brief summer, visitors to the Bush should be prepared for anything. Utqiaġvik and Prudhoe Bay may demand a parka: July highs there often don't hit 40°F (4.5°C). Along the Dalton Hwy and around Nome, the weather is famously variable. Intense heat (stoked by the unsetting sun) can be as much of a concern as cold.

National State & Regional Parks

One of the main attractions of Alaska is public land, where you can play and roam freely over an area of 348,000 sq miles, more than twice the size of California. The agency in charge of the most territory is the Bureau of Land Management (BLM; www.blm.gov), followed by the US Fish & Wildlife Service (USFWS; www.fws.gov) and the National Park Service (www.nps.gov).

Alaska's national parks are the crown jewels as far as most travelers are concerned, and attract more than two million visitors a year. The most popular units are Klondike Gold Rush National Historical Park, which draws 860,000 visitors a year, and Denali National Park, home of Denali, which sees around half that number. Other busy units are Glacier Bay National Park, a highlight of every cruise-ship itinerary in the Southeast, and Kenai Fjords National Park in Seward.

Alaska State Parks (www.alaskastateparks.org) oversees 123 units that are not nearly as renowned as most national parks, and thus far less crowded at trailheads and in campgrounds. The largest is the 2500-sq-mile Wood-Tikchik State Park, a roadless wilderness north of Dillingham that's bigger than the state of Delaware. The most popular is Chugach State Park, the 773-sq-mile unit that is Anchorage's after-work playground.

Both the BLM and the USFWS oversee many refuges and preserves that are remote, hard to reach and not set up with visitor facilities such as campgrounds and trails. The major exception is the Kenai National Wildlife Refuge, an easy drive from Anchorage and a popular weekend destination for locals and tourists alike.

For more pre-trip information, contact the Alaska Public Lands Information Centers (www.alaskacenters.gov).

Major Parks of Alaska

Park	Features	Activities
Admiralty Island National Monument	wilderness island, chain of lakes, brown bears, marine wildlife, cabin rentals	bear-watching, kayaking, canoeing
Chena River State Recreation Area	Chena River, alpine areas, granite tors, campgrounds, cabin rentals	backpacking, canoeing, hiking
Chugach State Park	Chugach Mountains, alpine trails, Eklutna Lake, campgrounds	backpacking, mountain biking, paddling, hiking
Denali National Park	Denali, brown bears, caribou, Wonder Lake, campground	wildlife viewing, backpacking, hiking, park bus tours
Denali State Park	alpine scenery, trails, views of Denali, campgrounds	backpacking, hiking, camping
Gates of the Arctic National Park & Preserve	Brooks Range, Noatak River, treeless tundra, caribou	rafting, canoeing, backpacking, fishing
Glacier Bay National Park & Preserve	tidewater glaciers, whales, Fairweather Mountains, lodge	kayaking, camping, whale-watching, boat cruises
Independence Mine State Historical Park	Talkeetna Mountains, alpine scenery, gold-mine ruins, visitor center	mine tours, hiking
Kachemak Bay State Park	glaciers, protected coves, alpine areas, cabin rentals	kayaking, backpacking, boat cruises
Katmai National Park & Preserve	Valley of 10,000 Smokes, volcanoes, brown bears, lodge	fishing, bear-watching, backpacking, kayaking
Kenai Fjords National Park	tidewater glaciers, whales, marine wildlife, steep fjords, cabin rental	boat cruises, kayaking, hiking
Kenai National Wildlife Refuge	chain of lakes, Russian River, moose, campgrounds	fishing, canoeing, wildlife-watching, hiking
Kodiak National Wildlife Refuge	giant bears, rich salmon runs, wilderness lodges, cabin rentals	bear-watching, flightseeing
Misty Fiords National Monument	steep fjords, 3000ft sea cliffs, lush rainforest, cabin rentals	boat cruises, kayaking, flightseeing
Tracy Arm-Fords Terror Wilderness Area	glaciers, steep fjords, parade of icebergs, marine wildlife	boat cruises, kayaking, wildlife-watching
Wrangell-St Elias National Park	mountainous terrain, Kennecott mine ruins, glaciers	backpacking, flightseeing, rafting, biking, mine tours

Environmental Issues

Alaska's vast tracts of pristine land and beloved status as America's last wild frontier mean that its environmental issues are, more often than not, national debates. These days the focus of those debates (and a fair amount of action) centers on the effects of global warming and resource management, especially the push for mining and drilling in reserve lands.

Land

The proposed Pebble Mine development in Bristol Bay has been one of the most contentious environmental issues of this century. The stakes are huge for all sides. Pebble is potentially the second-largest ore deposit of its type in the world, with copper and gold deposits estimated to be worth a staggering $500 billion. But the minerals would be extracted from near the headwaters of Bristol Bay and require a 2-mile-wide open pit that could pollute streams that support the world's largest run of wild salmon.

That issue saw an unlikely alliance of environmentalists, commercial fishers and Alaska Natives up in arms, and in 2013 the mine project was put on hold as investors pulled out. But under the Trump administration the Environmental Protection Agency (EPA) has allowed the Pebble Partnership to apply for a federal permit to begin work on the mine development. In September 2017, after meeting with Pebble Partnership CEO Tom Collier, EPA Administrator Scott Pruitt directed the agency to withdraw an Obama-era proposal to protect the Bristol Bay watershed from certain mining activities.

Oil exploration in the Arctic National Wildlife Refuge (ANWR) is another unresolved issue, despite a political battle that has raged in the lower 48 since the earliest days of the Reagan presidency. The refuge is often labeled by environmentalists as America's Serengeti, an unspoiled wilderness inhabited by 45 species of mammals, including grizzly bears, polar bears and wolves. Millions of migratory birds use the refuge to nest, and every spring the country's second-largest caribou herd, some 150,000 strong, gives birth to 40,000 calves there.

Though estimates of the amount of recoverable oil have dropped considerably in recent years, industry is still eager to jump in, and politicians continue to argue that ANWR can help the country achieve energy independence. At the time of research Senate Republicans were moving forward with the first legislative steps needed to allow drilling in ANWR.

Fisheries

The problems of resource exploitation are not restricted to oil, gas and minerals. After the king-crab fishery collapsed in 1982, the commercial fishing industry was rebuilt on pollack (also known as whiting), whose mild flavor made it the choice for imitation crab, frozen fish sticks, and fish sandwiches served at fast-food restaurants. Pollack are groundfish – fish that live on, in, or near the sea floor – and are a crucial species in the Bering Sea ecosystem. The Alaskan pollack catch constitutes the largest fishery in the country, and accounts for almost one-third of all US seafood landings by weight. The Marine Stewardship Council rates pollack caught from the eastern Bering Sea, Aleutian Islands and the Gulf of Alaska as a sustainable fishery.

Salmon is an incredibly important fishery to Alaskans on both a commercial and recreational level. The future of the species remains in question. During 2017, Bristol Bay, which produces 40% of the world's harvested sockeye salmon, experienced a record-breaking salmon run. On the flip side, the Kuskokwim River, an important source of king salmon, experienced one of the worst runs in history. The reasons for local fishery collapses remain a mystery, though theories about climate change and its many effects as well as overfishing have the most traction.

Native communities along the Arctic Alaska coast participate in sustenance-level hunting of bowhead whales, an activity with deep cultural roots. A complex social hierarchy determines who is allowed to captain and crew whaling boats, as well as the order of whale meat distribution. Whaling in Alaska is regulated at the state and federal level, with quotas set by the International Whaling Commission (IWC); from 2013 to 2018, indigenous Arctic communities in Alaska and Chukotka (Russia) were allowed to take 336 whales in total.

Rural Issues

Waste management is a hot issue in Alaska's rural communities, many of which are not connected to the rest of the state by convenient transportation routes. Though burning garbage is still a common way of reducing trash, as is dumping, more and more communities have begun to build recycling centers, practice composting and haul back to Anchorage whatever they can. A free program called Flying Cans takes bundled aluminum cans from rural communities to recycling plants in Anchorage via scheduled cargo flights. Energy-saving education programs are also making their way across the state, as are greenhouses. The latter are expected to have a positive impact on both nutrition and the amount of fuel used to supply rural villages with fresh produce.

For more information on environmental issues, contact these conservation organizations:

Alaska Sierra Club (www.alaska.sierraclub.org)

No Dirty Gold (www.nodirtygold.org) A campaign opposing abusive gold mining around the world.

Southeast Alaska Conservation Council (www.seacc.org)

Wilderness Society (www.wilderness.org)

Totem Bight State Park (p101), Ketchikan

DSHUMNY/SHUTTERSTOCK ©

Alaska Natives

Alaska Natives play an integral part in the Great Land's modern-day politics, culture and commerce. While their cultural imprint stretches back 10,000 years, present-day traditions and practices are evolving, dying off and transforming as the tide of Western influences sweeps through the state. Economically and politically, much of the work of the tribes happens on a village level, while the 13 Native corporations manage vast land and financial assets.

Village Life

Before 1940, Alaska Natives were in the majority. They now represent roughly 15% of the population. With 36,000 Alaska Natives, Anchorage is sometimes called the state's 'largest Native village.' Tribes once inhabited separate regions: the Aleuts and Alutiiqs lived from Prince William Sound to the Aleutian Islands; the Iñupiat, Yupik and Cupik occupied Alaska's northern and western coasts; the Athabascan populated the Interior; and the Tlingit, Haida, Eyak and Tsimshian lived along the southeast coasts. Urban migration has blurred lines.

Two-thirds of Alaska Natives live in villages within their ancestral lands. Though outwardly modern, the heart of village life is still the practice of subsistence hunting, fishing and gathering – depending on the community, 50% or more of village diets still come from subsistence food gathering. The situation is exacerbated in remote communities where outside foodstuffs are prohibitively marked-up due to the cost of transportation.

Though critical to rural economies, the customs and traditions associated with subsistence are also the basis of Native culture. Subsistence activities are cooperative, helping maintain community bonds, preserve traditional festivities and oral histories, facilitate a spiritual connection to the land, and provide inspiration and material for artists.

Language

Alaska has at least 20 distinct Native languages. Native language use varies: the last Eyak speaker died in 2008, Haida has only a handful of speakers remaining, but Yupik is still spoken by about half the population. Even so, few children are currently learning any Native language as their mother tongue, though there is mounting interest in ensuring Native-language preservation and instruction.

Many of the Native tribes have specialized vocabularies. For instance, modern linguists say the Iñupiat have about 70 terms for ice and the Yupik language has 50 words for snow.

Arts & Crafts

Alaska Natives produce much of the state's most creative work. Not content to rest on tradition, contemporary indigenous artists push boundaries and reinterpret old forms.

Traditionally, Native artisans gathered their materials in the fall and began work in December, when cold weather forced them to remain inside. Materials varied according to what the local environment or trade routes could supply, and included wood, ivory, bone, antler, birch bark and grasses.

Production of Native crafts for a Western market began in the 18th century with Iñupiat ivory carvers and, later, Aleut basket weavers, adapting traditional forms for collectors. Today, the sale of Native art comprises a large slice of the economy in many Bush communities.

Carving

Ivory carving is practically synonymous with the Iñupiat, though they will also use wood, bone and antler. In addition to sculptures depicting hunting scenes or wild animals, scrimshaw (known as 'engraved ivory') is also produced. These incredibly detailed etchings often present a vignette of daily life on a whale bone or walrus tusk.

Yupik carvings tend to have more intricate surface detailing, and feature stylized designs. Red clay paint is sometimes used for coloring.

Natives of the Southeast, such as the Haida and Tlingit, have a lively wood carving tradition that's heavy on abstractions based on clan symbols. Their totem poles are known worldwide but they are also masters at wood masks and bentwood boxes.

Purchasing ivory and bone crafts made from at-risk species is a personal decision for visitors to Alaska. Across the globe, it's a frowned-upon practice, particularly where ivory poaching poses serious risks to wildlife populations. In Alaska, it's a bit different. Alaska Natives are permitted to

AK REBEL

Samuel Johns, who also goes by the stage name AK REBEL, is an Anchorage-based rapper and hip-hop MC who regularly pens songs about issues impacting the Alaska Native community. Give him a listen if you want to hear a passionate, contemporary indigenous voice.

Alaska Native handicrafts display, Sitka National Historical Park (p124)

SUPAPAI/SHUTTERSTOCK ©

★ **Best Places to See Alaska Native Art**

Jilkaat Kwaan Cultural Heritage Center (p164)

Totem Heritage Center (p100)

Sitka National Historical Park (p124)

Alaska Native Heritage Center (p226)

Sealaska Heritage (p140)

hunt endangered species – and most experts say that Alaska Native harvests have no impact on populations of species like whales. They also use every part of the animal, rely on the meat for their subsistence lifestyle and make a little extra spending money by creating some amazing crafts from bone and ivory.

Dolls

All Native groups share a love of dolls, and traditionally used them in ceremonies, as fertility symbols, for play and for teaching young girls about motherhood. Modern doll-making is said to have begun in the 1940s in Kotzebue with the work of Ethel Washington, and continues today as one of the most vibrant Native art forms. Dolls can look realistic or be deliberate caricatures, such as the Chevak area 'ugly-faced' dolls with their wrinkled leather faces and humorous expressions.

Masks were traditionally used by Yupik and Iñupiat peoples for midwinter hunting festivals. Today you can find wonderful examples carved in wood and sewn from caribou.

Baskets

Perhaps no single form represents indigenous art better than basketry. Decorative patterns are geometric or reflect the region's animals, insects or plants. Athabascans weave baskets from alder, willow roots and birch bark; the Tlingit use cedar bark and spruce root; Yupik often decorate their baskets with sea-lion whiskers and feathers, and a few dye them with seal guts. Iñupiat are famous for using whale baleen, but this is in fact a 20th-century invention.

The Aleuts are perhaps the most renowned basket weavers. Using rye grass, which is tough but pliable, artists create tiny, intricately woven pieces that are highly valued.

Embroidery & Clothing

Athabascan women traditionally decorated clothing with dyed quills, but after Europeans introduced beads and embroidery techniques they quickly became masters of this decorative art. Their long, hanging baby belts are often purchased as wall hangings.

Both Haida and Yupik are renowned for *mukluks* (knee-high boots) and decorative parkas.

Challenges

There are 229 federally recognized tribes in Alaska, but no reservation system. In 1971 Alaska Natives renounced claims to aboriginal lands in return for 44 million acres of land, $962.5 million and 100 shares per person in regional, urban and village corporations.

Alaska Native totem symbol wood engraving

While the settlement was a cause of pride, it has done little for employment and household income.

There are many other social challenges. Few issues are as serious as alcohol abuse, which has led to a high rate of fetal alcohol syndrome, domestic violence, crime and suicide. Since 1980 the state has allowed local control of alcohol and dozens of villages have voted on some form of prohibition, with varying results. Needless to say, you shouldn't introduce alcohol to Native dry villages. Other challenges include recruiting sufficient teachers, police officers and medical professionals to the Bush, and improving the diet of Native people. One study in the *American Journal of Public Health* concluded there were lower risks of suicide in Alaska Native villages with more prominent traditional elders, job access, higher incomes and married couples.

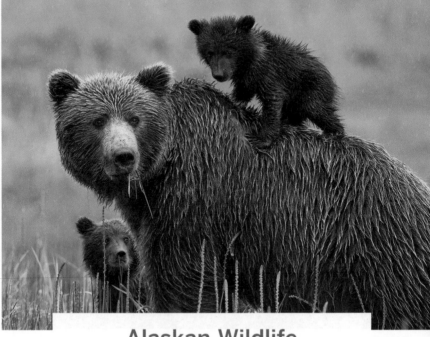

Alaskan brown bear with cubs

MARC LATREMOUILLE/CUMULUS/LONELY PLANET ©

Alaskan Wildlife

Alaska's vast landscape and waters allow the space for wild creatures to roam, and wildlife-watching is a major draw for visitors to the state. Spotting wildlife can be as dramatic as a flight over feeding grizzlies or as simple as a walk to see moose in an Anchorage park.

Land Mammals

Alaska boasts one of the earth's great concentrations of wildlife, and some species that are threatened or endangered elsewhere – brown bears, for example – thrive in the 49th state.

Bears

There are three species of bear in Alaska: brown, black and polar. Of these, you're most likely to see brown bears, as they have the greatest range.

Brown and grizzly bears are now listed as the same species *(Ursus arctos)* but there are differences. Browns live along the coast, where abundant salmon runs help them reach weights exceeding 800lb, or 1500lb in the case of the famed Kodiak. Grizzlies are browns found inland and subsist largely on grass. Normally a male weighs from 500lb to 700lb, and females half that. The most common way to identify any brown bear is by the prominent shoulder hump, easily seen behind the neck when the animal is on all fours.

Alaska has an estimated 30,000 brown bears, or more than 98% of the US population. In July and August you can see the bears fishing alongside rivers. In early fall they move into tundra regions and open meadows to feed on berries.

Though black bears (Ursus americanus), which may also be colored brown or cinnamon, are the USA's most widely distributed bruin, their range is limited in Alaska. They live in most forested areas of the state, but not north of the Brooks Range, on the Seward Peninsula, or on many large islands, such as Kodiak and Admiralty. The average male black weighs from 180lb to 250lb.

Polar bears (Ursus maritimus) dwell only in the far north and their adaptation to a life on sea ice has given them a white, water-repellent coat, dense underfur, specialized teeth for a carnivorous diet (primarily seals), and hair that almost completely covers the bottom of their feet. A male polar bear weighs between 600lb and 1200lb. Plan on stopping at the zoo in Anchorage, or taking a lengthy side trip to Utqiaġvik (Barrow) or Kaktovik, if you want to see one.

Moose

Moose are long-legged in the extreme, but short-bodied despite sporting huge racks of antlers. They're the world's largest members of the deer family, and the Alaskan species is the largest of all. A newborn weighs 35lb and can grow to more than 300lb in five months; cows weigh 800lb to 1200lb; and bulls 1000lb to more than 1600lb, with antlers up to 70in wide.

The moose population stands at around 175,000, and historically the animal has been the most important game species in Alaska. Some 20,000 are officially hunted each year.

Caribou

Although roughly 750,000 caribou live in Alaska across 32 herds, they are relatively difficult to view as they inhabit the Interior north up to the Arctic Sea. This is a shame as the migration of the Western Arctic herd, the largest in North America with almost 325,000 animals, is one of the great wildlife events left on earth. The herd uses the North Slope for its calving area, and in late August many of the animals cross the Noatak River and journey southward.

There have been steep declines in the state's caribou population recently; the Central Arctic herd's numbers have dropped by over 50%, for example. The reason for this remains a mystery, although wildlife biologists seem to agree that changing environmental conditions, partly attributable to climate change, are a factor.

Caribou range in weight from 150lb to more than 400lb. The animals are crucial to the Iñupiat and other Alaska Natives, who hunt them to support their subsistence lifestyle.

The best place to see caribou is Denali National Park.

Wolves

While gray wolves are struggling throughout most of the USA, in Alaska their numbers are strong despite predator control programs. In total, 7000 to 10,000 wolves live in Alaska, spread throughout almost every region of the state. Adult males average 85lb to 115lb, and their pelts can be gray, black, off-white, brown or yellow, with some tinges approaching red. Wolves travel, hunt, feed and operate in the social unit of a pack. In the Southeast their principal food is deer, in the Interior it's moose and in Arctic Alaska it's caribou.

★ **Best Places to See...**

Brown Bears Pack Creek (p136)

Moose Kenai National Wildlife Refuge, Denali National Park (p234)

Seals Tracy Arm, Prince William Sound (p200)

Whales Glacier Bay National Park & Preserve (p146)

Wild bull moose

JAN MIKO/SHUTTERSTOCK ©

Mountain Goats & Dall Sheep

Often confused with Dall sheep, mountain goats have longer hair, short black horns and deep chests. They range throughout the Southeast, fanning out north and west into the coastal mountains of Cook Inlet, as well as the Chugach and Wrangell Mountains. Good locations to see them include Glacier Bay and Wrangell-St Elias National Park.

Dall Sheep are more numerous and widespread, numbering close to 80,000, and live in the Alaska, Wrangell, Chugach and Kenai mountain ranges. They are often seen at Windy Corner, on the Seward Hwy, and in Denali National Park. Another good spot is on the Harding Icefield trail in Seward.

The best time to catch rams in a horn-clashing battle for social dominance is right before the mating period, which begins in November.

Lynx

This intriguing-looking feline has unusually large paws to help it move swiftly over snowpack as it hunts snowshoe hare, its primary food source. Lynx inhabit most forested areas of Alaska, but your chances of seeing one depend on the hare population, which fluctuates over an eight- to 11-year cycle.

Beavers & River Otters

Around lakes and rivers you stand a good chance of seeing river otters and beavers or, at the very least, beaver lodges and dams. Both animals live throughout the state, with the exception of the North Slope. Otters range from 15lb to 35lb, while beavers weigh between 40lb and 70lb, although 100lb beavers have been recorded in Alaska.

Fish & Marine Mammals

Whales

The three most common whales seen in coastal waters are the 50ft-long humpback, the smaller bowhead whale and the gray whale. Humpbacks are the most frequently seen on cruise ships and ferries, as they often lift their flukes (tails) out of the water to begin a dive, or blow every few seconds when resting.

Tour boats head out of almost every Southeast Alaska port loaded with whale-watching passengers. You can also join such trips in Kenai Fjords National Park and in Kodiak.

In northern Alaska, a different sort of whaling boat heads out for a different whaling season. Eleven indigenous communities on the Arctic Alaskan coast are allowed to take a certain number of bowhead whales per year (usually around 75 in total, out of a bowhead population of 10,000). These hunts are considered seminal to local traditional culture, and for basic food needs in sustenance communities.

At the Sitka WhaleFest (www.sitkawhalefest.org) in early November, visitors and locals gather to listen to world-renowned biologists talk about whales, and then hop on boats to go look for them.

Dolphins & Porpoises

Dolphins and harbor porpoises are commonly seen in Alaskan waters, even from the decks of public ferries. Occasionally, passengers will also spot a pod of orcas (killer whales), and sometimes belugas, both large members of the dolphin family. Orcas, which can be more than 20ft long, are easily identified by their high black-and-white dorsal fins.

The white-colored beluga ranges in length from 11ft to 16ft and weighs more than 3000lb. There are two populations of belugas in Alaska: the endangered Cook Inlet area population, and the Bering Sea area population. In the spring and fall, roughly May and September, pods of the Cook Inlet belugas feed in Turnagain Arm, right outside Anchorage. Lines of cars pull to the side of the Seward Hwy to watch these mammals surface; the best pullout is aptly named Beluga Point. The 74,500 belugas that live off Alaskan shores travel in herds of 10 to several hundred.

Salmon

Five kinds of wild salmon can be found in Alaska: sockeye salmon (also referred to as red salmon), king salmon (or chinook), pink salmon (or humpy), coho salmon (or silver) and chum salmon. For sheer wonders of nature it's hard to beat a run of thousands of salmon swimming upstream to spawn. From late July to mid-September, many coastal streams are so choked with the fish that at times individuals have to wait their turn to swim through narrow gaps of shallow water.

In the heart of Anchorage, Ship Creek supports runs of king, coho and pink. From a viewing platform you can watch the fish spawning upriver and also the locals trying to catch one for dinner. In downtown Ketchikan, you can watch salmon in Ketchikan Creek.

Seals

The most commonly seen marine mammal, seals are often found basking in the sun on ice floes. Six species exist in Alaska, but most visitors will encounter the harbor seal, whose range includes the Southeast, Prince William Sound and the entire Gulf of Alaska. The average male weighs 200lb, reached by a diet of herring, flounder, salmon, squid and small crabs.

The ringed and bearded seals inhabit the northern Bering, Chukchi and Beaufort Seas, where sea ice forms during winter. Steller sea lions, the largest member of the 'eared seals' family, range from Japan to California, but are divided from the Gulf of Alaska into two stocks: the endangered Western stock and the threatened Eastern stock. Females can weigh close to 800lb, while males can reach 2500lb. A day trip in Kenai Fjords National Park will take you to sea-lion haul-outs, where you can view a crowd of them resting on rocks.

Mosquitoes

Everyone knows the real state bird of Alaska is the mosquito. There are 35 bloodsucking species here, and they are relentless, especially on the North Slope, where they will swarm you the second you leave your car. Only ocean winds and DEET spray are preventative.

Walruses

Like the seal, the Pacific walrus is a pinniped (fin-footed animal) but this much larger creature is less commonly spotted. Walruses summer in the far northern Chukchi Sea and though they may number over 200,000, most visitors are likely to only encounter the tusks of these creatures in the carving of a Native artist.

Birds

Alaska's vast open spaces and diversity of habitat make it unusually rich in birdlife. Over 445 species have been identified statewide.

Bald Eagles

While elsewhere in the United States the bald eagle (a magnificent bird with a wingspan that reaches over 8ft) is on the endangered species list, in Alaska it is commonly sighted in the Southeast, Prince William Sound and Dutch Harbor in the Aleutian Islands.

Ptarmigan

The state bird is a cousin of the prairie grouse. Three species can be found throughout Alaska in high, treeless country.

Seabirds & Waterfowl

Alaskan seabirds include the crowd-pleasing horned and tufted puffins, six species of auklet and three species of albatross (which boast a wingspan of up to 7ft). The optimum way to see these is on a wildlife cruise to coastal breeding islands such as St Lazaria Island, home to 1500 pairs of breeding tufted puffins.

An amazing variety of waterfowl migrate to Alaska each summer, including trumpeter swans, Canada geese, eider, the colorful harlequin duck and five species of loon.

Tundra Species

Tundra birds such as wheateaters, Smith's longspurs, Arctic warblers, bluethroats and snowy owls are big draws for amateur twitchers. Prime viewing areas include Nome, Utqiaġvik and the Dalton and Denali Hwys.

Ravens

The largest member of the corvid family can be found – and heard – across Alaska, thanks to its distinctive 'quork' and deep gurgling caw. The raven is one of the most intelligent birds in the world, and has been observed using teamwork and tools and engaging in strategic planning. They are known for their acrobatic flights of fancy (literally), and many an Alaskan hunter has a tale of being led to their kill sites by ravens, who know a meal of viscera will be forthcoming. The raven is a major totemic animal for Alaskans of the Southeast Coast, who consider the bird to be both a creator and trickster.

Kayaker in an ice cave, Resurrection Bay, Seward (p207)

DOUG DEMAREST/DESIGN PICS/GETTY IMAGES ©

Adventure Activities

The Great Land is all about the Great Outdoors, with over 350 million acres of land, 28.8 million acres of waterways and 6640 miles of coastline. Plan your deep wilderness adventures well in advance – these can require permits, floatplanes and months of preparation. But short day hikes, paddles and flightseeing tours from the cruise ports provide an excellent sampling of one of the world's last great frontiers.

Hiking & Paddling

Much of Alaska's wilderness is hard to reach for visitors with limited time or small budgets. The lack of specialized equipment, the complicated logistics of reaching remote areas and lack of backcountry knowledge keeps many out of the state's great wilderness tracts such as the Arctic National Wildlife Refuge (ANWR). To experience such a remote and pristine place, you may need to shell out a premium amount of money to a guiding company.

But that doesn't mean you can't sneak off on your own for a trek into the mountains or a paddle down an icy fjord. There are so many possible adventures in Alaska that even the most budget-conscious traveler can take time to explore what lies beyond the pavement. Do it yourself and save.

Hikers on Mendenhall Glacier (p132)

★ **Best Outdoor Adventures**

Hiking in Juneau (p130)
Kayaking in Whittier (p198)
Rafting in Haines (p167)
Ziplining in Ketchikan (p98)
Glacier-trekking in Seward (p210)
Cycling in Haines (p166)

The best way to enter the state's wilderness is to begin with a day or half-day hike the minute you step off the cruise ship. Every port town has an extensive network of marked trails, many of them starting in the towns themselves. Visitor centers usually print basic free trail maps.

Hikes in Denali National Park (p234) are some of the best in Alaska, but they are largely trail-less (with no multiday hikes on trails). However, there is a network of well-marked trails in the park entrance area.

There is also a range of paddling opportunities, from calm rivers and chains of lakes for novice canoeists to remote fjords and coastlines whose rugged shorelines and tidal fluctuations are an attraction for more experienced open-water paddlers. Alaska is an icy paradise for kayakers. Double-bladed paddlers can easily escape into a watery wilderness, away from motorboats and cruise ships, and enjoy the unusual experience of gazing at glaciers or watching seal pups snuggle on icebergs from sea level.

Great Hiking Near Alaska's Cities

Even if you don't have any desire to hoist a hefty backpack, don't pass up an opportunity to spend a day hiking one of the hundreds of well-maintained and easy-to-follow trails scattered across the state. How good is the day hiking in Juneau? The trailhead for the Mt Roberts Trail is only five blocks from the state capitol, while the USFS (US Forest Service) maintains 29 other trails accessible from the Juneau road system. Anchorage is also blessed with numerous close-to-home trails. Drive 15 minutes from downtown and you can be at a treeline trailhead in Chugach State Park, where a path quickly leads into the alpine. Skagway, Girdwood, Seward and Sitka also have numerous trails close to main streets.

For the state's best close-to-town day hikes, hit the trail on one of these:

Mt Roberts Trail Great views, plenty of switchbacks, and extensive wildlife-watching, and it's all accessible from downtown Juneau.

Deer Mountain Trail Just arrived in Alaska? This 2.5-mile trail that runs from downtown Ketchikan to the top of Deer Mountain will whet your appetite for tying up your hiking boots at every stop.

Perseverance Trail (p131) Head out from Basin Rd in Juneau on this 3-mile hike, which takes in local history and spectacular scenery.

Turnagain Arm Trail An excellent hike through the Chugach National Forest that's only a few miles from Anchorage.

Mt Marathon Trail (p213) There are several ways to climb 3022ft-high Mt Marathon, which overlooks downtown Seward, but all end at a heavenly alpine bowl located just behind the peak.

Tours

If you lack the expertise to head outdoors on your own – or the logistics of visiting remote wilderness are too daunting – guiding companies will help you get there. Whether you want to climb Denali, kayak Glacier Bay or pedal from Anchorage to Fairbanks, there's an outfitter willing to put an itinerary together, supply the equipment and lead the way.

Useful Websites

Alaska Hike Search (www.alaskahikesearch.com) Includes details on trails around Anchorage and Southcentral Alaska.

Alaska Department of Natural Resources (www.dnr.state.ak.us/parks/aktrails) Has details on trails in every corner of the state.

Alaska Department of Fish & Game (www.adfg.alaska.gov) The excellent *Wildlife Notebook* covers all the state's major species of animals and birds that you may encounter on the trail or while paddling.

Knik Canoers & Kayakers (www.kck.org) With its tips, safety advice and contacts, this website is a great start for anybody thinking about a paddling adventure in Alaska.

SEAtrails (www.seatrails.org) SEAtrails provides brief descriptions and downloadable maps for more than 80 trails in 19 communities in Southeast Alaska.

Sitka Trail Works, Inc (www.sitkatrailworks.org) Detailed-coverage maps on almost 20 trails located around Sitka.

Trail Mix, Inc (www.trailmixinc.org) Trail information in and around Juneau.

Glacier Trekking & Ice Climbing

The glaciers may be melting, but glacier trekking is still a popular activity in Alaska. Most first-time glacier trekkers envision a slick and slippery surface, but in reality the ice is very rough and embedded with gravel and rocks that provide surprisingly good traction.

Glaciers are dangerous areas. Not only do they have ice-bridges and crevasses, they also move, meaning the surface changes from time to time. Dry glaciers have no snow on top, and are OK for limited travel without technical equipment. Wet glaciers may have snowbridges. Don't venture beyond the edge without a rope, ice axe and basic knowledge of glacier travel.

Your best bet is to hook up with a guiding company that offers glacier treks. On such outings you'll be outfitted with a helmet, crampons and an ice axe, and roped up for several miles of walking on the frozen surface.

Glaciers are also the main destination in Alaska for ice climbers in the summer. Icefalls and ice faces, where the glacier makes its biggest vertical descents out of the mountains, are where climbers strap on crampons and helmets and load themselves with ropes, ice screws and anchors. Inexperienced climbers should sign up for a one-day ice-climbing lesson, in which guides lead you to an ice fall and then teach you about cramponing, front pointing and the use of ice tools.

Outfitters that offer glacier trekking or ice-climbing excursions:

Above & Beyond Alaska (p142) A Juneau outfit that leads an eight-hour glacier trek and climb on Mendenhall Glacier.

Exit Glacier Guides (p213) A top operation, based in Seward, for exploring Kenai Fjords National Park's Exit Glacier.

Seeing Alaska From Above

Most flightseeing is done in small planes, holding three to five passengers, with the tours lasting, on average, one to two hours. A much smaller number of flights are taken by helicopter due to the high costs of operating the aircraft. With the rising price of fuel, expect to pay anything from $270 to $400 per person for a one-hour flight.

The following are some of Alaska's most spectacular flights:

Glacier Bay National Park (p146) From Haines; glaciers, Fairweather Mountains, maybe a whale or two.

Misty Fjords National Monument (p102) Two-hour flights that include a rainforest walk in this wilderness near Ketchikan.

Denali (p234) The bush pilots who fly climbers to the mountain will also take visitors around it for Alaska's most spectacular flightseeing tour.

Paddling

The paddle is a way of life in Alaska, and every region has either canoeing or kayaking opportunities or both. Southeast and Prince William Sound both offer spectacular kayaking opportunities.

Blue-Water Paddling

In Alaska, 'blue water' refers to the coastal areas of the state, which are characterized by extreme tidal fluctuations, cold water and the possibility of high winds and waves. Throughout Southeast and Southcentral Alaska, the open canoe is replaced with the kayak, and blue-water paddling is the means of escape into coastal areas such as Muir Inlet in Glacier Bay National Park or Tracy Arm-Fords Terror, south of Juneau.

If you do not know how to do a wet entry to a kayak (or know what a wet entry is), it's recommended that you travel with a guide. They know the tides, the wildlife and how to keep you safe.

Tidal fluctuations are the main concern in blue-water areas. Paddlers should always pull their boats above the high-tide mark and keep a tide book in the same pouch as their topographic map. Cold coastal water, rarely above 45°F (7°C) in the summer, makes capsizing worse than unpleasant. With a life jacket, survival time in the water is less than two hours; without one there is no time. If your kayak flips, stay with the boat and attempt to right it and crawl back in. Trying to swim to shore in arctic water is risky at best.

Framed backpacks are useless in kayaks; gear is best stowed in dry bags or small daypacks. Carry a large supply of assorted plastic bags, including several garbage bags. All gear, especially sleeping bags and clothing, should be stowed in plastic bags (or a dry bag if you have one), as water tends to seep in even when you seal yourself in with a cockpit skirt. Over-the-calf rubber boots are the best footwear for getting in and out of kayaks.

White-Water Paddling

Alaska's rivers vary, but they share characteristics not found on many rivers in the lower 48: water levels tend to change rapidly, while many rivers are heavily braided and boulder-strewn. Take care in picking out the right channel to avoid spending most of the day pulling your boat off gravel. You can survive flipping your canoe in an Alaskan river, but you'll definitely want a plan of action if you do.

Much of the equipment for white-water canoeists is the same as it is for blue-water paddlers. Tie everything into the canoe; you never know when you might hit a whirlpool or a series of standing waves. Wear a life jacket at all times. Many paddlers stock their life jacket with insect repellent, waterproof matches and other survival gear in case they flip and get separated from their boat.

Denali National Park (p234)

Ziplining

Alaska has an impressive and growing number of ziplines (canopy tours), including the largest in North America at Icy Strait Point (p150), a popular cruise-ship port. The state's ziplining capital is, undeniably, Ketchikan, with three canopies, but there are also rides in Seward and Juneau.

Cycling

With its long days, cool temperatures, lack of interstate highways and growing number of paved paths around cities such as Anchorage and Juneau, Alaska can be a land of opportunity for road cyclists.

Some roads do not have much of a shoulder – and many are quite rough even when paved – so cyclists should utilize the sunlight hours to pedal when traffic is light in such areas. It is not necessary to carry a lot of food, as you can easily restock on all major roads.

Good sources for cycling maps and news on events are Alaska's major bike clubs:

Arctic Bicycle Club (www.arcticbike.org)

Bike Anchorage (www.bikeanchorage.org)

Juneau Rides (https://juneaurides.org)

Hiker in Chugach State Park

HAGEPHOTO/GETTY IMAGES ©

Survival Guide

Directory A–Z

Customs Regulations

For a complete list of US customs regulations, visit the official portal for **US Customs & Border Protection** (www.cbp.gov). Click on 'Travel' to find out the basics.

Travelers are allowed to bring personal goods (including camping and hiking equipment) into the USA and Canada free of duty, along with food for two days and up to 100 cigars, 200 cigarettes and 1L of liquor or wine.

There are no forms to fill out if you are a foreign visitor bringing a vehicle into Alaska, whether it is a bicycle, motorcycle or car, nor are there forms for hunting rifles or fishing gear. Hunting rifles – handguns and automatic weapons are prohibited – must be registered in your own country, and you should bring proof of registration. There is no limit to the amount of money you can bring into Alaska, but anything over $10,000 must be registered with customs officials.

Keep in mind that laws protecting endangered species prohibit transporting products made of bone, skin, fur, ivory etc through Canada without a permit. Importing and exporting such items into the USA is also prohibited. If you have any doubt about a gift or and item you want to purchase, call the **US Fish & Wildlife Service** (US-FWS; ☎907-271-6198; www.fws. gov) in Anchorage or check the website.

Hunters and anglers who want to ship home their salmon, halibut or rack of caribou can do so easily. Most outfitters and guides will make the arrangements for you, including properly packaging the game. In the case of fish, most towns have a storage company that will hold your salmon or halibut in a freezer until you are ready to leave Alaska. When frozen, seafood can usually make the trip to any city in the lower 48 without thawing.

Discount Cards

Most museums, parks and major attractions will offer reduced rates to senior travelers and students, but most accommodations, restaurants and small tour companies will not.

● The best seniors card for US travelers to carry is issued by the **American Association of Retired Persons** (www.aarp.org).

● For student travelers, an **International Student Identity Card** (www.isic. org) will often result in discounted entry for attractions in cities and major towns.

● There are no Hostelling International chapters in Alaska so the Hostelling International card is of little use in the Far North.

Practicalities

Smoking There is no statewide smoking ban in Alaska but a growing number of cities including Anchorage, Juneau, Nome, Palmer, Skagway and Unalaska have a city ban on smoking in bars, restaurants and clubs.

Taxes There is no national sales tax in the USA and no state sales tax in Alaska, but towns have a city sales tax plus a bed tax.

Weights & Measures US distances are in feet, yards and miles. Dry weights are in ounces (oz), pounds (lb) and tons, and liquids are in pints, quarts and gallons. The US gallon is about 20% less than the imperial gallon.

Electricity

Voltage in Alaska is 120V – the same as everywhere else in the USA.

120V/60Hz

120V/60Hz

Embassies & Consulates

International travelers needing to locate the US embassy in their home country should visit the website of the **US Department of State** (http://usembassy.state.gov), which has links to all of them.

There are no embassies in Alaska, but there are a handful of foreign consulates in Anchorage to assist overseas travelers with unusual problems.

Gay & Lesbian Travelers

The gay community in Alaska is far smaller and much less open than in major US cities, and Alaskans in general are not as tolerant of diversity. In 1998 Alaska passed a constitutional amendment banning same-sex marriages. However, attitudes are slowly changing. A 2014 poll found 47% of Alaskan voters in favor of same-sex marriage.

In Anchorage, the only city in Alaska of any real size, there is **Identity Inc** (☎907-929-4528; www.identityinc.org), which has a gay and lesbian helpline, a handful of openly gay clubs and bars, and a weeklong **Pride-Fest** (http://alaskapride.org) in mid-June. The **Southeast**

Alaska Gay & Lesbian Alliance (www.seagla.org) is based in Juneau and offers links and travel lists geared to gay visitors. The list is short, however, because most towns do not have an openly active gay community. In rural Alaska, same-sex couples should exercise discretion.

Health

There is a high standard of hygiene found in Alaska, so most common infectious diseases will not be a significant concern for travelers. Superb medical care and rapid evacuation to major hospitals are both available.

Recommended Vaccinations

No special vaccines are required or recommended for travel to Alaska.

Environmental Hazards

The most dangerous health threat outdoors is hypothermia. Dress in layers topped with a well-made, waterproof outer layer and always pack wool mittens and a hat.

Due to Alaska's long summer days, sunburn and windburn are a primary concern for anyone trekking or paddling. Use a good sunscreen on exposed skin, even on cloudy days, and a hat and sunglasses for additional protection.

Alaska is notorious for its biting insects, including mosquitoes, black flies, no-see-ums and deer flies. Wear long-sleeved shirts, pants that can be tucked into socks, and a snug cap. Use a high-potency insect repellent and head nets in areas where there are excessive insects.

In recent years, paralytic shellfish poisoning (PSP) from eating mussels and clams has become a problem in Alaska. For a list of beaches safe to clam, check with the **Alaska Division of Environmental Health** (www.dec.alaska.gov/eh).

Availability & Cost of Health Care

The US has an excellent health-care system and health-care availability in Alaska is widespread in the main population centers. However, the cost of health care in Alaska, as in the rest of the USA, is extremely high.

Insurance

A travel insurance policy to cover theft, loss and medical problems is a smart investment for travelers. Coverage depends on your insurance and type of ticket but should cover delays by striking employees or company actions, or a cancellation of a trip. Such coverage may seem expensive but it's nowhere near the price of a trip to Alaska or the cost of a medical emergency in the USA.

Some policies offer lower and higher medical-expense options; the higher options are chiefly for countries such as the USA, which have extremely high medical costs. There is a wide variety of medical and emergency repatriation policies and it's important to talk to your health-care provider for recommendations on the best policy for you.

Worldwide travel insurance is available at www.lonelyplanet.com/travel-insurance. You can buy, extend and claim online anytime – even if you're already on the road.

Marijuana

Alaska became the third US state to legalize the use of recreational marijuana in February 2015 after a state ballot was held. Marijuana shops have been springing up through larger towns and cities since 2016, but it hasn't become Amsterdam quite yet. Wise up on the law before you arrive and use discretion at all times when imbibing.

The basic rules regarding the use of marijuana are as follows:

- You must be 21 years or over.

- Qualifying adults can possess up to one ounce of marijuana for personal consumption.

- You must buy it from a licensed facility.

- You can't smoke in public areas or on federal land (eg national parks and forests).

- It is illegal to drive while impaired.

- You can't take marijuana out of the state.

Internet Access

It's easy to surf the net, make online reservations or retrieve email in Alaska. Most towns, even the smallest ones, have free internet access available at public libraries. If you have a laptop or phone, free wi-fi is common in Alaska at bookstores, hotels, coffee shops, airport terminals and bars, although reception may be patchier than it is in the lower 48 United States. If you're not from the US, remember you will need an AC adapter and a plug adapter for US sockets.

Legal Matters

The use of drugs (except marijuana) is against the law and results in severe penalties, especially for cocaine, which is heavily abused in Alaska.

The minimum drinking age in Alaska is 21 and a government-issued photo ID (passport or driver's license) will be needed if a bartender questions your age. Alcohol abuse is also a problem in Alaska, and it's a serious offense if you are caught driving under the influence of alcohol (DUI). The blood alcohol limit in Alaska is 0.08% and the penalty for DUI is a three-month driver's license revocation. You may also be given a fine and jail time.

If you are stopped by the police for any reason while driving, remember there is no system of paying on-the-spot fines and bribery is not something that works in Alaska. For traffic violations, the officer will explain your options to you and many violations can often be handled through the mail with a credit card.

Money

Prices quoted are in US dollars unless otherwise stated. Keep in mind that the Canadian system is also dollars and cents but is a separate currency.

ATMs

In Alaska ATMs can be found everywhere: at banks, gas stations, supermarkets, airports and even some visitor information centers. At most ATMs you can use a credit card (Visa, MasterCard etc), a debit card or an ATM card that is linked to the Plus or Cirrus ATM networks. There is generally a fee ($1 to $3) that is charged for withdrawing cash from an ATM, but the exchange rate on transactions is usually as good if not better than what you will find anywhere else.

Cash

Hard cash still works. It may not be the safest way to carry funds, but nobody will hassle you when you purchase something with US dollars. Most businesses located along the Alcan in Canada will also accept US dollars.

US coins come in denominations of 1¢ (penny), 5¢ (nickel), 10¢ (dime), 25¢ (quarter) and the seldom seen 50¢ (half-dollar). Quarters are the most commonly used coins in vending machines and parking meters, so it's handy to have a stash of them on hand. Notes, commonly called bills, come in $1, $2, $5, $10, $20, $50 and $100 denominations.

Credit Cards

As in the rest of the USA, Alaskan merchants are ready and willing to accept just about all major credit cards. Visa and MasterCard are the most widely accepted credit cards, but American Express and Discovery cards are also widely used.

Places that accept Visa and MasterCard are also likely to accept debit cards. If you are an overseas visitor, check with your bank at home to confirm that your debit card will be accepted in the USA.

Tipping

Tipping in Alaska, like in the rest of the USA, is expected.

Bars If you order food at the table and it's brought to you, tip 15%, the same as at restaurants; 10% if you're having a drink or appetizer at the bar.

Restaurants From 15% for cafes and chain eateries to 20% for upscale restaurants.

Taxis 15%

Tour guides 10% for bus tour guides, 15% to 20% for wilderness guides on glacier treks or white-water-rafting trips.

Opening Hours

Banks 9am–4pm/5pm Monday to Friday; 9am–1pm Saturday (main branches).

Bars & Clubs City bars until 2am or later, especially on weekends; clubs to 2am or beyond.

Post Offices 9am–5pm Monday to Friday; noon–3pm Saturday (main branches open longer).

Restaurants & Cafes Breakfast at cafes/coffee shops from 7am or earlier; some restaurants open only for lunch (noon–3pm) or dinner (4–10pm, later in cities); Asian restaurants often have split hours: 11am–2pm and from 4pm.

Shops 10am–8pm/6pm (larger/smaller stores) Monday to Friday; 9am–5pm Saturday; 10am–5pm Sunday (larger stores).

Public Holidays

Public holidays for Alaskan residents may involve state and federal offices being closed, bus services curtailed, and store hours reduced.

New Year's Day January 1

Martin Luther King Day Third Monday in January

Presidents' Day Third Monday in February

Seward's Day Last Monday in March

Easter Sunday Late March or early April

Memorial Day Last Monday in May

Independence Day (Fourth of July) July 4

Labor Day First Monday in September

Columbus Day Second Monday in October

Alaska Day October 18

Veterans' Day November 11

Thanksgiving Day Fourth Thursday in November

Christmas Day December 25

Safe Travel

Alaska is a relatively safe place. The main dangers lurk in its extensive wilderness areas. These can be largely avoided by taking a few basic precautions.

• Alaska has an abundance of wild animals, even in urban areas. Carry pepper spray and avoid direct animal encounters.

Bears in Alaska

Too often travelers decide to skip a wilderness trip because they hear too many bear stories. Your own equipment and outdoor experience should determine whether you take a trek into the woods, not the possibility of meeting a bear on the trail. The **Alaska Department of Fish & Game** (☏ licensing 907-465-2376, main office 907-465-4100; www.adfg.alaska.gov) emphasizes that the probability of being injured by a bear is one-fiftieth the chance of being injured in a car accident on any Alaskan highway.

The best way to avoid bears is to follow a few common-sense rules. Bears charge only when they feel trapped, when a hiker comes between a sow and her cubs, or when enticed by food. Sing or clap when traveling through thick bush, and don't camp near bear food sources or in the middle of an obvious bear path. Stay away from thick berry patches, streams choked with salmon or beaches littered with bear droppings.

Set up the spot where you will cook and eat at least 30yd to 50yd away from your tent. In coastal areas, many backpackers eat in the tidal zone, knowing that when the high tide comes in, all evidence of food will be washed away.

At night try to place your food sacks 10ft or more off the ground by hanging them in a tree. Or consider investing in a lightweight bear-resistant container. A bear usually finds a food bag using its great sense of smell. Avoid odorous foods, such as bacon or sardines, in areas with high concentrations of bears, and don't take food, cosmetics or deodorant into the tent at night.

• Beware of glacier crevasses and calving icebergs.

• In these northern climes fickle weather can change on a dime. Come prepared for the worst, even in high summer.

Telephone

Telephone area codes are simple in Alaska: the entire state shares 907, except

Hyder, which uses 250. Phone numbers that begin with 800, 877 and 866 are toll-free numbers and there is no charge for using one to call a hotel or tour operator. If you're calling from abroad, the country code for the USA is 1.

Cell Phones

Cell (mobile) phones work in Alaska and Alaskans love them as much as everyone else in the USA. When calling locally in cities and towns, reception is excellent but overall, in a state this large, cell-phone coverage can be unpredictable and sporadic at times. The culprits in most cases are mountains.

Most travelers still find their cell phones to be very useful. Before you leave home, however, check your cell-phone provider's roaming agreements and blackout areas. It may be possible for international travelers to purchase a prepaid SIM card that can be used in their phones for local calls and voicemail. You can also purchase inexpensive cell phones from AT&T along with prepaid cards for calls.

Better still, with a wi-fi connection you can call using Skype or WhatsApp for free.

Time

With the exception of several Aleutian Island communities and Hyder,

a small community on the Alaska–British Columbia border, the entire state shares the same time zone, Alaska Time, which is one hour earlier than Pacific Standard Time – the zone in which Seattle, WA, falls. When it is noon in Anchorage, it is 4pm in New York, 9pm in London and 7am the following day in Melbourne, Australia. Although there is a movement to abolish it, Alaska still has Daylight Saving Time when, like most of the country, the state sets clocks back one hour in November and forward one hour in March.

Tourist Information

The first place to contact when planning your adventure is the **Alaska Travel Industry Association** (✆907-929-2842; www.alaskatia.org), the state's tourism marketing arm.

Almost every city, town and village has a tourist information contact center, whether it is a visitor center, a chamber of commerce or a hut near the ferry dock. These places are good sources of free maps and directions to the nearest hiking trail.

Most trips to Alaska pass through one of the state's three largest cities. All have large visitors bureaus that will send out city guides in advance.

For other tourist information:

Admiralty Island National Monument (✆907-586-8800; www.fs.fed.us/visit/destination/admiralty-island-national-monument)

Mountaineering Club of Alaska (http://mtnclubak.org)

National Park Service (✆907-983-2921; www.nps.gov/state/ak)

Tourism Yukon (✆800-661-0494; www.travelyukon.com)

USFS Glacier Ranger District (✆907-783-3242; www.fs.fed.us/r10/chugach)

Travelers with Disabilities

Thanks to the American Disabilities Act, cruise ships are equipped with wheelchair lifts and ramps, as are the Alaska Marine Highway ferries, the Alaska Railroad and many bus services. You can call the **Alaska Public Lands Information Center** (✆907-456-0527; www.alaskacenters.gov; 101 Dunkel St, Fairbanks; ⊗8am-6pm) to receive a map and campground guide to state and federal parks that have installed wheelchair-accessible facilities. Some wilderness guiding companies are experienced in handling wheelchair-bound clients on rafting and kayaking expeditions.

Access Alaska (www.accessalaska.org) Includes statewide tourist information on accessible services and sites.

Challenge Alaska (📞907-344-7399; www.challengealaska.org) A nonprofit organization dedicated to providing recreation opportunities for those with disabilities.

Flying Wheels Travel (📞877-451-5006; www.flyingwheels travel.com) A full-service travel agency specializing in disabled travel.

Society for Accessible Travel & Hospitality (📞212-447-7284; www.sath.org) Lobbies for better facilities and publishes *Open World* online magazine.

Download Lonely Planet's free Accessible Travel guides from http://lptravel.to/AccessibleTravel.

Visas

It is your responsibility to make sure you have the correct travel documentation before you board your cruise ship.

Since September 11, the US has continually fine-tuned its national security guidelines and entry requirements. Double-check current visa and passport regulations before arriving in the USA, and apply for visas early to avoid delays. Overseas travelers may need one visa, possibly two: for citizens of many countries a US visa is required, while you may also need a Canadian visa.

Canadians entering the USA must have proof of Canadian citizenship, such as a passport; visitors from

countries in the Visa Waiver Program may not need a visa. Visitors from all other countries need to have a US visa and a valid passport. Check the website of the **US State Department** (www.travel.state.gov) for full details.

Note that overseas travelers should be aware of the process to re-enter the USA. Sometimes visitors get stuck in Canada due to their single-entry visa into the USA, used up when passing through the lower 48. Canadian immigration officers often caution people whom they feel might have difficulty returning to the USA. More information about visa and other requirements for entering Canada is available on the website of the **Canada Border Services Agency** (www.cbsa-asfc.gc.ca).

Visa Application

Apart from Canadians and those entering under the Visa Waiver Program, foreign visitors need to obtain a visa from a US consulate or embassy. Most applicants must now schedule a personal interview, to which you need to bring all your documentation and proof of fee payment. Wait times for interviews vary, but afterward, barring problems, visa issuance takes from a few days to a few weeks. If concerned about a delay, check the websites of the **US State Department** (www.travel.state.gov), which provides a list of wait times calculated by country.

Your passport must be valid for at least six months longer than your intended stay in the USA. You'll need a recent photo (2in by 2in) and you must pay a $160 processing fee, plus in a few cases an additional visa-issuance fee (check the State Department website for details). In addition to the main nonimmigration visa application form (DS-156), all men aged 16 to 45 must complete an additional form (DS-157) that details their travel plans.

Visa applicants are required to show documentation of financial stability, a round-trip or onward ticket and 'binding obligations' that will ensure their return home, such as family ties, a home or a job.

Visa Waiver Program

The Visa Waiver Program (VWP) lets citizens of some countries enter the USA for tourism purposes for up to 90 days without having a US visa. Currently there are 36 participating countries in the VWP, including Austria, Australia, Belgium, Denmark, Finland, France, Germany, Iceland, Ireland, Italy, Japan, the Netherlands, New Zealand, Norway, Spain, Sweden, Switzerland and the UK.

Under the program you must have a round-trip or onward ticket that is nonrefundable in the USA, a machine-readable passport (with two lines of letters, numbers and '<<<' along the bottom of the passport information page) and be able to show evidence of financial solvency.

Citizens of VWP countries must register online prior to their trip with the **Electronic System for Travel Authorization** (ESTA; https://esta.cbp.dhs.gov/esta), an automated system used to determine the eligibility of visitors traveling to the US. There is a $14 fee. Beware, there are several bogus ESTA websites.

Women Travelers

While most violent crime rates are lower here than elsewhere in the USA, women should be careful at night in unfamiliar neighborhoods of cities such as Anchorage and Fairbanks or whenever hitching alone. Use common sense; don't be afraid to say no to lifts that are offered.

If camping alone, have pepper spray and know how to use it.

Alaska Women's Network (www.alaskawomensnetwork.org) Has listings of women-owned travel agencies across the state.

Women's Flyfishing (www.womensflyfishing.net) Alaska's premier outfitter for women-only fly-fishing trips and a great web resource for women arriving in Alaska with a fly rod.

Behind the Scenes

Acknowledgements

Climate map data adapted from Peel MC, Finlayson BL & McMahon TA (2007) 'Updated World Map of the Köppen-Geiger Climate Classification', Hydrology and Earth System Sciences, 11, 1633–44.

This Book

This 1st edition of Lonely Planet's *Cruise Ports Alaska* guidebook was curated by Brendan Sainsbury and researched and written by Brendan Sainsbury, Catherine Bodry, Adam Karlin, John Lee and Becky Ohlsen. This guidebook was produced by the following:

Destination Editor Alexander Howard

Product Editor Alison Ridgway

Senior Cartographer Alison Lyall

Book Designer Mazzy Prinsep

Assisting Editors Bridget Blair, Paul Harding, Victoria Harrison, Jenna Myers

Assisting Book Designers Meri Blazevski, Michael Weldon

Cover Researcher Campbell McKenzie

Thanks to Liz Heynes, Elizabeth Jones, Kate Mathews, Kathryn Rowan, Tony Wheeler

Send Us Your Feedback

We love to hear from travelers – your comments keep us on our toes and help make our books better. Our well-traveled team reads every word on what you loved or loathed about this book. Although we cannot reply individually to postal submissions, we always guarantee that your feedback goes straight to the appropriate authors, in time for the next edition. Each person who sends us information is thanked in the next edition, the most useful submissions are rewarded with a selection of digital PDF chapters.

Visit lonelyplanet.com/contact to submit your updates and suggestions or to ask for help. Our award-winning website also features inspirational travel stories, news and discussions.

Note: We may edit, reproduce and incorporate your comments in Lonely Planet products such as guidebooks, websites and digital products, so let us know if you don't want your comments reproduced or your name acknowledged. For a copy of our privacy policy visit lonelyplanet.com/privacy.

Index

Symbols & Map Key

Look for these symbols to quickly identify listings:

- ◎ Sights
- ✦ Activities
- ⊖ Courses
- ⊙ Tours
- ✦ Festivals & Events
- ✖ Eating
- ⊖ Drinking
- ✦ Entertainment
- ⊟ Shopping
- ⓘ Information & Transport

These symbols and abbreviations give vital information for each listing:

- 🖋 Sustainable or green recommendation
- **FREE** No payment required

- 🕿 Telephone number
- ⊙ Opening hours
- P Parking
- ⊝ Nonsmoking
- ✳ Air-conditioning
- @ Internet access
- 🛜 Wi-fi access
- 🏊 Swimming pool
- 🚍 Bus
- 🛳 Ferry
- 🚊 Tram
- 🚆 Train
- 🖺 English-language menu
- 🥗 Vegetarian selection
- 👪 Family-friendly

Find your best experiences with these Great For... icons.

- Art & Culture
- Beaches
- Budget
- Cafe/Coffee
- Cycling
- Detour
- Drinking
- Entertainment
- Events
- Family Travel
- Food & Drink
- History
- Local Life
- Nature & Wildlife
- Photo Op
- Scenery
- Shopping
- Short Trip
- Sport
- Walking
- Winter Travel

Sights

- 🄑 Beach
- 🄑 Bird Sanctuary
- 🄑 Buddhist
- 🄑 Castle/Palace
- 🄑 Christian
- 🄑 Confucian
- 🄑 Hindu
- 🄑 Islamic
- 🄑 Jain
- 🄑 Jewish
- 🄑 Monument
- 🄑 Museum/Gallery/ Historic Building
- 🄑 Ruin
- 🄑 Shinto
- 🄑 Sikh
- 🄑 Taoist
- 🄑 Winery/Vineyard
- 🄑 Zoo/Wildlife Sanctuary
- 🄑 Other Sight

Points of Interest

- ⓒ Bodysurfing
- ⊕ Camping
- ⊜ Cafe
- ⊜ Canoeing/Kayaking
- • Course/Tour
- ⊗ Diving
- ⊖ Drinking & Nightlife
- ⊗ Eating
- ✦ Entertainment
- ⊛ Sento Hot Baths/ Onsen
- ⊟ Shopping
- ⊕ Skiing
- ⊜ Sleeping
- ⊜ Snorkelling
- ⊙ Surfing
- ⊛ Swimming/Pool
- ⊛ Walking
- ⊛ Windsurfing
- ⊕ Other Activity

Information

- 🅢 Bank
- 🄑 Embassy/Consulate
- ⊕ Hospital/Medical
- @ Internet
- ⊗ Police
- ⊠ Post Office
- ⊘ Telephone
- 🄑 Toilet
- ⓘ Tourist Information
- • Other Information

Geographic

- 🄑 Beach
- ⊢< Gate
- ⊕ Hut/Shelter
- ⊕ Lighthouse
- ⊕ Lookout
- ▲ Mountain/Volcano
- ⊕ Oasis
- ⊕ Park
-)(Pass
- 🄑 Picnic Area
- 🄑 Waterfall

Transport

- ✈ Airport
- Ⓑ BART station
- ⊗ Border crossing
- ⓣ Boston T station
- 🚍 Bus
- Cable car/Funicular
- Cycling
- Ferry
- Ⓜ Metro/MRT station
- Monorail
- P Parking
- 🄑 Petrol station
- 🅢 Subway/S-Bahn/ Skytrain station
- ⊜ Taxi
- Train station/Railway
- Tram
- ⊜ Tube Station
- Ⓤ Underground/ U-Bahn station
- • Other Transport

John Lee

Born and raised in the UK, John grew up in the lengthy shadow of London, then succumbed to the lure of Canada's West Coast in 1993 to begin an MA in Political Science at the University of Victoria. Regular trips home to Britain ensued, along with stints living in Tokyo and Montreal, before he returned to British Columbia to become a full-time freelance writer in 1999. Now living in Vancouver, John specializes in travel writing and has contributed to more than 150 different publications around the world. You can read some of his stories (and see some of his videos) online at www.johnleewriter.com. John has worked on around 25 Lonely Planet books, including *Canada, British Columbia, Western Europe, Vancouver* and *Europe on a Shoestring*.

Becky Ohlsen

Becky is a freelance writer, editor and critic based in Portland, Oregon. She writes guidebooks and travel stories about Scandinavia, Portland and elsewhere for Lonely Planet. After a few years of studying her adopted hometown of Portland from the copy desk at an alternative weekly newspaper, Becky spent the requisite year bumming around Europe on the mega-cheap. This did nothing to quell her urge to run off exploring new places every couple of months; quite the opposite. Aside from Scandinavia, she has spent time roaming around the UK, Panama, Mexico, Hong Kong, Beijing and most of the US.

Our Story

A beat-up old car, a few dollars in the pocket and a sense of adventure. In 1972 that's all Tony and Maureen Wheeler needed for the trip of a lifetime – across Europe and Asia overland to Australia. It took several months, and at the end – broke but inspired – they sat at their kitchen table writing and stapling together their first travel guide, *Across Asia on the Cheap*. Within a week they'd sold 1500 copies. Lonely Planet was born.

Today, Lonely Planet has offices in Franklin, London, Melbourne, Oakland, Dublin, Beijing and Delhi, with more than 600 staff and writers. We share Tony's belief that 'a great guidebook should do three things: inform, educate and amuse'.

Our Writers

Brendan Sainsbury

Originally from Hampshire, England, Brendan has traveled all over Alaska from Ketchikan in the south to Deadhorse in the north by bus, train, kayak, bicycle, ferry, airplane and his own two feet. Memorable moments have included taking a bus up the Dalton Highway from Fairbanks to the Arctic Ocean, catching a ferry through the off-the-grid Alaskan peninsula to the Aleutian Islands, and running the Chilkoot trail in the footsteps of the Klondike 'stampeders' in a day. Now based in Vancouver, Canada, Brendan has contributed to more than 50 Lonely Planet guides including six editions of *Cuba*.

Catherine Bodry

Catherine is based in Anchorage, Alaska, but spends much of her time in Southeast Asia. As a writer, she's covered Alaska, Thailand and China, among other destinations. A lover of mountains, she spends as much time as possible in or near hills, whether it's running, hiking, camping, berry picking, rafting or just gazing at them. For Lonely Planet, she's contributed to about a dozen guide and trade books including several editions of *Alaska*, as well as *Canada, Thailand* and *Pacific Northwest Trips*.

Adam Karlin

Adam has contributed to dozens of Lonely Planet guidebooks, covering an alphabetical spread that ranges from the Andaman Islands to the Zimbabwe border. As a journalist, he has written on travel, crime, politics, archaeology, and the Sri Lankan Civil War, among other topics. He has sent dispatches from every continent barring Antarctica (one day!) and his essays and articles have featured in the BBC, NPR, and multiple non-fiction anthologies. Adam is based out of New Orleans, which explains his love of wetlands, food and good music. Learn more at http://walkonfine.com or Instagram @adamwalkonfine.

More Writers

STAY IN TOUCH LONELYPLANET.COM/CONTACT

AUSTRALIA The Malt Store, Level 3, 551 Swanston St, Carlton, Victoria 3053 ☎03 8379 8000, fax 03 8379 8111

IRELAND Digital Depot, Roe Lane (off Thomas St), Digital Hub, Dublin 8, D08 TCV4, Ireland

USA 124 Linden Street, Oakland, CA 94607 ☎510 250 6400, toll free 800 275 8555, fax 510 893 8572

UK 240 Blackfriars Road, London SE1 8NW ☎020 3771 5100, fax 020 3771 5101

 twitter.com/lonelyplanet　facebook.com/lonelyplanet　instagram.com/lonelyplanet　youtube.com/lonelyplanet　lonelyplanet.com/newsletter